simply incredible FLAVOR

The ultimate **healthy cooking** flavor guide book

chef mark anthony

SIMPLY INCREDIBLE FLAVOR

©2018 by Mark Anthony

All rights reserved.

ISBN 13: 978-0-9828791-7-7

ISBN 10: 0-9828791-7-2

Layout and cover design: Lanette Steiner

To order books, request information, or comment, please contact:

MARK ANTHONY

Address: Box 6103 . South Bend, IN 46660

Email: tvchefmarkanthony@gmail.com

Printed in the United States of America

8757 County Road 77 . Fredericksburg, OH 44627
p. 888.473.6870

introduction

WELCOME TO THE WORLD OF SIMPLY INCREDIBLE FLAVOR. We have stretched beyond the knowledge of any cookbook on the market to bring you the simplicity of developing extraordinary flavors. And what's even more amazing, is that these flavors are all plant strong and healthy. Eating healthier does not mean you have to give up on taste. In fact we are going to show you how to get more flavor from a plant strong lifestyle than you could ever imagine.

You may be considering ways to flavor a particular food, like rice, beans, tofu, grains, potatoes. Or you may be looking for a particular type of cuisine. This book has your answers. And even more important is that this book gives you the answers without a bunch of complicated recipes that are impossible to make. These recipes are easy!

It's all about flavor. It's all about the spices. And it's all about making your life healthier and easier. Prepare yourself for a wide variety of ways to get the most amazing flavors the world has ever imagined.

We are also going to educate you about the intelligence of flavor by teaching you the way tastebuds work. Everything from salty to sweet is explained in a simple to understand format. There are also the elements of texture, and smell. What about the sensation of oil? Or how does heat and cold affect spices?

There is far more to cooking than just throwing the potatoes into the pot. And we are here to show you the easy way to bring flavor to a whole new level.

This book is more that just a cookbook! It has a depth of knowledge that will expand your culinary talents to the level of Master Chef, without having to spend $50,000.00 on a 3-year degree. So enjoy these recipes and implement the concepts that will make your kitchen life so much easier and reward you with the Simply Incredible Flavor that you deserve.

Part of the moving force behind this book and the foods we have selected are based on the scientific knowledge brought to us through these extraordinary doctors and their books.

THESE BOOKS ARE A MUST READ FOR LEARNING HOW TO GET HEALTHY:

How Not To Die by Dr. Michael Greger

The Starch Solution by Dr. McDougall

Reversing Diabetes by Dr. Neal Barnard

The Low Carb Fraud by T. Colin Campbell

The Low Carb Myth by Dr. Ari Whitten and Wade Smith

They all teach that we need to eat more carbs and less oils. But don't forget, they need to be the whole complex carbs, not the simple processed carbs. Eat the potato, not the potato chip.

HOW TO
use this book

We have created effortless ways to achieve many flavors of the world. And we are doing it with simplicity. The trick to creating foods from other cultures is to first determine what foods are native to that culture. So we have comprised a comprehensive list of the primary foods native to every major cuisine. Now that could be a long list so we custom spotlighted the most common ingredients. We then take it one step further and share with you the most popular pairings.

We also did the same thing with the healthiest foods in the world. We know that we need to eat more complex carbohydrates. But if you haven't learned how to season them well, then you may not enjoy them enough to make them part of your regular diet. We have chosen the most nutritious complex carbs and included all the foods and seasonings to pair them with. This concept will help you develop Simply Incredible Flavor.

FIRST: you will find a lists of ingredients for a particular region, or cuisine.

SECOND: you will find Simply Incredible Pairings. When you combine these particular ingredients, you will achieve Simply Incredible Flavor.

Example:

chili peppers + garlic + onions

chili peppers + peanuts + tomatoes

THIRD: you will find some great recipes that capture that particular region or food

GOOD These items go well with this food.	BETTER Even better pairing.	BEST The WOW factor!
allspice	**cream sauces**	**DILL**
apples	**mushrooms**	**SOUR CREAM**
bay leaf	**SIMPLY INCREDIBLE PAIRINGS** bay leaf + dill + nutmeg + onion	
breads		

TABLE of CONTENTS

YOUR FIVE SENSES, PLUS TWO NEW ONES! » 9

YOUR FIVE TASTEBUDS, PLUS TWO NEW ONES! » 25

SPICES + HERBS » 49

MOST POPULAR SPICE BLENDS AND MIXES » 63

CHEF'S SECRETS

    Cooking Without Oil » 65

    Water Sauté » 67

    Egg Substitutes » 69

    Must Have Products » 71

FLAVORING FOR THE WORLD'S HEALTHIEST FOODS » 77

According to the experts, complex carbs are the healthy foods that we should be eating the most of every day. This section will expand your ability to create amazing, flavorful, healthy dishes.

Barley » 78

Beans, black » 85

Beans, pinto » 96

Beans, red kidney » 102

Beans, white » 109

Chickpeas » 117

Corn » 127

Lentils » 132

Oats » 140

Potatoes » 149

Potatoes, sweet » 175

Quinoa » 180

Rice » 194

Tofu » 210

Whole Grains » 225

Winter Squash » 234

FLAVORING FOODS FROM AROUND THE WORLD » 243

This section is going to become one of your most valuable cooking tools.

African » 244

American

    Barbecue » 251

    Cajun » 258

    Hawaiian » 264

    Native American » 270

    Southern » 277

    Tex-Mex & Southwest » 282

Asian » 291

    Chinese » 292

    Japanese » 297

    Thai » 304

Belgian » 311

Caribbean » 315

French » 323

German » 329

Greek » 335

Hungarian » 342

Indian » 349

Irish » 357

Italian » 363

Latin American » 371

Mediterranean » 380

Middle Eastern » 390

Mexican » 401

Russian » 413

Spanish » 419

Swedish » 428

Index » 437

Your Five Senses
PLUS TWO NEW ONES!

Welcome to the amazing world of senses. We are going to dive right into these five known senses plus two additional senses not normally thought of, until now. That's right! I am going to explain two other senses that affect your tastebuds and flavor receptors in more ways than we had ever imagined. This is not the 'Sixth-Sense' as portrayed in that old 1999 suspense movie. These are actual senses, that have a powerful impact on how you perceive and taste food.

Before we explore the bonus senses, let's go through the standard five. We all know the five senses of sight, hearing, taste, touch and smell. And what an amazing job they do. When we look at the absolute miracle of these five senses we will certainly discover what a blessing they are. They really are a gift from God for us to enjoy. Like anything in this world, they can all be twisted and used for evil as well as good. But for the purposes of health and flavor, we are going to focus on the elements that will affect our taste, dining, and healthy living experiences.

The first thing that I want to point out about the five senses is that their main purpose is for protection. Every sense is a mechanism to keep us safe from danger. As we go through these senses, I will show you how each one of them is designed for safety.

And of course all five senses are connected to many dopamine receptors. That is why we can actually experience joy from the activities of these senses. Otherwise, the experiences would be only that, an experience. One that would not be filled with any joy, or pleasure. In fact these dopamine receptors are integrated into a lot of our daily business, including motivation, pleasure, memory, and learning. And amazingly, these dopamine receptors are also connected to fine motor controls, neurological processes, and even nerve functions.

On the flip side, when we experience the pain and suffering of negative emotions and feelings, it can produce harmful effects through endorphins, cortisol secretions, and other damaging characteristics.

So as you can see, these five senses are more than just senses. They serve a far greater purpose. And while a whole book could be written just on senses, I will move forward to the relevant elements that affect our taste and also affect the way we think about food.

When it comes to food and flavor, which is the focus of this book, we need first keep in mind a couple of factors that are necessary to achieve Simply Incredible Flavor. Because flavor can be complex.

The first and most important lesson we need to embrace is the fact that Simply Incredible Flavor starts with thoughts of the finished product. You don't have to have the entire result carved in stone, but it's a good idea to have a vision. We will need to work backwards in our head from time to time in order to establish the order of production.

If I'm going to make a salad, my first thought is….. I'm going to make a salad. And then we need to decide what we need to prep in order to make a salad. And if you are going to make it all in one bowl, you will have to prepare the foundation first. This is because you are going to want to put the cut vegetables on top of the base of lettuce. Sounds simple enough, right? Well, not so fast. There are a couple of factors to consider before ending up with a boring result. What about salad dressing? What if you are doing a sizzling salad with some delicious sautéed Butler Soy Curls? This is where we need to consider the order of what we are preparing. We certainly wouldn't want the hot vegan soy curls sitting on a salad while you prepare a dressing. Maybe you will want to make that in advance so that it is well chilled.

The reason I wanted to point out these elements first is because the vision of the final product will certainly delegate the order of production. We will be digging into a lot more amazing strategies for preparation throughout this book.

What we are going to create, and the order of production needs to consider all the senses. Will the food be hot or cold? Or maybe a combination of both. What is going to be the color that we will visually find appealing. And maybe there is a certain smell that will create a more appetizing experience.

Now you know why it is important to cultivate an understanding of how your senses will affect the final product. Keep in mind that spectacular foods are going to start with a vision. And incorporating all of your senses into this vision, then applied to your cooking will help you create Simply Incredible Flavor.

Taste

SENSE 1

Taste, or the more formal term, gustation, is simply the capability of the body to detect the taste of a substance. It is actually designed as one of the bodies most in-tune defense mechanisms. Think about it. You can taste if something is rotten and most poisons are relatively easy to detect. God gave us all the senses as a defense, to keep us safe and protect us.

For example, imagine the reaction you would experience if you were to taste bleach, or chlorine. Your body would also get that exact same reaction from alcohol or tobacco. Unfortunately people don't take those first warning flags seriously enough. Their tastebuds become desensitized to the harmful elements. And quite often, the body actually develops a taste for something that was originally determined, by the body, as something to stay away from.

Let's also face the fact that there are a lot of messed up tastebuds. We are being bombarded by chemicals and pesticides. Most of these toxins are certainly taking their toll on our tastebuds, desensitizing them to the point that the healthy foods we should be eating are lifeless and bland.

Animal products are also taking their toll on our ability to taste. When we eat animal products, the fat and cholesterol coats our tastebuds so that we are not able to discern flavors nearly as well as we could without all that animal fat. So if you really want to taste food, and really want to experience what food is supposed to taste like, eliminate all the animal products out of your diet. When your tastebuds are free from the fat coating, they will start functioning the way they are supposed to and you will develop a taste for fresh, healthy foods.

I'm living proof of this. Being a huge meat and dairy consumer was definitely taking it's toll on my tastebuds. I really didn't notice it until I went all vegan, with no animal products whatsoever. It does take a month or two for your tastebuds to be transformed and start doing the job their supposed to be doing. I started craving oatmeal which is something I would never have eaten before. I now eat salads with no dressing on them whatsoever. I never would have thought that was possible. But you see, my tastebuds are working. Vegetables are bursting with flavor and I love them. Even plain oatmeal is appealing. Of course, I do love to jazz it up but with my tastebuds in working order I can use a fraction of the sweetener that would be considered normal. It is a win win in every way to eliminate all the animal products out of your diet. And then, you will really experience the flavor you have been missing in your diet.

When it comes to taste, there are a couple of elements that we must first consider. Taste itself, is actually determined by a combination of the five senses and the tastebuds themselves are not able to provide a full range of tastes without the other senses.

Taste really is a combination of senses. Have you ever had a cold, and wondered why food just didn't taste the way it should? That's because your sense of smell is distorted. If you were to lose your taste functions of the tongue, that would be termed 'Ageusia'. And while your taste buds could not sense sweet, sour, salty, bitter, or savory, you will still be able to taste the food through the sense of smell. Likewise, if you were to lose your sense of smell, termed 'Anosmia' and still have your tastebuds working, food will still have flavor, it would just be extremely dull.

I learned early on to never experiment with test recipes when I have a cold or sickness that would impair my senses. The last thing I want to do is create a recipe, and then find out later that it wasn't quite right because I had decreased senses. Of course we do need to understand that every single body is a little bit different, even when it comes to taste. What might be the absolute perfect recipe for you, might not be a good recipe for someone else. Some people hate onions; if my wife had her way, onions would never be found in the kitchen. And that is just one of the hundreds of ingredients that every single person will have a different opinion on.

This is one of the reasons why I teach concepts. Because when you learn the concept of how to cook, then you can develop the flavors that are right for you. I always think of any recipe as a base, a place to start, and then develop your own creations. In fact most of my recipes are to serve as a guide. While they will all taste great to me, you may want to do a little tweaking for your particular tastebuds.

In our next chapter we will go over the actual tastebuds, but for now, we need to understand that even though technically taste is not affected by any of the other senses, flavor is. As we continue, do keep in mind how valuable all the senses are to creating Simply Incredible Flavor.

Sight

SENSE 2

The gift of sight is certainly one of God's greatest creations. We have all heard that old saying that we eat with our eyes, and this is so very true. We need to understand that sight alone simply does not bring us any actual flavor whatsoever. Our mind can be easily tricked. Just look at a box of strawberry pop tarts. We see the wonderfully colorful packaging of beautiful strawberries, and then we taste the pop tart, enjoying that delicious strawberry stuffed pastry. But wait! There are no strawberries in the pop tart whatsoever. That's right, they're made with specific chemicals! And with the visual connection, your mind will think strawberry. Some manufacturers will add the slightest amount of strawberry in order to be able to market it as 'Made with real Strawberries' Even though it's 1% strawberries, and 99% filler and chemicals. But just seeing that 'Made with real Strawberries' on the label, will give you an even stronger reenforcement of the flavor.

Sight can go along way when it comes to the purchasing power of food. We purchase with our eyes. Most fruits and vegetables have been specifically designed to look beautiful. But yet have you noticed that many of the foods now really don't have the flavor that we expect. That's because when it comes to looks, the flavor of the food is not always reflected in appearance.

I'll never forget the joy of picking apples as I grew up in the midwest where they were abundant. We would travel to Uncle Richard's farm to get apples. Now Richard wasn't even an apple farmer, but he had about 6 of the best apple trees for miles around. And let me tell you, these apples were ugly. Ugly as an apple could ever be, with pits and deformities, even the color was an ugly brown. But oh how tasteful they were. Now if these apples were in the grocery stores, nobody would buy them. People associate beauty with flavor, even though that is not always the case.

Sight would certainly have to be the greatest of all the senses when it comes to the absorption of information. Just look at the countless hours we use our eyes for everything from reading, to sightseeing. And when it comes to food, we could spend many hours discovering what sight does to our perception of flavor.

I would like to show you a couple of pictures to give you an example of the power of sight.

First we have this burnt piece of toast. Just looking at it, you already know what it is going to taste like.

Lets look at this next picture of mouthwatering citrus oranges and juice. Once again, you can actually feel your mouth salivating just by looking at a picture.

There is huge marketing power in pictures. Nothing sells food more than an appetizing photo. We need to need to understand that presentation is key to making things taste good. Color is very important, and the best thing about a vegan lifestyle, is that we have the most colorful foods to work with.

Another visual element is the cognitive or post-sensory function of memory. This too is a mystery that I would credit to our Creator. In a nut shell, the visual cortex part of the brain is where objects and images are recognized.

What does this mean when it comes to flavor? Well, it allows the mind to know what food should taste like, based on prior experiences. This can have a great effect on our perception, causing us to be more selective as our expectations of taste are based upon this memory.

For instance, if your mom always served you burnt eggs, you will be accustomed to the flavor of burnt eggs and would expect that flavor when you are served eggs. In fact this particular post-sensory function is a creativity killer. My mom always made us over-easy eggs, and for forty years, that's what I would eat, without variation. My chili tastes exactly like my moms chili. And I had to break away from that complacency in order to make other flavors of chili. To this day I still find myself trending towards the flavors that I was accustomed to growing up. My food resembles what my mom's food used to look like. Fortunately my mom was a fantastic cook, and it is still reflected in my style.

Have you ever had a bad experience with food? I got sick as a child by riding on a four way ferris-wheel. Following that, the only thing I was allowed to consume was peach juice. After a couple of days I was actually allowed to eat a peach. This went on for over a week. It took a good ten years before I ever ate another peach. Even today, I get flashbacks every time I see a peach. Past experiences that are recorded in your mind go a long way to determine your perception of flavor.

You can use this phenomena to your advantage. When you get a flavor that really tastes great in a recipe, your mind will take you right back to it. And after a couple of times, your cooking will become pretty consistent as to what that recipe is supposed to taste like, even when you prepare it without using a recipe.

I still remember my mom's wonderful cinnamon rolls. We could smell the cinnamon and it would attract our attention, but it wasn't until we saw the cinnamon rolls that the anticipation really grew. While all the other senses can produce a partial cognitive memory, it's the visual that really brings the memories back.

I would suggest that when you create a great recipe of your own, take a picture of it. In today's world of technology, there are lots of apps and programs to file recipes. Personally, I still like the simple binders. Just slip a picture into the sleeve, and your memory will kick in when you are ready to make it again.

Hearing

SENSE 3

While hearing may be considered the least of the senses affecting flavor, you will be surprised how hearing actually has an influence on our perception of food. Hearing or 'audition' is the sense of sound perception. Technically it is all about vibrations. Vibrations turned into nerve pulses.

My culinary experiences have used sound in many ways. In fact in the production kitchens, it was sometimes a lack of sound that informed me that the preparation of food was complete. Especially when it came to deep fried fish. The minute I would drop the battered or breaded fish into the fryers, it would create a loud bubbling effect, then it would tone down for a while, and then suddenly the bubbling sound would stop. That's when I knew the fish was done. And the same effect occurs with chicken. And even some vegan foods too. Basically when the food is cooking, moisture escapes, and when this moisture hits the oil it evaporates. When the moisture has all been released, the food is done. These types of signals take time to learn, and it is only by practice that you can achieve an ear for cooking.

Think about some sizzling fajitas. I love serving fajitas on a hot steel plate. When we hear that food as it is presented in front of us, it certainly increases our dining and flavor experiences.

What would chips be without the crunch? The sound you hear when you bite into them triggers a preconceived expectation of what that food should taste like.

I know what a particular food is suppose to sound like, because I have had that food experience before. And if the sound isn't the same, I notice. Is it stale? or over cooked?

Smell

SENSE 4

According to many sources, we have as many as 388 different receptors that can detect a plethora of scents which have the potential to signal the brain. The sense of smell is also another 'chemical' sense. As all the senses are designed for protection, only taste and smell can detect a chemical alert. And if you smell chemicals, big warning flags appear. Interestingly enough, our olfactory receptor neurons in the nose die and regenerate regularly. Often, as we age they quit or slow in their regenerating and we end up with anosmia, or the inability to smell.

When it comes to cooking, the smell or olfaction, plays a huge role. Generally the very first activation is burning . As part of the warning senses, it cautions us of danger. Unfortunately humans have developed an affinity for burnt food. Just look at the fire roasted red peppers, dark brown burnt onions, and burnt cheese even has an appealing flavor.

The problem with overcooking food is that it can create potential toxins and carcinogens. This risk is greatly increased with the addition of oils. And in fact, all meats that are cooked in a pan or on a grill are known to be carcinogenic. Since meat has fat throughout the flesh, it is impossible to cook it without increasing the cancer growth, unless you boil it. But it's not just meats. Many foods will experience the same carcinogens when burned.

Trust the instincts that God has given us. Stay away from the chemically enhanced processed foods. Avoid burning your food. Find other ways to increase flavor and generate that appetizing aroma.

Take garlic for example. It has great aroma. And if you want to take it to an extreme, heat is the solution to cause the garlic aroma to expand. But don't burn it. Just a little water sauté or oven roasting will make the garlic bloom.

Have you even noticed when you have a cold, food just doesn't taste the same? That's because the sense of smell is not working properly.

Allergies and pesticides are other possible factors that can affect your tastebuds. Every single time I go to the California farm belt, I sneeze constantly. I really don't know if it's a pollen in the air, or just the fact that with all that produce, they are spraying an awful lot of chemicals. But it's been consistent. Four tours in a row, and every single time the same thing happens with no relief until I leave. And it does affect my taste.

So as you can see, the sense of smell can have big effects on the flavor of food. As we continue, I will show you ways to take the flavor of the food we eat to the extreme. Even by simply creating an aroma that will make your mouth water.

Touch

SENSE 5

Touch is another sense that many people don't affiliate with flavor. And in reality most of our touch receptors are in our skin or hair follicles. Technically called somatosensation, we have these receptors in our mouth, tongue, and throat too. These receptors can detect the textures of the food we eat.

This is why we always want to be aware of textures. There is a huge variety of textures that can be detected. Some through the hands when we handle food and even more so in the mouth when we eat food. Here is also where we get that traditional perception where, by past experiences, we think we know what texture a food should have. And if that food does not have that texture, it can be disappointing. And this isn't a bad thing, take lettuce for example. We know what the lettuce should feel like in our mouth, and if it has been sitting for too long it will become wilted. Even though none of the other senses will pick up on the product that could already be rotten, the sense of touch will detect it. It's certainly another one of our God given defense mechanisms. We can often feel when a product develops slime on it, and it would certainly be a key indicator that botulism or other harmful bacterias are present.

On the good side, in this book we are going to look at the textures that will enhance your food. Quite often, I am looking for ways to add texture to food to increase the sensation. Salads can be bumped up with crunchy croutons and that's great. But let's add a smooth sensation with some canned beets or avocado. Even salad dressings can provide an incredibly important texture factor. Salad dressing as thick as jello would be a problem.

The texture of the food can also cause your tastebuds to be clogged. Too much flour, too many dry oats. Most people will not be able to eat a bowl of dry oats, regardless how you spice it up.

So as you can see, touch has a lot to do with the flavor and enjoyment of food. We need to first be aware of what most people are expecting, and then see if it can be enhanced without overdoing it.

NOW FOR THE
new senses...

THE SENSE OF
Thought

SENSE 6

This is not the mystical sense that some people claim to possess. But it does connect to the sense of thought, because it actually is 'The Sense of Thought'. When it comes to eating, the sense of thought has a lot to do with our acceptance or rejection of many things, even before we ever smell, see, or taste food.

For example: If I were to suggest a delightful cherry cheesecake, smothered with flambé June berries in a mango reduction, your mouth could actually start tasting the food before we ever presented it to you. As far as you know, it could be the worst cheesecake ever created. And on the other hand, marinated slugs, sautéed in a swamp water brine topped with cricket sprinkles, would probably turn you off so fast that you wouldn't even try it. Even if the flavor was actually incredibly delicious. Your sense of thought has already determined it as inedible.

Consider the sense of thought for a moment as you read a menu. Your mind determines flavors just by reading the description of the entree; Sizzling Fajitas, with red bell peppers and sweet onions, marinated with cajun seasonings, and served with beans and fried rice. Even without the picture, your mind has already determined flavor, and your body has already experienced a physical reactions.

You see, the mind is a very powerful influence when it comes to food and flavor.

The Sixth Sense of thought is largely influenced by our heritage. More often than not, children mimic the lifestyle they grew up with. Obesity, alcoholism and addictions may become generational issues. I grew up with the unhealthy eating habits that the rest of my family adopted and breaking out of those traditions was a challenge. Becoming a healthy vegan quite likely has saved me from diabetes, heart disease and cancer that others in my family have experienced. We were all eating the same chicken, bacon & eggs, hamburgers, milk and cheese, and junk foods that our parents fed us. I expect that I will always have to be mindful and deliberate about choosing the right foods to eat and not falling into the traditional habits I grew up with.

If you are living under the same condition as my family, press forward and overcome. Transforming your life will not only break that generational curse adapted from your parents, it will set a new course for future generations.

The Sixth Sense is also powerful when it comes to people being creatures of habit and convenience.
Bad habits are hard to break especially in today's world of fast food. Quite often there is a false perception of time. I can order a pizza to be delivered in 30 minutes, or I can prepare a meal in half the time. For people who dine out, it may take an hour or more to travel to the sit down restaurant of your choice and have a nice meal. It would not take near the time if you stay at home and cook. And if you do some big batch cooking, you can have meals ready in minutes.

The problem lies in the fact that many people will justify their actions in every way possible, in order to continue living as they please. This is true in many lifestyle decisions. People will succumb to their distorted appetite, rather than submit to what is right and what is good. Quite frankly, in the world we live in, you can find anything on the Internet to justify whatever you want to do, anything you want to believe, or everything you want to eat.

But the bottom line here is that we are often filled with the lies and deceptions that Satan and the world has presented before us. This sixth sense of thought can create a perception of, 'convenience tastes good'. It really does have an effect on how we conduct ourselves, and how we react to the elements in life that are placed before us. The truth of the matter is that most of the foods we encounter today are designed for addiction. Fast food restaurants hire scientists to make their food addictive. These people do not care about your health, and most will do whatever it takes to increase sales. The products they are now trying to sell us are filled with chemicals and we don't even know the extent of harm being done to our bodies when we consume them.

If we take a moment to think about flavor, which is the topic of this book, we must realize that the flavors and appetite that you have right now, are not necessarily your own. More often than not, they are influenced by someone else. Anyone who is a meat eating, cheese loving, processed food consuming individual, is living a lifestyle not necessarily picked by themselves. Their sense of thought, is not really 'their' sense of thought, but one which has been adapted through the influence of others.

When asking most animal consuming individuals to adapt a vegan plant strong lifestyle, it will immediately activate the sixth sense of thought with a pre-determination of a horrible, tasteless, health-depriving nightmare, before they would ever take one bite.

On the other hand, a healthy vegan person who has eaten an array of whole foods that are animal free would cringe at the thought of eating anything so gross as a piece of meat or a glass of animal milk.

In all reality, the real blessing here is that the sixth sense of thought can be trained. And fortunately it can be retrained. If you have been eating an unhealthy lifestyle, it can be reversed. With a little time, commitment, and array of delicious vegan options, you too will transform your sense of thought to adapting the healthy lifestyle you should have been living all along.

THE SENSE OF
Spiritual Discernment

SENSE 7

This sense will always play a role in your life. Although it may not be acknowledged by scientists, it is as real as any of the other senses. In fact it is a sense that has great development potential. The big difference between the sixth sense and the seventh sense is that one is spiritual and one is not. The sixth sense is simply a sense that is an uncontrolled 'reaction' of mind, whereas the seventh sense is a deliberate, thoughtful process and an impression from a higher power.

Think for a moment about morality. Think about right from wrong. We are generally wired to know good from evil and many of our convictions can be traced back to our childhood and how we were raised. Even generations of character development can be traced. What I will believe to the day I die, is that God has given us the Holy Spirit to convict upon us what is right from wrong.

Certainly the best way to develop this Seventh Sense is through prayer and study; praying for discernment. Interestingly enough, the Seventh Sense of Spiritual Discernment is something that Satan is always attacking. He will attack all the senses, but none more than the discernment needed to make good decisions.

A simple example is where Satan will impress upon people that it is okay to lie. Most people know that it is wrong to lie. The Bible says that it is a sin to lie. It's even one of the Ten Commandments that you shall not bear false witness. When a person lies, there is an immediate sense of wrong doing, but over time, one who constantly lies, develops a guilt free conscience. And the sense given by God is replaced with a false justification provided by Satan.

Within the food industry is the greatest of lies and deceptions. There is a need for people to make poor decisions in order for the food industry to make big profits. These companies have become experts at marketing food and beverages to make us think that unhealthy things are okay to consume. Then when you continue to consume these unhealthy products, your mind becomes clouded and unable to discern the way it should. It truly does! Especially when it comes to animal products and sugar. These are often used together and keep you from being clear minded, your brain cells become coated and your appetite rules over good judgment.

This is why I always encourage people to pray for discernment. It is one of the most valuable gifts that we can ever receive from God. With discernment, you can recognize the worldly concepts that you have been tricked into believing. You will start seeing the world in a whole new light, God's light. And it is this God given

discernment, that the food producers are feverishly trying to destroy. Because the smarter people are, the less likely they are to consume unhealthy processed foods. You are going to get healthier physically and you are going to get healthier mentally, and then you are going to have a better connection with God, which will help you make even better decisions. Body, Mind and Spirit. It really is connected all together in a mighty way.

Think about this, When you're tempted to eat a 1,000 calorie, fat laden, sugary dessert, what is going through your mind? Let me guess: "I know I shouldn't eat it. This isn't good for me." The reality is that God is impressing on you to resist. Do you feel guilty after eating it? Of course you do, some more than others. I truly believe that it is a Seventh Spiritual Sense. And once again, these senses are designed by our Creator to help keep us safe and free from harm. People will either listen to these senses, or not and suffer the consequences. Spiritual sense is a protector for our bodies. We just need to listen and obey. I am so thankful I started listening and obeying that still small voice telling me to change my unhealthy lifestyles. Otherwise I might not even be here today.

Interestingly enough, eating is a behavior that comes with reward. People eat unhealthy and receive the immediate reward. That is a difficult temptation to overcome. Especially in today's society, with the constant demand for immediate gratification. But there is a better reward waiting for you when you do resist. You won't get your reward instntly, but with perseverance it will come. As Dr. Hans Diehl says, "Health isn't everything, but without it, everything is nothing." What we put into our mouth is the singular most important factor in how good we feel.

Looking at all of the senses, we can start to understand the role they are all going to play in the rest of this book. I point these out in such great length because flavor has more to do with than just the tastebuds. Connecting the body, mind, and spirit will provide a comprehensive eating experience.

When you are preparing a meal, consider the following questions. Then begin cooking with Simply Incredible Flavor.

THE SIMPLY INCREDIBLE QUESTIONS

OCCASION: What is the main reason for preparing a meal?

WEATHER: What type of foods should be prepared?

DATES: Is it a holiday, or seasonal occasion?

FLAVOR: What does your sense of thought tell you to prepare?

VOLUME: Is this a full meal or snacks?

PRESENTATION: How will you stimulate the sense of vision?

EXTRA: What can you do to show that your guests/family are special to you?

Your Five Tastebuds
PLUS TWO NEW ONES!

Every single one of us has a different set of tastebuds. No two are exactly alike. Some people tend to favor the spicy, while others like the savory or sweet.

With this reality, comes the truth that there is no perfect recipe that will satisfy every palate. I can make the perfect recipe for me and love it, while my wife won't eat a bite.

Here is your first lesson in creating Simply Amazing Flavor. Keep it simple. The less complicated you make it, the more people will love it. I have worked in a lot of restaurants and I have noticed that the more elaborate the chefs made the dishes, the more complaints we would have. Yes, some of them would have spectacular flavor, but the more complex the recipe, the more individuals would say that the dish didn't taste right to them.

There is a rule of thumb in the most successful restaurants in the world of every culture and that is: stick to the basics. If you expand the basics with a little creativity, you're probably going to be fine and have success. Go an extreme and you will definitely have failures.

Because of my profession, I will often go three steps beyond what should ever be done. But in the process, I learn more that I can share with you. So stick to the basics, then add your own flair. Put a little wow factor in the dish that will set your recipe apart from the standard acceptable version.

There are five standard senses to the tastebuds plus two more that I am adding.

THE FIVE COMMON TASTES ARE,

SWEET   SOUR   SALTY   SAVORY   BITTER

But that is just not enough for me.

Ok, DRUM ROLL please………. The two added senses of taste are about to be revealed. First is the 'Taste of Heat'. And I'm not talking about temperature heat, I'm talking spicy heat.

Yes the 'Taste of Heat'! Certainly one of the most important elements in cooking. The taste buds will pick-up on heat faster than any other taste. Heat is an important factor to the tastebuds, and it actually is a sense that we need to be aware of when it comes to culinary excellence.

Think about this, when you experience heat, it's not a flavor. Yes, there are flavors in heat, but it's not connected with the degree of heat. Some foods have a lot more heat with relatively no flavor whatsoever. In fact you can get the exact flavor in some dishes with or without the spicy heat. In all reality, the degree of heat can also change the flavor, where changing the flavor will seldom change the degree of heat.

As we continue, you will see where this element of heat will be an extremely valuable tool in creating Simply Incredible Flavor. Just think about garlic, for example. There are really mild forms of garlic and then there are garlics that will burn your tongue. You can take a spicy garlic, and sauté it. It will lose the heat, but increase the garlic flavor. Look at how our bodies react to heat. People who eat something extremely spicy will actually start sweating, their face will turn red. Even if the heat is coming from a spice seed that has no flavor.

Are you beginning to understand the concept of heat and flavor? I suggest keeping this in mind when you are creating any recipe. What is your desired degree of heat? You consider this with salt, and with sugar. And when you start doing this with heat, you will start getting Simply Incredible Flavor.

The second added sense is a little more subtle but extremely important to understand when it comes to how the tastebuds work, and that is the 'Taste of Fat'. Fat absolutely needs to be added to the equation of how the tastebuds work. Fat affects the tastebuds in more ways than one. The oils we cook with may have different flavors when it comes to savory, salty, or bitter.

Then there is the element of texture. Technically the scientists will attempt to put this into the sense of 'touch'. And with good reason. We feel textures, we don't taste textures. If something is gritty, or smooth, we feel it. And if something is greasy, we will certainly feel it too.

There is also an aroma that can be picked up from oil, especially when the oil or fat is burned. Take a steak. Would it really be that good without the fat? Without the charred fat? Fat is flavor. It is not necessarily always the flavor of the fat, but the way the fat is manipulated to create a new dimension to the food all together.

So call it what you will; call it the touch sense, or call it a flavor detecting tastebud. I'm simply calling it the fat tastebuds. Because fat is in a league of it's own.

When you coat your tastebuds with fat, they cannot do their job nearly as well as they can if the fat is not present. Amazingly, the fat from animal products can coat your tastebuds for weeks. And that will really affect the way your food tastes. Eliminating the animal products is probably the best thing you could possibly do in order to get your tastebuds working right and get the true flavor of the food the way God created it.

And the taste of fat goes way beyond just your flavor experience. It will affect your entire body. People who are not accustomed to eating any fat, and then eat something that is really fatty often have immediate

digestive issues. High fat diets cause acne breakouts and clogged cells that keep the body from getting the right amount of oxygen they need. Then there are the blocked arteries, and killer diseases like cancer, and heart disease and stroke. Type 2 Diabetes develops as a direct result of dietary fat. That's right! Reversing diabetes is simply a matter of eliminating fats.

In the next chapter, we will be going over all of the tastebuds, and how we can use them to get Simply Incredible flavor.

SWEET   SOUR   SALTY   SAVORY   BITTER   FAT   HEAT

TASTEBUD FACTS

So is there an account for good taste? The fact is that genes influence our taste. Give two preschoolers a piece of broccoli. One child eats it and the other takes a bite and pushes it away with disgust. Why? Well, researchers decided to create the concept of taste genetics and identified two categories, tasters and non-tasters. Eventually they expanded the non-tasters and tasters to include super-tasters, and bitter-tasters.

This is where I again get a real kick out of the so called 'science'. 'Nutrigenetics' is the new buzzword in the industry for the study of how the tastebuds work. in addition, 'nutrigenomics' refers to the influence of diet on genes, mainly related to health and disease states such as obesity, cancer, and heart disease.

Most dietitians work on the premise that eating is a behavioral issue determined by culture, background, individual life experiences and even religion. But now there are indications that genes have a huge role in diet, and yet they are weak on showing the correlation that diet has on genes. The main purposes of the field of nutrigenetics is for the manufacture and sale of processed foods. Their focus is to determine how to make food more palatable, and more addictive. Or in many cases, how can we shut down the tastebuds so that people will not be able to detect the taste of the chemicals used for preserving the food. Maybe we could shut down one part of a tastebud to manipulate an enhanced reaction.

Remember that the body would put up a warning flag if it was to detect any chemicals that would be harmful. But through science, these particular receptors can actually be shut off by simply adding another chemical. But then we might need to add another chemical to hide that one. And the trail of experimenting continues until the perfect combination is met to create the most addictive product without the detection of the chemicals used to create it.

Now here is the big kicker. The more animal fats that surround your tastebuds, the less flavor they will be able to detect. This factor also plays a role in the needed seasonings. I was a big meat and cheese eater, and when I went vegan, it was very difficult to eat. The food I was eating tasted horrible. Oatmeal, beans, rice, who wants to eat these things? It helped that I knew a little about how to season food. But many people would consider healthy food equivalent to eating cardboard. That's one of the reasons for this book; to show you how to incorporate Simply Incredible Flavor into your food. Still the point that I need to make here is the fact that the manufacturers and restaurants deliberately manipulate the food, intentionally adding additional fat and chemicals to their products in order to block the tastebuds from doing their job.

Before I changed my diet, I would never eat salads. In fact, the only way I would eat lettuce is if it were on a cheeseburger. Amazingly, now I eat salads with no dressing on them what so ever. It really does take about a month for your tastebuds to clear up. Then, when they're not smothered with all that animal fat, your tastebuds will start doing the job they're supposed to be doing. Everything will taste so much better.

You will also be able to detect the presence of food that you should not be eating. Greasy food will not have such an appealing taste. And not only will your tastebuds clear up, you will get that animal fat off the receptors that detect smell. Now I cringe at the offensive smell that permeates from a butcher shop. When you eliminate all those animal fats, and reduce even so called healthy fats, even your nose receptors will clear up, giving you a far better sense of smell which will enhance your flavor experience.

Eliminating animal fats will result in all of your food tasting different. Beans will have flavor, rice will have flavor, even plain tofu will actually have flavor. I initially added a lot more flavor to foods than I do now. If you're a meat eater, you will definitely need to jack up the spices for a little while. Just keep taking those steps. Major steps will result in major success in no time at all.

Let's get on to more depth about the seven tastes.

SWEET   SOUR   SALTY   SAVORY   BITTER   FAT   HEAT

Sweet

TASTE 1

I could write an entire book on the subject of sweet. But for the sake of time, we are going to cover just the basics and what you need to know. First of all, the sweet tastebuds which have been traditionally known to be on the tip of your tongue, are actually all over your tongue, and even on the roof of your mouth. This also applies to the other taste buds as well. While they may have a predominantly stronger presence in one area or another, none of them are exclusively confined to any particular region. These sweet tastebuds are extremely weak in detecting anything other than sweet. Sweet is sweet. And while these tastebuds can detect variations of sweetness, most of the differences detected between different sweeteners is discovered through a multitude of tastebud receptors.

Brown sugar tastes like brown sugar because of the bitter detection from the bitter buds. The sweetness of an orange is detected by the nose, which will send the signal to your brain, determining it's an orange sweetness. Of course without the sense of smell, you will be simply detecting a sweetness. Keep this in mind when creating healthy sweet treats without the sugar. Sugar free sweeteners such as Stevia, or xylitol can give you a sweet sensation, but when you add some zest, or molasses, or even a concentrated essential oil, then you will create Simply Incredible Flavor.

There is a big difference between the type of sugars, and the type of sweeteners. And there are countless sugar substitutes. Most people growing up prior to the 70's, never had artificial sweeteners. And interestingly enough, when those chemically created sweeteners came out, we knew they were fake. I could literally taste the chemical compounds and a warning signal went to my brain cautioning my body to react. As I mentioned before, that's the body's natural warning system to inform us of poisons. It's just like counterfeit money, Most people are so familiar with money that they can spot a counterfeit. Experts are trained to know everything there is to know about the real money, so that when they do come across a fake, to them it sticks out like a sore thumb.

Today, the children are growing up on chemical sweeteners. Their body has never experienced the real thing exclusively in order to have a comparative understanding. They have literally become desensitized to these dangerous chemicals from birth. And unlike counterfeit experts, the current generation has grown up on so many different combinations of chemical sweeteners and real sweetness that their taste buds will have much more difficulty telling the difference.

We also must understand that the food manufacturers have been studying the human body for years. Chemically altered foods are far more advanced today than they ever were when artificial sweeteners first entered the food chain.

THE THREE MAJOR FORMS OF SUGAR

The three major forms of sugar are sucrose, fructose, and lactose. Sucrose comes primarily from sugar cane or sugar beets. Fructose come from fruits and starchy plants. And lactose comes from dairy products. A simple way to remember would be, if it ends in -ose, it's a type of sugar. There are many other sugar names like maltose and dextrose.

Before we go any further in this complex understanding of sugar and the tastebuds, I should quickly explain 'glucose'. Glucose is generally known for its foundation of the 'Glycemic Index (GI). This index measures how much your blood glucose levels increase in the two to three hours after eating foods. While every body can react a little differently, table sugar, or sucrose, has a GI of 60.

So when it comes to sucrose, glucose, and fructose there are some common characteristics. Probably most important is, they can all be fuel for your body. Energy for your cells. They also store away as fat if the body doesn't burn them up.

Like all complex sugars, sucrose breaks down into glucose and fructose. The glucose is transported by insulin to the cells for energy. Complex sugars like sucrose or lactose also break down into fructose. And this is where it gets confusing because isn't fructose a natural sugar from fruits and plants? Well it is, but we still don't want a massive amount of fructose either. Fructose doesn't even spike blood glucose levels the way other sugars do. But don't be fooled. Because fructose travels to the liver where it gets converted into triglycerides. These triglycerides are fats that are directly associated to heart disease. And for all you people who want to lose weight, excess fructose converted to triglycerides, not burned, actually increase the size of your fat cells and allow you to gain weight even quicker.

So now that you know how sugars are broken down in the body, let's look at some of the different sweeteners that we use in cooking to get Simply Incredible Flavor.

TYPES OF SWEETENERS

White Sugars

Brown Sugars

Liquid Sugars

Sugar Alcohols

Sugar Substitutes

Natural Sugars

WHITE SUGARS

Regular white table sugar is primarily made from cane and or sugar beets. While it is a sucrose type of sugar, the basic components are 50% glucose and 50% fructose. These sugars provide empty calories and zero nutritional value.

Also be aware of the 'Crystalline Fructose'. This is a finer sugar that is used in your pre-packaged goods such as cakes, puddings, gelatin, and powdered drinks. This specially manufactured sugar is made totally from fructose, and can certainly have more harmful health effects.

BROWN SUGARS

Brown sugars can vary in processing methods. The benefit is that brown sugars have not had the molasses chemically or physically removed. The least processed brown sugar would be the Panela or Rapadura sugars, that still have the minerals and enzymes in tact.

Light and Dark Brown Sugars are generally cane sugars that chemically remove the molasses and then reintroduce the molasses syrup. This is what gives it a unique flavor.

Light brown sugars are generally used for baking cakes, glazes and condiments. While the dark brown sugar is used when a more robust flavor is needed, such as baked beans, and gingerbreads. Both light and dark brown sugars can be equally substituted cup for cup in most recipes.

Brown Palm Sugar is different in both texture and flavor from the brown cane sugars. It may still contain trace minerals and generally does not have a strong molasses flavor.

Evaporated Cane Juice is exactly that, filtered and clarified cane juice that is heated to evaporate the moisture and leave you with granular crystals. These crystals retain their molasses and give it a stronger flavor.

Sucanat contains less sucrose which makes it not nearly as sweet. It cannot simply replace regular sugar in equal parts for recipes. The texture is grainy and can also cause problems with baking.

Turbinado Sugar is a lightly processed raw sugar, where only the surface molasses has been rinsed off This sugar can be a easily substituted for regular sugar in equal portions and does not have the extreme molasses flavor. The most popular brand would be 'Sugar in the Raw'.

Muscovado Sugar is a very dark brown sugar with strong molasses flavor. Minimally processed, this sugar is slightly coarser and stickier than regular brown sugar.

Demerara Sugar is a much lighter brown sugar with large golden crystals. Most popular in England, these crystals are often used in teas, coffees, or hot cereals.

Rapadura Sugar is the least processed of all the cane sugars. This brick formed and dried sugar cane juice is healthier than any other sugar and is rich in dietary iron. In many other countries it is the cheapest sweetener available, yet in America, the novelty of healthy sugar has inflated the price to ridiculous levels.

Palm Sugar is the old school sugar, dating back thousands of years. Originally made from the sap of Palmyra Palm, this sugar has migrated into Date Palms, and Coconut Palm trees. You will find a lot of Asian recipes using palm sugars because of their availability and wonderful molasses flavor.

Date Sugar is the tricky one to pay attention to. Palm sugars from date trees will be sold as date sugar, when in reality there are no dates in the sugar. There is 'real' date sugar available that is made from pulverized dried dates. The difference is that real date sugar will not dissolve in water, where the palm sugar sold as date sugar will.

LIQUID SUGARS

The most popular form of liquid sugar is the dreaded High-fructose Corn Syrup (HFCS), now officially renamed simply "Fructose", and it's running mate Corn Syrup. They are not the same. HFCS is comprised of 45% glucose and 55% fructose, while corn syrup is simply glucose.

In a nut shell, corn syrup glucose is dumped directly into your bloodstream, ready for your tissues to soak it up and use it as energy. But when it comes to HFCS, the fructose is absorbed in your small intestine but sent off to your liver for processing before it hits your bloodstream. When too much fructose enters your liver, whatever cannot be processed will be converted into fat. This can causes major problems for most people.

But don't be fooled by thinking that corn syrup is good for you. Both are added sugars that the body has trouble processing. It is worth mentioning that many cancers love to fuel up on any of these sugars for their midnight snack.

Unfortunately high fructose corn syrup (Fructose) is a relatively inexpensive sweetener that is used in thousands of processed foods. The financial gain from using this product, at the expense of health, has contributed to the increase of obesity, cancers, heart disease, and Type II Diabetes.

Avoiding High Fructose Corn Syrup is strongly recommended, and even regular corn syrup should be avoided. Sticking to more natural sugars would be a far better choice for sweet options.

Agave Syrup has been heavily marketed as a healthy natural alternative to sugar, when in reality it is a highly processed syrup that has even been banned by the Glycemic Index Institute because of its consistently harmful results on studied participants. Agave syrups can contain in excess of 90% fructose, and this does not occur naturally. You might as well call it High Fructose Agave Syrup. It is that similar to HFCS. Agave is not even naturally sweet, but through the science of manufacturing, a money gem was created. I've personally used it and had it in many recipes when it first came on the market. But as I have learned more about the dangers of it, I have since taken it out of my recipes.

Yacon Syrup is native to South America. This syrup is derived from the roots of the Yacon plant, and some studies source it as a good source of antioxidants.

The big plus here is that it is glucose-free, making it attractive to diabetics. But don't jump for joy yet. This sweetener has large amounts of fructose, so the same concerns about the health effects of fructose apply.

You can use Yacon syrup in place of maple syrup or molasses, and works well to sweeten beverages. Yet there is also the price factor, at sometimes $20.00 per 8 oz jar, it is definitely a more expensive option.

Rice Syrup is a natural sweetener which is made from cooked brown rice, turning the rice starches into sugars. It can have a little nutty flavor with a very light sweetness, so experiment first when substituting for honey or molasses. It does well for desserts and fruit, and a lot of baking needs. I think you will be pleased with the pleasant taste.

Molasses is used primarily in baking because of its deep rich flavor. This deep brown to black syrup is generally the by product of the processing of beet sugar or cane sugar. It is still made up of glucose and fructose, and has the same amount of calories as sugar. Gingerbread just wouldn't be the same without it.

Maple Syrup is definitely a syrup choice for me. Fewer calories than honey with a higher concentration of minerals, and even a source of zinc and manganese.

When you tap a maple tree, sap it flows as a clear and almost tasteless syrup. When 39 gallons of syrup are boiled and the water is evaporated, you end up with one gallon of delicious maple syrup. Boil out more water and you can create maple cream, maple butter, or maple sugar.

Maple syrup is graded and for those who are familiar with the different grades, you may know that the grading system has recently changed. Currently there is simply Grade A which is divided into four different categories from Golden Light Amber to Very Dark Amber.

Honey can come in several forms such as honey comb, honey powder, raw, pasteurized and as many flavors as there are flowers. Some vegans claim that honey is an animal product, while others understand that this byproduct carries no harmful animal protein, cholesterol, or fat. With 64 calories per tablespoon, it is definitely not a weight loss product.

Standard grocery store honey has been heated and filtered. While creating a more consistent product with a longer shelf life, it also destroys vitamins and enzymes. Since all honey is mainly glucose and fructose, we need to take caution just the same as any other sugar products.

You may also be interested in the Manuka honey made from the Manuka flowers in New Zealand. They are thought to have the highest nutrition and greatest healing power. True differences you can experience or great marketing for higher profit? You be the judge. Personally, I love every single type of honey just the same.

Sorghum Syrup was a popular inexpensive sweetener produced from the sorghum cane grown across much of the southern United States. But the manufacturing processes of sugar cane and beet sugar became far more cost effective. It is experiencing a comeback with the health conscious because sorghum is highly-nutritious, gluten-free, and an ancient cereal grain that is minimally processed into syrup. It is also thought to contains lots of antioxidants, vitamins and trace minerals.

Sorghum syrup has a very unique mild flavor, making it a great substitute for molasses, honey or maple syrup.

SUGAR ALCOHOLS
Xylitol, Erythritol, Mannitol, Sorbitol and Glycerine (Glycerol)

Sugar Alcohols can occur naturally in plants. Many are chemically or biologically extracted such as sorbitol from corn syrup or mannitol from seaweed. The easy rule of thumb to remember sugar alcohol is names ending in 'ol' such as Xylitol, Erythritol, or Glycerol.

There are pro's and con's to sugar alcohols. First, they are not completely absorbed by the body. Because of this, they don't elevate blood sugar levels and that can be a big plus for diabetics. But because they are not completely absorbed, sugar alcohols can ferment in the intestines. This can cause bloating, gas, or diarrhea, and can also cause problems for people with IBS or digestive issues.

Sugar alcohols don't promote tooth decay like sugar does, so you will find them in a lot of the sugar free gum and mints. And even though they have less calories, they are generally not as sweet. Some are less than 60% of the sweetness of sugar, thus making them difficult to work with when it comes to cooking.

And remember that sugar alcohols like Xylitol are extremely toxic for dogs.

Swerve is the latest 'natural sweetener' to hit the market. Swerve is made from a combination of erythritol, oligosaccharides and natural flavors. It has excellent baking and cooking functionality, and even has the ability to brown and caramelize!

Unfortunately it is still a highly manufactured sweetener made from sugar alcohol. The jury is still out when it comes to it's actual safety. As you will find with many products, profit can swing recommendations. Then, in a few years, when independent groups start testing the product, evidence may contradict prior advice

SUGAR SUBSTITUTES

There has been an array of sugar substitutes introduced over the years. All of them try to introduce claims of being better than sugar. Whether it be calorie free, or natural, they all come with questionable downsides.

Saccharin is the oldest artificial sweetener often sold under the name Sweet & Low. It is most commonly used in diet soft drinks and candies. You can also find it in medicine and toothpaste to improve the flavor.

Aspartame is sold under a number of different product names, including Equal and NutraSweet. It too is used to sweeten diet soft drinks and candies. It is 180 times sweeter than sugar. When heated, it looses a lot of its sweetness, and there is also a unpleasant aftertaste.

Sucralose is sold under the name Splenda. It is made from refined sugar which has a molecule of chlorine artificially added to it so it is not properly absorbed by the body.

All three of these are completely artificial, chemical sweeteners. They are generally made by highly complex manufacturing processes with fossil-fuels. Each one of them has been linked to cancer, digestive problems, and chronic illnesses in numerous studies. I would recommend avoiding all of them.

NATURAL SUGARS

Here is just a small handful of my favorite ways to get truly natural sweetness. There are many deceptive claims of 'natural' in marketing, but I'm sure you will get the message when you see where I go to satisfy my sweet tooth. And don't forget all the dried fruits too. Raisins, dates, and dried cherries are a great source of truly natural sugars.

MY TOP TEN SWEETS

» APPLES

Rather it be crunching into a fresh apple, or breaking it down into applesauce, apples have a lot of sweetness for the calories.

» BANANAS

This on-the-go fruit is a good source of fiber, potassium, and vitamin C. And brown bananas are a lot sweeter. That's when the starches turn into sugars.

» BEETS

Beets are easy to prepare and can help you maintain your blood sugar while satisfying your need for good sugar.

» CARROTS

Boiled or fresh, carrots pack a lot of satisfying crunch, along with good sugar.

» DATES

As one of the sweetest fruits, dates are rich in carbohydrates and provide your body with a tasty source of energy.

» GRAPES

What a wonderfully sweet alternative to processed sugars. Not only sweet, but also packed with antioxidants.

» HONEY

Honey is definitely one of my favorite ways to get sweetness. Sweeter than refined sugar, you may need less to obtain the desired taste.

» PINEAPPLES

When you crave something sweet, try pineapple! It packs a lot of sugar in small amounts.

» PRUNES

Prunes are a great source of antioxidants as well as potassium. This fiber rich dose of sweetness makes it a super good choice.

» STEVIA

One of my favorite all time sweeteners is stevia. This zero calorie leaf is 15 to 30 times sweeter than sugar. Be careful, If you use too much, it can leave a bitter taste. It comes in powders of white or green, liquids of every flavor, and you can even buy 10 pound bags of whole dried stevia leaves which are great for tea.

Salty

TASTE 2

Evidence suggests that too much salt is bad for you. But on the flip side, not enough salt can be very harmful too. Salt enhances the flavor of food and adding salt to food actually helps certain molecules in the food be more easily released into the air. This helps with the aroma which is important in our perception of taste. That's right, salt makes food smell better.

Salt also has been shown to help suppress the bitter taste. So adding a bit of salt won't just enhance the flavor but will also decrease the bitter taste perception in any given food. For instance, this is one of the reasons why salt is often sprinkled on grapefruit before eating.

Adding salt to sweet or sour things will not suppress sweet or sour flavors as with bitter flavors, but it will help balance out the taste a bit by making the perceived flavor less one dimensional. It expands the sensation, for example: sugary candies or lemons.

Adding salt to water will raise the temperature it boils at and lower the temperature it will freeze at. This is helpful in cooking pastas. And can aid in making both frozen beverages and ice-cream.

TOP 10 TYPES OF SALT

Table Salt: Is refined salt mined from underground salt deposits. Table salt contains more sodium chloride than sea salt. (97% to 99%) This is what you usually find in salt shakers at dining tables and in restaurants. Most table salts contain additives, anti-caking agents, and iodine, an essential nutrient.

Kosher Salt: Kosher salt would have to be considered the chef's choice for salt. It dissolves easily, and compliments smooth flavor when whole. And because of it's unique mildness, it is actually quite forgiving if you happen to add a little too much. Kosher salt, originates from either the sea or the earth. It is so named for its use in the preparation of meat according to Jewish dietary guidelines.

Sel Gris: This salt is harvested from salt evaporation ponds. Named 'grey salt' in French. It is also known as Celtic sea salt. It is a coarse sea salt. Moist, granular, and chunky, Sel Gris is used as both a cooking salt and finishing salt. It's great for roasted root vegetables.

Gros Sel: The French named 'large salt'. Keep it in a salt grinder for freshly ground sea salt.

Flake Salt: Flake salt is used as a finishing salt for fresh foods such as salads.

Fleur de Sel: In French 'The Flower of Salt'. This delicate, irregular crystals gently dissolve, making it a great finishing salt. Try it on vegetables.

Hawaiian Sea Salt: This salt can be fine or coarse grained and can be either red or black. Red Hawaiian sea salt gets its color from a natural mineral called 'Alaea', a volcanic red clay, while black Hawaiian sea salt gets its color from the addition of charcoal. It is full of trace minerals, and works great for a visual appeal as well as a dissolving salt.

Smoked Salt: This salt is slow-smoked over a wood fire to infuse the crystals with a deep, smokey flavor. This makes it ideal for grilled vegetables.

Seasoned Salt: Seasoned salt is exactly that, seasoned salt. There are countless varieties of seasoned salts out there and every one may be used to create a unique flavor. You can also make your own seasoned salts at home.

Himalayan Salt: Hand-mined from the ancient sea salt deposits in the Pakistan Khewra Salt Mines, Himalayan salt is rich in minerals and believed to be one of the purest salts available. It ranges in color from pure white to shades of pink and deep red. You may see it hand cut into slabs and used as a surface for serving food. Due to its ability to hold specific temperatures for an extended period of time, these slabs can be used for anything from serving cold ice cream to cooking vegetables. Himalayan salt can also be used as a cooking or finishing salt and is also popular for use in spa treatments. It is simply a great all around salt.

Sour

TASTE 3

Sour foods brighten a dish, and create that Simply Incredible Flavor that may have been lacking. Think of a splash of lime on an avocado or guacamole. Even tomatoes and many berries add the sourness needed to perk up a dish. The first thing we will probably need to look at is some of the foods that bring on the sour.

THE TOP SOUR FOODS

ASCORBIC ACID:
it tastes like unsweetened Vitamin C and is great for adding a punch of sour orange flavor without the liquid.

CITRIC ACID:
use citric acid as you would salt – a pinch here and there can add a dramatic tartness to anything. This a great secret weapon for Simply Incredible Flavor!

CRANBERRIES

GRAPEFRUIT JUICE

KIMICHI

KUMQUATS

LEMONGRASS

LEMONS

LEMON JUICE

LIMES

LIME JUICE

LEMONS, PRESERVED

PICKLES OR PICKLE WATER

RHUBARB

SAUERKRAUT

SOUR CREAM

TART ORANGE JUICE

TAMARIND: everyone should keep some tamarind on hand. It adds a great complex sourness that goes very well with things like dried chilies.

TOMATO

VINEGARS: It's great to have a few vinegars in your pantry. Vinegars I recommend include apple cider, balsamic, and rice.

WHAT'S THE DIFFERENCE BETWEEN SOUR AND BITTER?

Many people are confused about this area, and how it affects your culinary flavors. Bitterness is more harsh, while sour is not near as sharp.

Some people really need a hands on training test. For starters, you could take a grapefruit and taste it. The grapefruit will be sour. Now try a piece of the rind, which will be bitter, and chew in it. Do this several times and you will notice the differences. This is a great learning tool to help understand your tastebuds.

WHEN TO ADD MORE SOURNESS:

If the dish tastes too sweet or spicy or too bland, You can add a little sour to balance it out.

HOW TO FIX A DISH THAT'S TOO SOUR:

Add sweetness. For vegetables, try roasting or grilling them. The heat cuts some of the bitterness, and can smooth them out.

Savory

TASTE 4

Savory taste, or 'Umami', the technical term, is described as the tastebuds of broth or meaty flavors. Interestingly enough these taste receptors are specific to 'glutamate'. But don't fear that you need to consume a bunch of monosodium glutamate (MSG), we will get plenty of this delightful glutamate without some manufactured chemical.

MSG gets a bad rap in America where only certain people have a bad reaction to it. I personally have slight unpleasant side effects. Other people get much worse reactions. In other countries, like Asia for example, people can eat it every day without ever having problems.

Then there was the rumor put out there that glutamate and hundreds of other foods we eat are excitotoxins. A term coined and claiming to cause brain damage. The fear mongers sold millions of dollars worth of books and pills stating if you don't take their pills, you're going to die. While there was some truth to the manufactured glutamate, the natural glutamates were shown to have none of the damages these carnival doctors were pushing. It was simply truth mingled with error in order to scare people into sales.

In reality there are hundreds of studies showing the absolute necessity of glutamate for the body and brain function. It actually aids these receptors and neurotransmitters in the brain and all over the body.

Vegetables offer satisfying savory flavors. They contain large amounts of glutamic acid or other specific amino acids. Their extreme savory capabilities are what makes them so popular with chefs who want to create Simply Incredible Flavor.

THE BEST SAVORY FOODS

Foods high in glutamic acid or other specific amino acids

- » ALMONDS
- » APRICOTS
- » ASPARAGUS
- » AVOCADOS
- » BANANAS
- » BARLEY
- » BEANS, ALL
- » BROCCOLI
- » CACAO

- » CARROTS
- » CAULIFLOWER
- » CASHEWS
- » CHICKPEAS
- » CORN
- » CHIA SEEDS
- » GARLIC
- » GRAINS, WHOLE
- » GRAINS, SPROUTED

- » GRAPE JUICE
- » HEMP SEEDS
- » LEGUMES
- » MUSHROOMS
- » MUSHROOMS, SHITAKE
- » ONION
- » PEAS
- » POTATOES, ALL
- » PUMPKINS

- » RICE, ALL
- » RYE
- » QUINOA
- » SOY
- » TOMATO
- » WALNUTS
- » WHEAT
- » WHEAT GLUTEN

Bitter

TASTE 5

Defined: having a strong and often unpleasant flavor that is the opposite of sweet. Bitter is often avoided because of the initial shock. Just look at cranberries, or cocoa, or even kale. But interestingly enough, bitter food equals healthy food. In most cases, you will find benefits to bitter food, HUGE benefits!

Bitter food helps in the absorption of nutrients. They help cleanse the body with sulfur-based compounds that produce the natural detoxification the body needs. They actually help fight free radicals in the body and boost the immune system.

A great dieting reality is that bitter food also stimulates the metabolism, helping your body lose weight, with green tea topping the list.

Culinary wise, bitter balances the tastebuds especially when it comes to sugar, actually helping the sweets from being too overpowering. And bitter greens can actually be addictive. The more we eat, the more we want. You might get an overload of bitter at one sitting telling you that's enough, which is a physical defense mechanism but then in no time at all, you want more.

POPULAR BITTER FOODS AND HERBS

- ARUGULA
- BARLEY
- BASIL
- BITTER MELON
- CHOCOLATE, DARK
- CILANTRO
- COFFEE
- DANDELION
- DILL
- EGGPLANT, JAPANESSE
- FENUGREEK SEEDS
- HORSERADISH
- JICAMA
- KALE
- LEAFY GREENS
- LETTUCE
- PARSLEY
- RADISH
- SESAME
- TURMERIC
- WATERCRESS

Fat

TASTE 6

Fat is the flavor that has attracted chefs for centuries. The problem is that most chef's have a weakness when it comes to cooking anything healthy, especially when it comes to avoiding oil. The best doctors in the world will tell you that your daily consumption of fat calories should be less than 10%. Some doctors recommend as low as 5%.

Many doctors now know that fat is the cause of type 2 diabetes. And if you have type 2 diabetes, it can be reversed in a matter of weeks by simply eliminating all animal products and reducing the consumption of oils, including olive oil and coconut oil.

There are good fats and there are bad fats. But we can not simply assume that because it is a good fat, we should over indulge. There are essential fats, and non essential fats. In all reality what you need to do is eat the olive not the olive oil. Eat the coconut, not the coconut oil. Eat the corn, not the corn oil.

According to the USDA, the national average in America for the consumption of edible oils is 10.2 pounds per person - per month. That's over 1,200 calories a day that the average person consumes, just in oil alone. That's not counting all the fat in the animal meats, and milk, and cheese. You see we are getting absolutely bombarded by fats. Especially in the manufactured foods, and restaurant chains who hire scientists to do whatever it takes to make their food addictive. And guess what? The fat makes food addictive.

When it comes to cooking, fat is flavor. And I will suggest that you get your fats from the whole foods, and not the processed foods. And if you need to use a little oil, use very little. There are alternatives to using oil. Applesauce and mashed bananas are great substitutes for getting moisture into your baked items without using oils. Do a water sauté, rather than an oil sauté. And I love to use avocados for spreads.

FATS TO USE IF YOU MUST

USE CAUTIOUSLY

» **AVOCADOS**

» **COCONUT**

» **CORN**

» **FLAX SEEDS**

» **NUTS, ALL**

» **OLIVES**

» **SUNFLOWER SEEDS**

RARELY USE

» **AVOCADO OIL**

» **COCONUT OIL**

» **FLAX SEED OIL**

» **NUT BUTTERS, ALL**

» **OLIVE OIL**

NEVER USE

» **ANIMAL FATS**

» **VEGETABLE OILS, ALL**

Heat

TASTE 7

There are two different types of 'heat' when it comes to achieving Simply Incredible Flavor. The first is temperature. Temperature is critically important. Pay attention to the temperature outside, hot soups go well on a cold winter day, and cold crisp fruits and vegetables are tastier in the summer months. Then there is the traditional familiarity of what temperature food is supposed to be served, Hot, warm, cool, or cold.

Second there is the other 'heat' which is the heat that is an actual tastebud, and not the temperature kind of heat. There is a lot more to it than just dumping hot sauce on your food. Many spices may be used to create heat.

Let's take a quick look at culture: In Chinese cuisine, Szechuan food tends to be spicy from chili oil and Sichuan peppers. In Japanese cuisine, spicy condiments such as wasabi and shichimi are popular heat sources. Thai dishes also use a lot of chiles. South Indian cuisine tends to be much spicier than North Indian with lots of red chiles and dried chili powder. Jamaican food uses scotch bonnet peppers. Mexican culture makes use of hot peppers such as habanero and jalapeño. Cajun dishes use spice blends with cayenne, paprika and chile peppers. And most every culture uses garlic which can have some heat. Simple black and white pepper is one of the easiest ways to provide a little heat. Ginger is spicy too, but doesn't have a long lingering heat on the palette.

 I want to caution you to start small. You can always add more spice later but you can't take it away if you put in too much. It might also be a good idea to serve the heat on the side rather than mixed in the dish. That way every person can heat it up to their own liking.

The last concept is to balance the heat. Many Mexican dishes will be served with sour cream to 'cool it down'. Spicy Indian food might be served with cucumbers. Coconut milk goes great with curry. And Cajun beans will generally always be served on a mild rice.

HERE ARE SOME OF MY FAVORITE HEAT SOURCES

» ALLSPICE

» BIRDS EYE CHILI PEPPERS

» BLACK PEPPER

» CAYENNE PEPPER

» CHILI OIL

» CHILE PEPPERS

» CINNAMON, KORINTJE

» CRUSHED RED PEPPER

» CURRY POWDER

» CHILE POWDER

» FRANKS OR DURKEY RED HOT

» GARLIC

» GINGER

» HORSERADISH

» HABANERO PEPPERS

» HARISSA

» JALAPENO PEPPERS

» NEW MEXICO CHILI PEPPERS

» PEPPERS

» POBLANO PEPPERS

» RED PEPPER

» SALSAS

» SERRANO PEPPERS

» SRIRACHA

» TABASCO

» WASABI

» WHITE PEPPER

Spices + HERBS

There are hundreds of herbs and spices but these are the basics. And in all reality, this is all you need to achieve Simply Incredible Flavor. Sometimes people try to complicate cooking far too much. And regardless of whether you use fresh or dried, these are still the best pairings.

 Allspice

A dried ground fruit from a West Indian tree. Similar to cloves; more pungent and deep flavored. Best used in spice mixes, and baking.

GOOD — These items go well with this food.

- beans
- beats
- cabbage
- Caribbean cuisine
- carrots
- chickpeas
- chili peppers
- cloves
- coriander
- curry
- eggplant
- English cuisine
- garlic
- grains
- Indian cuisine
- ketchup
- mace
- Mexican cuisine
- mushrooms
- mustard
- Native American Cuisine
- nutmeg
- nuts
- oats
- onions
- pepper
- pineapple
- rice
- rosemary
- salsa
- sauces
- sauerkraut
- soups
- spinach
- sweet potatoes
- thyme
- tomatoes
- turnips
- vegetables
- wheat

BETTER — Even better pairing.

- **baked items**
- **breads**
- **cake**
- **cinnamon**
- **fruits**
- **ginger**
- **Latin American cuisine**
- **Middle Eastern cuisine**
- **squash, winter**

BEST — The WOW factor!

- **APPLES**
- **PUMPKIN**

Basil

The most popular uses for basil include making pesto, marinara sauce, and tomato sauce. You can get fresh basil, dried basil or even basil oil which is very concentrated. Any way you use it, basil is a sure winner.

GOOD — These items go well with this food.

- Asian cuisine
- beans
- broccoli
- capers
- chile peppers
- chives
- cilantro
- cinnamon
- coconut
- corn
- cream
- cucumbers
- curry
- eggplant
- fennel
- French cuisine
- ginger
- honey
- lime
- marjoram
- mint
- mustard
- olives
- onions
- parsley
- pasta sauces
- peaches
- peas
- pepper
- pineapple
- potatoes
- rice
- rosemary
- salads
- salt
- sauces
- spinach
- squash
- thyme

BETTER — Even better pairing.

- **carrots**
- **vegetables**
- **vinegar**
- **watermelon**
- **zucchini**

BEST — The WOW factor!

- **AVOCADOS**
- **BELL PEPPERS**
- **CHEESE**
- **GARLIC**
- **ITALIAN CUISINE**
- **LEMON**
- **MEDITERRANEAN CUISINE**
- **OLIVE OIL**
- **OREGANO**
- **PASTA**
- **PESTO**
- **PIZZA**
- **SOUP**
- **TOFU**
- **TOMATOES**

 Bay Leaf

Adds a woodsy background note. Great for more than just soups and sauces.

GOOD — These items go well with this food.

- allspice
- apples
- cauliflower
- celery
- chestnuts
- corn
- dates
- French cuisine
- garlic
- grains
- Indian cuisine
- lemon
- Mediterranean cuisine
- onions
- parsley
- pears
- polenta
- rosemary
- sage
- sauces
- spinach
- squash
- thyme

BETTER — Even better pairing.

- **lentils**
- **tomato**
- **vegetables**

BEST — The WOW factor!

- **BEANS**
- **BROTHS**
- **POTATOES**
- **RICE**
- **SOUPS**
- **STEWS**
- **TOMATO SAUCES**

Caraway Seed

This sweet and sour taste is great for soda bread, sauerkraut, and potato salad and so much more.

GOOD — These items go well with this food.			BETTER — Even better pairing.	BEST — The WOW factor!
apples	fruits	stews	German cuisine	**BREADS**
cabbage	garlic	thyme	goulash	**POTATOES**
carrots	Indian cuisine	tomatoes	Hungarian cuisine	
coleslaw	onions	turnips	sauerkraut	
coriander	rye	vegetables		
cumin	soups	wheat		

Cardamom

This warm, aromatic spice is widely used in Indian cuisine. It's also great in baked goods when used in combination with spices like cinnamon and clove.

GOOD — These items go well with this food.			BETTER — Even better pairing.	BEST — The WOW factor!
anise	cloves	pears	coriander	**CINNAMON**
apples	cumin	peas	dates	**INDIAN CUISINE**
apricots	curry	pepper	ginger	**RICE**
Asian cuisine	grapefruit	pistachios	lemon	
baked goods	honey	saffron	orange	
bananas	lentils	squash		
caraway	lime	stews		
carrots	paprika	sweet potatoes		
chickpeas	parsnips	vanilla		
chocolate	pastries	vegetables		
citrus		walnuts		

Cayenne Pepper

Made from dried and ground red chili peppers. Add a sweet heat to anything. Tastes hotter the more it is cooks.

GOOD — These items go well with this food.			BETTER — Even better pairing.	BEST — The WOW factor!
basil	Indian cuisine	soups	corn	**CAJUN CUISINE**
beans	lemon	stews	Creole cuisine	**FAJITAS**
bell pepper	Mexican cuisine	vegetables	garlic	
chili	oil		potatoes	
chocolate	onion		tomatoes	
cilantro	rice			
coriander	salt			
cumin	salt, seasoned			
eggplant	sauces			

Chervil

Delicate anise flavor. Great raw in salads or as a finishing garnish. Not to be used cooked.

GOOD — These items go well with this food.			BETTER — Even better pairing.	BEST — The WOW factor!
basil	lemon	potatoes	**asparagus**	**LETTUCE**
beans	marjoram	shallots	**carrots**	**SALADS,**
cream	mint	soups, cream	**chives**	**POTATO, MACARONI**
dill	mushrooms	spinach	**French cuisine**	
fennel	mustard	squash	**tarragon**	
herbes de Provence	parsley	thyme	**tomato sauce**	
leeks	peas	vegetables	**tomatoes**	

Chives

Delicate onion flavor, great as a garnish.

GOOD — These items go well with this food.			BETTER — Even better pairing.	BEST — The WOW factor!
avocados	garlic	sauces	**Chinese cuisine**	**POTATOES**
basil	herbs	stews	**pasta**	**SOUPS**
butter, substitutes	marjoram	tarragon	**rice**	**SOUR CREAM**
cheese	onions	thyme		
cilantro	paprika	vegetables		
cream	parsley	vinegar		
dill	salads	zucchini		
fennel				

Cilantro

From the coriander plant, cilantro leaves have a pungent, herbaceous flavor. Used in Caribbean, Latin American, and Asian cuisine. Best served fresh, not cooked.

GOOD — These items go well with this food.			BETTER — Even better pairing.	BEST — The WOW factor!
African cuisine	garlic	parsley	**chives**	**AVOCADOS**
Asian cuisine	ginger	potatoes	**coconut milk**	**CHILI, WHITE BEAN**
basil	Indian cuisine	salads		**CHILI PEPPERS**
beans	legumes	sauces		**CHUTNEY**
bell peppers	lentils	scallions		**LEMON**
butter, substitutes	lime	soups		**RICE**
cardamom	mayonnaise	soy sauce		**SALSA**
Caribbean cuisine	Mediterranean cuisine	stews		**TOMATOES**
carrots	Mexican cuisine	tamarind		
coconut	Middle Eastern cuisine	Tex-Mex cuisine		
corn	mint	Thai cuisine		
cucumbers	onions	vegetables		
cumin	orange	vinegar		
curries				
dill				

Cinnamon

There are dozens of types of cinnamon, Here are the top four:

Ceylon - This is the only variety that many other countries refer to as cinnamon.

Cassia - This evergreen tree is the sister to cinnamon often sold 'as cinnamon' in America, even though it's not actually cinnamon. It doesn't have near the punch of real cinnamon.

Korintje - This is my favorite cinnamon, with a far higher oil content than Cassia. Smooth, yet packs a huge punch. The best bang for the buck.

Saigon Cinnamon - Saigon cinnamon is actually an evergreen tree indigenous to Southeast Asia. Despite its name, Saigon cinnamon is more closely related to cassia than to cinnamon,

GOOD — These items go well with this food.			BETTER — Even better pairing.	BEST — The WOW factor!
allspice	curry	nutmeg	**barbecue**	**APPLES**
apricots	eggplant	nuts	**blueberries**	**BAKED ITEMS**
berries	fennel	pastries	**cloves**	**BANANAS**
breads	fruits	pies	**orange**	**CHOCOLATE**
butter	garlic	plums	**pancakes**	**COCOA**
cardamon	ginger	pumpkins	**pears**	**CUSTARDS**
cherries	Indian cuisine	raisins	**pecans**	**DESSERTS**
chili peppers	Latin cuisine	rice	**vanilla**	**FRENCH TOAST**
chili powder	lemon	squash	**waffles**	**OATS**
cookies	mace	tomatoes		**SUGAR**
coriander	maple syrup	turmeric		
couscous	mole	vegetables		
cumin				

Cloves

Sweet and warming spice. Used often in baking, and can add a nice complexity to barbecue sauces and rubs.

GOOD — These items go well with this food.			BETTER — Even better pairing.	BEST — The WOW factor!
allspice	cumin	onions	**chocolate**	**APPLES**
almonds	curry	pumpkin	**cinnamon**	**BARBECUE**
Asian cuisine	fennel	squash	**ginger**	**ORANGE**
baked items	fruits	star anise	**honey**	
bay leaf	garlic	stews		
beets	German cuisine	sweet potatoes		
cabbage	Indian cuisine	tamarind		
cardamom	lemon	tomatoes		
carrots	mace	turmeric		
chili peppers	Mexican cuisine	vegetables		
cookies	nutmeg	walnuts		
coriander	oil			

Coriander

Earthy, lemony flavor. Used in a lot of Mexican and Indian dishes. Toast coriander seeds to release their flavor.

GOOD — These items go well with this food.					BETTER — Even better pairing.
allspice	chili	fennel	mushrooms	pickles	chili peppers
anise	cilantro	fruits	African cuisine	plums	garlic
apples	cinnamon	ginger	nutmeg	potatoes	lentils
baked items	citrus	Indian cuisine	nuts	rice	soups
basil	cloves	Latin cuisine	oil	saffron	stews
beans	coconut	mace	onions	salsas	
cardamom	corn	Mediterranean cuisine	orange	stuffing	
carrots	cumin	Mexican cuisine	pastries	sugar	
cayenne	curry	mint	pears	tomatoes	
chickpeas			pepper	turmeric	

Cumin

Smoky and earthy. Used in a lot of Southwestern and Mexican cuisines, as well as North African, Middle Eastern, and Indian.

GOOD — These items go well with this food.			BETTER — Even better pairing.	BEST — The WOW factor!
allspice	cloves	paprika	chickpeas	BEANS
anise	fennel	peas	chili powder	CHILI
apples	fruits	pepper	coriander	LENTILS
baked items	honey	saffron	couscous	MEXICAN CUISINE
bay leaf	hummus	sauerkraut	curry	POTATOES
beets	Indian cuisine	squash	eggplant	RICE
bread	mace	sugar	garlic	
cabbage	mint	tahini	soups	
cardamom	mustard	tamarind	Southwest cuisine	
carrots	nutmeg	thyme	stews	
cayenne	onions	turmeric	Tex Mex cuisine	
chili peppers	orange	vegetables	tomatoes	
cinnamon	oregano			

Curry

There are curry powders, curry sauces, and curry leaves. While there are differences between them, these ingredients will go well with all of them. Curry powers and sauces would be added early in the cooking, while the leaves should be added at the end of the cooking process or use in the cold dishes.

GOOD — These items go well with this food.				BETTER — Even better pairing.	BEST — The WOW factor!
allspice	coconut	lime	salad	cream	ASIAN CUISINE
butter, substitutes	coriander	mace	sauces	onions	INDIAN CUISINE
cardamom	cumin	mayonnaise	stews	potatoes	RICE
cashews	dill	mushrooms	tamarind	salt	TOFU
cayenne	fennel	nutmeg	Thai cuisine	soups	
chile peppers	garlic	oil	tomatoes	vegetables	
cilantro	ginger	paprika	turmeric		
cinnamon	lemon	pepper	zucchini		
cloves		saffron			

Dill

Dill is always better fresh rather than dried, yet I do dry any extra dill and use it later when I need a little flavored garnish. It is great in breads and salads.

GOOD — These items go well with this food.				BETTER — Even better pairing.	BEST — The WOW factor!
avocados	cauliflower	cream sauce	onions	cream	CUCUMBERS
basil	celery	eggplant	parsley	vegetables	GREEK CUISINE
beans	cheese	garlic	peas		LEMON
beets	chives	green beans	rice		MAYONNAISE
breads	cilantro	Mediterranean cuisine	sauces		PICKLES
broccoli	coriander	Middle Eastern cuisine	sour cream		POTATO SALAD
cabbage	corn	mint	squash		POTATOES
capers	cream cheese	mushrooms	tofu		SALADS
carrots		mustard			TOMATOES

Fennel

Lightly sweet and licorice flavored. Great for giving vegan breakfast sausage an authentic sausage flavor.

GOOD — These items go well with this food.					BETTER — Even better pairing.	BEST — The WOW factor!
anise	cucumbers	leeks	parsley	stuffing	almonds	BUTTER, SUBSTITUTES
asparagus	eggplant	lettuce	pecans	tarragon	apples	LEMON
basil	endive	lime	pickles	thyme	arugula	OLIVES; BLACK, GREEN
bay leaf	garlic	mint	rice	vegetables	Mediterranean cuisine	PEPPER
beets	ginger	nutmeg	rosemary	vinegar	potatoes	SALT
bell pepper	Italian cuisine	oil	scallions	walnuts	tomatoes	SAUSAGE
carrots	herbs	onions	shallots	watercress		
chives	honey	orange	soups	zucchini		
cream		paprika	spinach			

Fenugreek

This herb smells like maple syrup while cooking, But it has a rather bitter, burnt sugar flavor. Found in a lot of Indian and Middle Eastern dishes.

GOOD — These items go well with this food.			BETTER — Even better pairing.	BEST — The WOW factor!
cauliflower	lentils	spinach	cardamom	CURRY
cinnamon	maple syrup	stews	garlic	INDIAN CUISINE
cloves	mayonnaise	tomatoes	oil	RICE
coriander	mint	turmeric	potatoes	
cumin	peas	vegetables		
fennel	pepper			
legumes	soups			

Garlic

Garlic powder is made from dehydrated garlic cloves and can be used to give dishes a softer garlic flavor. Fresh garlic will tend to present stronger and even hotter notations. Cooking garlic will increase the flavor, but reduce the spicy heat.

GOOD These items go well with this food.				BETTER Even better pairing.	BEST The WOW factor!
almonds	chili peppers	lentils	saffron	mushrooms	**LEMON**
barbecue	Chinese cuisine	lime	sage	onions	**OLIVE OIL**
basil	chives	mayonnaise	sauces	pasta	**POTATOES**
bay leaf	cilantro	Mediterranean cuisine	shallots	tomato	**SALT**
beans	cumin	Mexican cuisine	soups	tomato sauce	**TOFU**
beets	curry	mustard	soy sauce		**VINEGAR**
bread	eggplant	oil	spinach		
broccoli	fennel	oregano	tarragon		
cabbage	ginger	paprika	Thai cuisine		
Cajun cuisine	Indian cuisine	pesto	thyme		
cayenne	Italian cuisine	rice	vegetables		
cheeses	leeks	rosemary	zucchini		

Ginger

Fresh or dried, ginger has a spicy, zesty bite that can be used with a wide spectrum of foods and regions.

GOOD These items go well with this food.				BETTER Even better pairing.	BEST The WOW factor!
allspice	citrus	oats	saffron	apples	**ASIAN CUISINES**
almonds	cloves	oil	shallots	basil	**CREAM**
anise	coconut	onions	soups	chocolate	**CURRY**
apricots	coriander	orange	star anise	cilantro	**GARLIC**
bananas	eggplant	papaya	stews	cinnamon	**HONEY**
bay leaf	fennel	peaches	stock	cranberries	**ICE CREAM**
bell pepper	figs	peanuts	strawberries	cumin	**LEMON**
beverages	grapefruit	pepper	sweet potatoes	mint	**LIME**
blueberries	hazelnuts	persimmons	tarragon	molasses	**NOODLES**
butter	Indian cuisine	plums	tomatoes	pears	**SOY SAUCE**
cardamom	leeks	prunes	turmeric	pumpkin	**SUGAR: WHITE, BROWN**
carrots	mangos	raisins	vanilla	salt	**TOFU**
cashews	maple syrup	raspberries	vegetables	scallions	
celery	mushrooms	rhubarb		squash	
chili peppers	nutmeg	rice			

Mace

From the same plant as nutmeg, but tastes more subtle and delicate. Great in savory dishes, especially stews.

GOOD These items go well with this food.						BEST The WOW factor!
allspice	cardamom	cloves	Indian cuisine	sauces		**NUTMEG**
Asian cuisine	carrots	coriander	ketchup	soups		
baked items	cheeses	cream	onions	spinach		
beans	cherries	cumin	paprika	stuffing		
broccoli	chocolate	curry	pepper	sweet potatoes		
butter	chowders	ginger	potatoes	thyme		
cabbage	cinnamon	hazelnuts	pumpkin	vegetables		

Marjoram

Marjoram is popular in Mediterranean and North American cooking. Add to vegetables, tomato based dishes, and stuffings. Chop the leaves, but do not use the stems. Best when added at the end of the cooking time.

GOOD — These items go well with this food.			BETTER — Even better pairing.	BEST — The WOW factor!
artichokes	French cuisine	pizza	onions	BASIL
asparagus	garlic	sage	rice	LEMON
bay leaf	Italian cuisine	salads	soups	OREGANO
beans	Mediterranean cuisine	savory	thyme	POTATOES
beets	Middle Eastern cuisine	spinach	tomato	ROSEMARY
butter, substitutes	mushrooms	squash	tomato sauce	
carrots	African cuisine	stews		
chives	olive oil	stuffing		
corn	pasta	tofu		
cucumbers	peas	vegetables		
		zucchini		

Mint

There is dried and fresh. Spearmint or peppermint. And this is a general list of some of the best ways to use mint for Simply Incredible Flavor.

GOOD — These items go well with this food.				BETTER — Even better pairing.	BEST — The WOW factor!
apples	cinnamon	lavender	pumpkin	berries	BEANS
Asian cuisine	cloves	lentils	radishes	citrus	CHOCOLATE
basil	coconut	lettuce	raspberries	cucumbers	DESSERTS
beets	cream	lime	rice	honeydew	FRUITS
cantaloupe	cumin	mango	rosemary	Mediterranean cuisine	GREEK CUISINE
cardamon	curries	marjoram	squash	Mexican cuisine	LEMON
carrots	dill	mushrooms	Thai cuisine	Middle Eastern cuisine	SALADS
cashew	eggplant	olives	tomatoes	pineapple	STRAWBERRIES
chile peppers	garlic	onions	vanilla		SUGAR
chives	ginger	parsley	vegetables		TABBOULEH
chutney	honey	plums	watermelon		
cilantro	Indian cuisine	potatoes			

Nutmeg

Sweet and pungent. Great in baked goods, but also adds a warm note to savory dishes.

GOOD — These items go well with this food.			BETTER — Even better pairing.	BEST — The WOW factor!
allspice	coriander	pasta	cinnamon	APPLES
baked items	cumin	pastries	cloves	CHEESES
berries	green beans	pears	cookies	CREAM
broccoli	honey	pepper	fruits	CREAM SAUCES
butter, substitutes	Latin American cuisine	raisins	ginger	DESSERTS
cabbage	lemon	squash	Indian cuisine	RICE
cardamon	mace	stuffing	Italian cuisine	SAUCES, WHITE
Caribbean cuisine	mushrooms	sugar	milks	SPINACH
carrots	nuts	thyme	pasta sauces	
cauliflower	onions	tomatoes	potatoes	
chickpeas	oranges	tomato sauces	pumpkin	
chocolate	parsnips	vanilla	sour cream	

Nutritional Yeast Flakes

Very different from bread yeast, this can be sprinkled on or in sauces, pastas, and other dishes to add a nutty, cheesy, savory flavor.

GOOD – These items go well with this food.			BETTER – Even better pairing.	BEST – The WOW factor!
almonds	cucumbers	pepper	cashews	AVOCADOS
artichokes	curries	rice	cauliflower	BUTTER, SUBSTITUTES
basil	eggplant	risotto	greens	CHEESE
beans	garlic	salads	squash	CREAM SAUCES
bell peppers	lentils	sour cream		POPCORN
broccoli	lemon	spinach		POTATOES
cabbage	mushrooms	tomato		SALT
carrots	oil	tomato sauces		TOAST
chili peppers	onion	vegetables		TOFU
cream	pasta	zucchini		

Oregano

Fresh or dried, oregano has a distinct flavor all its own. Robust, and lemony, yet these flavors can range from the milder Italian oregano to the bolder Greek oregano. Then there is also the Mexican oregano that is hotter and generally budded together with a lot more seeds.

GOOD – These items go well with this food.			BETTER – Even better pairing.	BEST – The WOW factor!
artichokes	greens	stews	chili	BASIL
arugula	marjoram	stuffings	chili peppers	BELL PEPPERS
beans	mushrooms	thyme	chili powder	GREEK CUISINE
beef	olive oil	tofu	garlic	LEMON
broccoli	onions	zucchini	Italian cuisine	PASTA
broths	paprika		Mediterranean cuisine	PASTA SAUCES
capers	parsley		Mexican cuisine	PIZZA
cheeses	pepper		olives	SOUPS
chives	rosemary		potatoes	TOMATO
cucumbers	sage		salads	TOMATO SAUCES
cumin	sauces			VEGETABLES
eggplant	squash			

Paprika

Sweet, Hot or Smoked. This can add a sweet note and a red color. Or a nice smoky flavor. Used in stews and spice blends.

GOOD – These items go well with this food.			BETTER – Even better pairing.	BEST – The WOW factor!
allspice	curries	oregano	cream	HUNGARIAN CUISINE
barbecue	garlic	pepper	goulash	ONIONS
bell peppers	ginger	rosemary	rice	POTATOES
butter, substitutes	hummus	saffron	sour cream	SPANISH CUISINE
Cajun cuisine	Indian cuisine	salads: pasta, potato		
caraway	legumes	salt		
cardamom	lemon	sauces		
casseroles	marjoram	soups		
cauliflower	mayonnaise	stews		
cheeses	mushrooms	thyme		
chili	olive oil	turmeric		
		vegetables		

Parsley

Flat-leaf or curly varieties, this very popular herb is light and grassy in flavor.

GOOD — These items go well with this food.			BETTER — Even better pairing.	BEST — The WOW factor!
avocados	dill	pesto	carrots	BUTTER, SUBSTITUTES
basil	eggplant	rosemary	stews	CORN
bay leaf	lentils	salads	tomato	GARLIC
beans	Mediterranean cuisine	sauces	tomato sauces	HERBS
bulgur wheat	Middle Eastern cuisine	stuffing	vegetables	LEMON
capers	mushrooms	tarragon		PASTA
cauliflower	olive oil	thyme		POTATOES
chile peppers	onions	vinegar		RICE
chives	pasta sauces	zucchini		SOUPS
cream	pepper			TABBOULEH

Peppercorns

Peppercorns come in a variety of colors (black, white, pink, and green being the most popular). These are pungent and pack a heat. They are different that simple ground pepper and carry a far more aromatic and deeper flavor.

GOOD — These items go well with this food.			BETTER — Even better pairing.	BEST — The WOW factor!
avocados	curries	parsley	vinegar	GARLIC
bay leaf	fennel	pineapple		POTATOES
beans	lentils	sage		RICE
butter, substitutes	mint	sauces, white		
chocolate	mustard	tomatoes		
cream	nutmeg	vegetables		

Rosemary

Strong and piney. Great with beans, and potatoes, soup and sauces.

GOOD — These items go well with this food.			BETTER — Even better pairing.	BEST — The WOW factor!
apples	focaccia	pasta	bell peppers	BEANS
apricots	fruit	peas	butter, substitutes	GARLIC
asparagus	grains	pizza	cabbage	LEMON
baked items	grapefruit	polenta	eggplant	OLIVE OIL
bay leaf	grapes	sauces	grilling	ONIONS
breads	honey	savory	Italian cuisine	POTATOES
Brussel sprouts	lavender	spinach	marjoram	SOUPS
carrots	lentils	squash	Mediterranean cuisine	STEWS
cauliflower	lime	sweet potatoes	mushrooms	TOMATOES
celery	milks	thyme	oregano	
chives	mint	vinegars	rice	
cream	orange		risotto	
fennel	parsley		sage	
figs	parsnips		tomato juice	
			tomato sauces	

Saffron

Saffron has a subtle but distinct floral flavor and aroma that hits sour, sweet, and bitter taste-buds all at the same time. It also gives foods a bright yellow color. A little goes a long way, so there is no need to add extra.

GOOD — These items go well with this food.			BETTER — Even better pairing.	BEST — The WOW factor!
anise	coriander	nutmeg	couscous	RICE
artichokes	corn	onions	fennel	RISOTTO
asparagus	cream	orange	garlic	SPANISH CUISINE
basil	cumin	paprika	ginger	
bread	curries	sauces	mayonnaise	
cardamom	eggplant	soups	Mediterranean cuisine	
carrots	fruits	spinach	potatoes	
cheeses	ice cream	squash		
cinnamon	Indian cuisine	stews		
citrus	Italian cuisine	tomatoes		
cloves	mushrooms	vegetables		

Sage

Pine-like flavor, with more lemony and eucalyptus notes than rosemary. Found in a lot of northern Italian cooking.

GOOD — These items go well with this food.			BETTER — Even better pairing.		BEST — The WOW factor!
apples	cream	oranges	bread	stews	BEANS
asparagus	fennel	oregano	eggplant	tomato	CHEESE
bay leaf	Greek cuisine	pears	garlic	tomato sauces	CORN
blueberries	Italian cuisine	pumpkin	ginger		ONIONS
butter, substitutes	legumes	salad: pasta, potato	lemon		PASTAS
cabbage	Mediterranean cuisine	Spanish cuisine	marjoram		POTATOES
caraway	mint	squash	olive oil		STUFFINGS
carrots	mushrooms	thyme	rice		
cherries		vegetables	rosemary		
chickpeas			soups		
citrus					

Star Anise

Whole star anise can be used to add a sweet licorice flavor to sauces and soups. Not to be confused with anise, star anise is a star shaped fruit from evergreen trees, where anise is a Mediterranean plant of the parsley family.

GOOD — These items go well with this food.				BETTER — Even better pairing.	BEST — The WOW factor!
allspice	cumin	lemon	root vegetables	cinnamon	CHINESE CUISINE
baked items	curry	lemongrass	scallions	ginger	CHINESE FIVE SPICE
cardamom	fennel	lime	soy sauce	pineapple	PEARS
chestnuts	figs	mace	stews	raspberries	TEAS
chile peppers	fruits	mangos	sweet potatoes	soups	VANILLA
chili powder	garlic	nutmeg	tamarind		
chocolate	Indian cuisine	orange	turmeric		
citrus	kumquats	pepper	vegetables		
cloves	leeks	plums			
coriander		pumpkin			

Sumac

Zingy and lemony, sumac is a Middle Eastern spice that's great in marinades and spice rubs.

GOOD — These items go well with this food.			BETTER — Even better pairing.	BEST — The WOW factor!
allspice	garlic	pine nuts	avocados	MIDDLE EASTERN CUISINE
cheeses	Indian cuisine	pomegranates	beets	SALT
chile peppers	lemon	rosemary	chickpeas	
chili powder	lime	salads	lentils	
coriander	mint	tomatoes	onions	
cucumber	orange	vegetables	pepper	
cumin	oregano		sesame seeds	
eggplant	paprika		thyme	
fennel	parsley			
ginger				

Tamarind

Technically a fruit, tamarind trees produce an abundance of long, curved, brown pods filled with small brown seeds, surrounded by a sticky pulp that dehydrates naturally into a sticky paste. Most popular in foreign cuisines, it will soon be a staple in your cupboard.

GOOD — These items go well with this food.				BETTER — Even better pairing.	BEST — The WOW factor!
African cuisine	cilantro	honey	peanuts	chile peppers	BEVERAGES
allspice	cinnamon	lentils	pears	chili powder	DESSERTS
almonds	cloves	lime	potatoes	chutney	INDIAN CUISINE
Asian cuisine	cumin	mango	sauces	coconut	MARINADES
bananas	curries	mint	soups	coconut milk	RICE
beans	dates	mushrooms	soy sauce	Latin American cuisine	STEWS
cabbage	fennel seeds	oil	star anise	Middle Eastern cuisine	SUGAR
cardamom	fruits	onions	Thai cuisine	mustard	
chickpeas	garlic	orange	vegetables	turmeric	
Chinese cuisine	ginger	peaches			

Tarragon

Tarragon has a sweet flavor with a slight licorice essence. Can be eaten raw in salads or used to flavor tomato dishes. Carrots love tarragon. It is best used at the end of a cooking process, just before serving.

GOOD — These items go well with this food.				BETTER — Even better pairing.	BEST — The WOW factor!
apples	celery	lentils	pepper	chile peppers	CARROTS
apricots	cheese	lime	rice	chili powder	LEMON
artichokes	chives	marjoram	salads	chutney	ONIONS
asparagus	corn	melon	savory	coconut	POTATOES
basil	cream	mint	shallots	coconut milk	SAUCES
beans	dill	mustard	soup	Latin American cuisine	TOMATOES
beets	fennel	olive oil	spinach	Middle Eastern cuisine	VINEGAR
broccoli	French cuisine	parsley	squash	mustard	
capers	garlic	pasta	stocks	turmeric	
cauliflower	leeks	peas	vegetables		
			zucchini		

Thyme
Adds a pungent, woodsy flavor. Great as an all-purpose seasoning.

GOOD — These items go well with this food.			BETTER — Even better pairing.	BEST — The WOW factor!
allspice	fennel	olive oil	**cabbage**	**BASIL**
apples	fruits, dried	orange	**carrots**	**BAY LEAF**
beans	garlic	paprika	**green beans**	**CORN**
bell peppers	Greek cuisine	parsley	**vegetables**	**LEMON**
broccoli	gumbo	parsnips		**MARJORAM**
Brussels sprouts	herbes de Provence	pastas		**MUSHROOMS**
Caribbean cuisine	honey	pears		**OREGANO**
casserole	Italian cuisine	peas		**POTATOES**
celery	jerk seasoning	pepper		**ROSEMARY**
chile peppers	lavender	rice		**SAVORY**
chives	leeks	sage		**SOUPS**
cloves	legumes	salads		**STEWS**
coriander	lentils	Spanish cuisine		**TOMATO SAUCE**
cranberries	Mediterranean cuisine	spinach		**TOMATOES**
curries	Middle Eastern cuisine	stocks		
dates	mint	stuffing		
dill	mustard	tarragon		
eggplant	nutmeg	vinegar		
		zucchini		

Turmeric
Sometimes used for its yellow color more than its flavor. It has a mild woodsy flavor.

GOOD — These items go well with this food.			BETTER — Even better pairing.	BEST — The WOW factor!	
Asian cuisine	cumin	paprika	**mustard**	**CURRY**	**SOUPS**
beans	eggplant	spinach	**potatoes**	**PEPPER**	**TOFU**
Caribbean cuisine	fennel	stew	**tamarind**	**RICE**	
chili peppers	garlic	Thai cuisine			
cilantro	ginger	vegetables			
cloves	Indian cuisine				
coconut	lentils				
coconut milk	Middle Eastern cuisine				
coriander	African cuisine				

MOST POPULAR
Spice Blends & Mixes

ADOBO - *(Latin American)* An all-purpose seasoning that contains garlic, oregano, pepper, and other spices; used in Mexican and other Latin American cuisines.

BAHARAT - *(Middle Eastern)* Black pepper, cumin, cinnamon, and cloves. Used to flavor soups, tomato sauces, lentils, rice pilafs, and couscous.

BEBERE - *(African)* Hot peppers, black pepper, fenugreek, ginger, cardamom, coriander, cinnamon, and cloves. Other ingredients may include cumin, allspice, nutmeg, paprika, onion, or garlic. Used to flavor slow-cooked stews.

BOUQUET GARNI - *(French)* Thyme, parsley, and bay leaf. Used to flavor broths and soups.

CHILI POWDER - *(Mexican)* Ground chilis, cumin, oregano, cayenne, and lots of optional extras to make this seasoning uniquely yours. Use for chili, stew, beans and tacos.

CHINESE FIVE-SPICE POWDER - *(Asian)* Star anise, Szechuan peppercorns, fennel, cassia, and clove. Adds sweetness and depth to savory dishes.

CURRY POWDER - *(Indian)* Typically includes turmeric, coriander, cumin, fenugreek, and red pepper, but mixes can vary. Used primarily to quickly flavor curry sauces.

DUKKAH - *(Egyptian)* Includes nuts (most often hazelnuts), sesame seeds, coriander, and cumin.

FINES HERBES - *(French)* A blend of four fresh or dry herbs, such as chervil, chives, tarragon, and parsley.

GARAM MASALA - *(Indian)* Typically includes cinnamon, cardamom, cloves, cumin, coriander, nutmeg, and pepper. Sweeter than curry powder. Also used to season curry sauces.

HARISSA - *(Middle Eastern)* Made from smoked red peppers and widely featured in Tunisian and other North African cuisines.

HERBES DE PROVENCE - *(French)* Usually savory. Contains rosemary, marjoram, thyme, and sometimes lavender. Use as a marinade or dry rub for vegetables.

JERK SPICE - *(Jamaican)* A mixture including red and black pepper, allspice, cinnamon, and thyme.

KHMELI SUNELI - *(Georgian)* A mix of warm, nutty, grassy, and bitter spices like fenugreek, coriander, savory, and black peppercorns.

OLD BAY - *(American)* Celery salt, mustard, red and black pepper, bay leaves, cloves, allspice, ginger, mace, cardamom, cinnamon, and paprika. It is traditionally used for sea food, but works great in potato salads and soups.

PICKLING SPICE - *(Russian)* Includes bay leaf, yellow mustard seeds, black peppercorns, allspice, and coriander. Used for pickling vegetables in vinegar.

POULTRY SPICE - *(Native American)* An aromatic, woodsy combination of sage, thyme, and other herbs and spices. can be used for stuffings and vegetables

PUMPKIN PIE SPICE MIX - *(American)* Cinnamon, nutmeg, ginger, and cloves. Used for seasoning pumpkin pie, but also great in other spiced baked goods, and oatmeal.

QUATRE EPICES - *(French)* Meaning "four spices," this blend typically includes ground black and/or white pepper, cloves, nutmeg, and ginger.

RAS EL HANOUT - *(Moroccan)* Cardamom, clove, cinnamon, paprika, coriander, cumin, mace, nutmeg, peppercorn, and turmeric. Use as a simple condiment.

TOGARASHI - *(Japanese)* A condiment made from spices including chile pepper, citrus peel, sesame seeds, and seaweed.

ZA'ATAR SEASONING BLEND - *(Middle Eastern)* great all around blend consisting of sumac, thyme, roasted sesame seeds, marjoram, oregano, and salt.

Chef's Secrets

COOKING TIPS: COOKING WITHOUT OIL

Question:
What has 120 calories per tablespoon and is 100% fat?

Hint… No fiber, no water content, and virtually no nutritional value.

If your guess is oil, you are correct.

Scientist and doctors alike have discovered that oil is the #1 cause of Type 2 Diabetes. And it is a leader in causing both obesity and heart disease. Both animal fats, and processed oils are something we need to avoid - so today, I am going to give you some strategies on how to cook without all the oil.

BAKING: Oil helps with browning in the oven, but it's not necessary. Vegetables will brown on their own. Looking them on lower temperatures, and slower helps too. And you can always broil things to get quicker crispiness. Parchment paper or a little water in the bottom of the pan can prevent sticking.

SAUTÉING: When you sauté vegetables, there is no need to sauté in oil. You can get the same effect by doing a water sauté or using vegetable broth. The next page shows you exactly how to do that.

STEAMING: Steaming is one of the simplest and healthiest ways to cook. No oil needed. And when the steaming is done, sprinkle with your spices or seasonings, and presto, you have Simply Incredible Flavor without the oil.

SUBSTITUTING:

» If the oil is required for moisture in baking, try bananas.

» Applesauce and other pureed fruits, work great for oil substitutes.

» Pumpkin and squash purees work well also.

» Instead of oil, try using vegetable broth or water.

» Blended cashews, have good fats that can be substituted for oil.

» Blended Tofu, is a fine oil substitute for baking.

» Properly seasoning food makes the tastebuds completely forget about the fat.

Chef's Secrets

COOKING TIPS: HOW TO WATER SAUTÉ

Sautéing Vegetables

Browned onions have excellent flavor and can be used alone or mixed in with recipes to make a dish with Simply Incredible Flavor.

To do a Water Sauté:

1. Place 1 1/2 cups of chopped onions in a large nonstick frying pan with 1 cup of water.

2. Cook over medium heat, stirring occasionally, until the liquid evaporates and the onions begin to stick to the bottom of the pan.

3. Continue to stir for a minute, then add another 1/2 cup of water, loosening the browned bits from the bottom of the pan.

4. Cook until the liquid evaporates again.

5. Repeat this procedure 1 or 2 more times, until the onions are as browned as you like.

You can also use this technique to brown carrots, green peppers, garlic, potatoes, shallots, zucchini, and many other vegetables.

For Additional Sautéing Flavor Use:

» lemon juice

» lime juice

» Mexican salsas

» red or white wine (I use nonalcoholic)

» sherry (I use nonalcoholic)

» soy sauce or Tamari

» tomato juice

» vegetable broth

» vinegar, rice or balsamic

For even more great taste:

Add spices and herbs, liquid smoke or smoked salt, ginger root, dry mustard, fennel seeds, and especially GARLIC.

Chef's Secrets

COOKING TIPS: EGG SUBSTITUTES

APPLESAUCE OR MASHED BANANA: you can use applesauce or banana in recipes where there is already a leavening agent, and the eggs are only used for moisture. Use ¼ cup applesauce or mashed banana in place of 1 egg.

AQUAFABA BEAN BRINE: This is the liquid from a can of chickpeas. It is a great egg substitute for baked goods. You don't even have to whip it. But if you do, it will capture air in a similar way that egg white does for the light and fluffy recipes. Use 1/4 cup per egg.

ARROWROOT POWDER: Arrowroot powder is a starch which acts as a binder in recipes for baked goods as well as puddings. Arrowroot won't leaven baked goods, so you will only want to use it in recipes which already call for baking soda and baking powder. For binding purposes only, use 2 Tbsp arrowroot powder in place of the egg. To bind and get the moisture properties of the egg, mix the arrowroot powder with equal parts water first.

BAKING SODA AND VINEGAR: Baking soda and vinegar bubble up when you mix them together. This is a perfect way to add some fluff and airiness to your baked goods without relying on eggs. Mix 1 tsp of baking soda with 1 tsp of white vinegar to replace 1 egg.

CHIA SEEDS: Just mix 1-2 Tbsp of chia seeds with hot water and let it sit a while before mixing it in with the rest of the ingredients. Chia seeds (and flax) are also great vegan sources of Omega 3.

ENER-G EGG REPLACER: All egg replacer products are made up of a combination of starches and leavening ingredients, so it does a pretty good job of mimicking eggs in baked recipes. It is one of the best options to use if you want a fluffy, airy baked recipe like sponge cake. You can even use Ener-G Egg Replacer to make vegan quiche.

FLEGGS: Is a term coined for the mixture of 1 Tbsp ground flax seed mixed with 3 Tbsp hot water. It will not trap air like eggs do, so this won't work well in recipes likes angel food cake or crepes. Fleggs also doesn't act as a leavening agent, so only use fleggs in recipes which call for added agents to make the food rise and get fluffy.

SILKEN TOFU: In some recipes, the eggs are only there to add moisture. If this is the case, then you can substitute ¼ cup silken tofu for 1 egg.

VEGAN SUBSTITUTES FOR EGG WASH: include vegetable oil, non-dairy milk, butter substitutes, or light corn syrup thinned with water.

Chef's Secrets

MUST HAVE PRODUCTS: BRAGG

Two of my favorite staples that I keep in my kitchen are Bragg Liquid Aminos, and Bragg Apple Cider Vinegar. These are organic, non-GMO items that are PACKED with nutrients. And the best part - they taste absolutely spectacular. So if you want to achieve Simply Incredible Flavor, these products are absolutely necessary.

BRAGG LIQUID AMINOS

Use this anywhere you use soy sauce.

16 AMINO ACIDS

- Alanine
- Arginine
- Aspartic Acid
- Glutamic Acid
- Glycine
- Histidine
- Isoleucine
- Leucine
- Lysine
- Methionine
- Phenylalanine
- Proline
- Serine
- Threonine
- Tyrosine
- Valine

Great on Salads, Veggies, Rice & Beans, Tofu, Tempeh, Potatoes, Popcorn, Dressings, Gravies & Sauces, Casseroles, Stir-fries and So Much More.

Bragg Apple Cider Vinegar

» Rich in enzymes & potassium

» Support a healthy immune system

» Helps control weight

» Promotes digestion & ph Balance

» Helps soothe dry throats

» Helps remove body sludge toxins

» Helps maintain healthy skin

» Helps promote youthful, healthy bodies

» Soothes irritated skin

» Relieves muscle pain from exercise

I love the Bragg line of products, and they have more items such as Salad Dressings, Olive oil, and seasonings, For more info and products, just check out their website at *www.Bragg.com*.

Chef's Secrets

MUST HAVE PRODUCTS: BUTLER SOY CURLS

Butler has a couple of great products that are essential for your pantry.

Their Soy Curls are a fantastic substitute to use in great Fajitas, Sandwiches, Sizzling Stir Fry, Soups, Salads, Casseroles, Barbecue, and so much more!

SOY CURLS™ ARE: 100% Natural, Contain the whole soybean, High in protein, Good source of fiber, Gluten-free, Vegan, Non-GMO - no chemical pesticides, Grown & made in the USA, 0 trans fats, No sodium, No cholesterol.

They also have other great products. Their Jerky is simply the best jerky you will ever find. And their Chicken Style Seasoning is unique product that brings a creaminess as well as great flavor.

Their website is: www.ButlerFoods.com

I can't recommend their products enough. THEY'RE SIMPLY THAT GOOD!

Chef's Secrets

MUST HAVE PRODUCTS: MCKAY'S

I am partial to McKay's. They have two of the best seasonings you will ever find. There is a Beef Style and a Chicken Style seasoning and both have a vegan option. You will find yourself using them often.

» Low in cholesterol

» Gluten-free (helping people with Celiac Disease)

» Hydrogenation-free

» Available in vegetarian/vegan non-dairy varieties

» No animal byproducts

» Low trans fat

» Low sugar

» Meatless—no meat or meat byproducts

» Offered with No MSG Added

» Offered with No GMO

These products are widely available, or you can visit their website at: www.McKays-seasoning.com

MCKAY'S SOUP SEASONINGS can be used as a delicious seasoning for a variety of foods or can be mixed with hot water to drink as a broth or used as soup—the possibilities are endless!

USE MCKAY'S SOUP SEASONING FOR SOME OF THESE GREAT IDEAS:

» Add hot water to make hot bouillon or broth for soup

» Great in all your favorite vegan entrées

» Season potatoes (hot or cold)

» Popcorn flavoring

» Macaroni salad

Chef's Secrets

MUST HAVE PRODUCTS: LEAHEY GRAVY

Leahey Foods is one of my most highly recommended companies for saving time in the kitchen and getting Simply Incredible Flavor. Their most popular products are their gluten free No Chicken Gravy, and their gluten free No Beef Gravy. They are the best!

But That's not all. They also carry Macaroni & Cheese, a wide variety of soups and even quick and easy cookie mixes.

Check out their website at www.leaheyfoods.com

Chef's Secrets

MUST HAVE PRODUCTS: BETTER THAN BOUILLON

Better Than Bouillon is a product that I have been using for years. I can tell you as an ex-meat eater, their vegan chickenless and beefless bouillon taste like the real thing. I have cases of these at home, because I use them that often. So if you want Simply Incredible Flavor, get the vegan Better Than Bouillon stocked in your pantry.

Better than Bouillon Vegetarian Bases are Vegan certified. Contain 1/3 less sodium than other bouillons, are Fat Free, Non-irradiated, Dairy Free-lactose / No Whey / No caseinate

SEASONED VEGETABLE BASE A rich base that's made by combining real sautéed onions, celery, and carrots. This is the perfect starting point to create vegetable broth, minestrone soup or add it to rice for more flavor.

NO BEEF BASE A paste that produces a standard base with beef flavor that can be used in soups, gravies, and meat stocks.

NO CHICKEN BASE A paste that produces a standard base with chicken flavor that can be used in soups, gravies, and meat stocks.

ROASTED GARLIC BASE Our Roasted Garlic Base is made with real Roasted Garlic and natural juices. It gives your favorite recipe a deliciously savory flavor.

Their website is www.betterthanbouillon.com

FLAVORING THE
World's Healthiest Foods

According to the experts, complex carbohydrates are the healthy foods that we should be eating the most of every day. This section will provide you the resources to make them taste great.

We have created for you the most effortless ways to achieve any flavor in the world. The trick to creating Simply Incredible Food is to first determine what food to use. You have in your hands an extensive list of all the foods that go with every major carb.

HOW TO USE THIS SECTION

FIRST: you will find a lists of ingredients for a particular region, or cuisine.

SECOND: you will find Simply Incredible Pairings. When you combine these particular ingredients, you will achieve Simply Incredible Flavor.

Example:

chili peppers + garlic + onions

chili peppers + peanuts + tomatoes

THIRD: you will find some great recipes that capture that particular region or food

GOOD These items go well with this food.	BETTER Even better pairing.	BEST The WOW factor!
allspice	cream sauces	**DILL**
apples	mushrooms	**SOUR CREAM**
bay leaf	**SIMPLY INCREDIBLE PAIRINGS** bay leaf + dill + nutmeg + onion	
breads		

Barley

The grain of barley is used to make medicine. Barley is used for lowering blood sugar, blood pressure, and cholesterol, and for promoting weight loss. It is also used for digestive complaints including diarrhea, stomach pain, and inflammatory bowel conditions. One cup of barley has 32 grams of dietary fiber and 52% of the RDA for carbs making it one of the highest of any food.

Barley

GOOD These items go well with this food.		BETTER Even better pairing.	BEST The WOW factor!
apples	scallions	**celery**	**CARROTS**
butter substitutes	squash	**garlic**	**MUSHROOMS**
bay leaf	thyme	**onions**	**SALT**
ginger	tomatoes	**sage**	**SOY SAUCE**
leeks	vegetable stock	**savory**	
lemon	walnuts		
olives			
oregano			
parsley			
peppers			
potatoes			

SIMPLY INCREDIBLE PAIRINGS

barley + garlic + mushrooms
barley + garlic + soy sauce
barley + carrots + celery + onions
barley + carrots + savory
barley + tomatoes + onions

BARLEY RECIPES

Slow Cooker Vegetable Barley Soup

Simply Incredible Flavor couldn't be easier. Just throw everything into the crockpot and walk away. Healthy. Delicious. Nutritious.

Ingredients

6 cups vegetable broth

3 cups water

1 - 14 oz can diced tomatoes

3/4 cup pearl barley

1 yellow onion, chopped

3 carrots, cut into ½-circles

3 stalks celery, chopped

1 sweet potato, peeled, cut into ¾-inch pieces

4 garlic, cloves, minced

2 cups frozen green beans

1 tsp paprika, smoked

1 Tbsp dried oregano

1 tsp dried thyme

1/2 tsp salt

1/2 tsp pepper, ground

1/4 cup minced flat-leaf parsley

Directions

1. In a large (6-quart) slow cooker, add all of the ingredients, except for the parsley.

2. Cook on low until the barley is tender, about 8 hours.

3. Just before serving, stir in the parsley.

Servings: 8

Prep time: 10 mins

Cook time: 8 hours

Total time: 8 hours

BARLEY RECIPES

Mushroom Barley Soup

One of the best pairings you can have is barley with mushrooms and garlic. And this recipe is a sure winner for Simply Incredible Flavor.

Ingredients

2 Tbsp vegetable oil, or water sauté

1 large onion, chopped

2 lbs mushrooms, sliced

2 cloves garlic, minced

3 qt. mushroom or vegetable stock

1 1/4 cups pearl barley

3 celery stalks, including leaves, chopped thin

2 large carrots, chopped small

2 Tbsp soy sauce

3 bay leaves

Salt and pepper to taste

Directions

1. In a large heavy bottom stock pot on medium-high heat, sauté the onions for about 5 to 7 minutes, until golden.

2. Add the mushrooms and sauté for another 5 minutes. If it is sticking to the bottom of the pan, even better.

3. Add the garlic and stir in for one minute.

4. Add the remaining ingredients and bring to a boil.

5. Simmer uncovered until barley is tender, for about one hour.

6. Remove bay leaves and serve.

Servings: 8

Prep time: 10 mins

Cook time: 1 hour

Total time: 1.2 hours

BARLEY RECIPES

Butternut Squash Barley Risotto

This is a healthy version of risotto. It replaces the traditional Arborio rice with barley. Which is high in soluble fiber and it helps lower cholesterol. I swapped out the traditional butter for very little olive oil. And I use a white non-alcoholic wine. The rest of the cooking method remains the same so your final dish is still creamy, with a delightful texture and Simply Incredible Flavor.

Ingredients:

1 small butternut squash, peeled, seeded and cut into 1/2 inch cubes

4 Tbsp olive oil

Salt and freshly ground pepper, to taste

4 cups vegetable broth

2 garlic cloves, minced

2 shallots, minced

1 Tbsp sage, fresh chopped

1 tsp thyme, fresh chopped

1 cup pearl barley

1/2 cup white wine
(I used the Fre Moscato non-alcoholic wine)

1/2 cup vegan parmesan cheese

Directions:

1. Preheat oven to 400 degrees. Line a baking sheet with parchment paper.

2. In a bowl, toss the squash with 2 tablespoons of olive oil.

3. On the baking sheet, place the squash in a single layer, and season with salt and pepper.

4. Roast for about 35 minutes, stirring once until tender and caramelized. Set aside.

5. In a small saucepan heat the broth over low heat.

6. In a large saucepan over medium heat, sauté the garlic, shallots, thyme and sage. Season with salt and pepper. Stir for about 1 minute, until fragrant.

7. Add the barley and cook for about 2 minutes, stirring often, until toasted.

8. Add the non-alcoholic wine and cook, stirring occasionally, until it is evaporated.

9. Reduce the heat to medium-low and add 1 cup of the broth, stirring often, until the liquid is completely absorbed. About 5 minutes.

10. Continue to add the remaining broth, 1 cup at a time, allowing the liquid to be absorbed before adding more.

11. When the barley is tender and the risotto is creamy, stir in the squash and cheese.

12. Remove from heat and season with salt and pepper.

13. Serve immediately.

Servings: 6

Prep time: 20 mins

Cook time: 1 hour

Total time: 1.4 hours

BARLEY RECIPES

Cold Barley Kalamata Salad

This is a cool refreshing way to get your fiber and healthy carbs all in one meal. The combination of vegetables with olives gives it a Simply Incredible Flavor.

Ingredients

1 1/2 cups barley, uncooked

1 cup corn, kernels fresh or frozen

2 plum tomato, seeded, diced

1/2 cup green onions, chopped

1/2 cup yellow bell pepper, diced

1/4 cup parsley, fresh chopped

25 Kalamata olives, pitted and chopped

For the Sauce

3 Tbsp fresh lemon juice

2 Tbsp olive oil

1 garlic clove, minced

zest of one lemon

1/4 tsp salt

pinch pepper

Directions for Sauce:

Mix the ingredients well and set aside for flavors to blend.

Direction for Salad

1. Cook barley according to package directions, omitting salt.

2. Drain and rinse with cold water. Drain and cool completely.

3. Place barley in a large bowl and add the remaining ingredients.

4. Add the sauce, mixing well. Serve, or chill.

5. Garnish with vegan Parmesan cheese, or parsley.

Servings: 6

Prep time: 10 min.

Cook time: 30 min.

Total time: 45 min.

BARLEY RECIPES

Pareve Cholent

A JEWISH BARLEY STEW.

This soup was often made for Sabbath meals, started the night before.

Ingredients

8 cups vegetable stock

2 cup dry kidney beans

1 cup dry white beans

1 cup barley

3 large potatoes, peeled and cubed

3 large sweet potato, peeled and cubed

2 large onion, chopped

4 garlic cloves, minced

1 1/2 cups ketchup

1/2 cup barbecue sauce

1/2 cup soy sauce

1/2 cup brown sugar

2 Tbsp onion powder

2 Tbsp paprika

1 tsp pepper

Directions

1. Place all ingredients into a large crockpot. Mix well.

2. Cook on high for 1 hour.

3. Then reduce heat to low and continue cooking overnight until the beans are tender. 10+ hours.

Servings: 8

Prep time: 20 mins

Cook time: 11 hour

Total time: 11 hours

Beans, black

One cup of black beans 29 grams of dietary fiber and 40 grams of total carbs. They are a staple in every healthy kitchen. I can eat them straight out of the can. We cook large batches with a little salt and then freeze them in bags.

Beans, black

GOOD These items go well with this food.		BETTER Even better pairing.	BEST The WOW factor!
allspice	orange zest	**chili powder**	**CHILI PEPPERS**
apples	oregano	**cilantro**	**ANCHO**
avocados	parsley	**lemon**	**CHIPOTLE**
bay leaf	pepper	**onions**	**JALAPENO**
bell peppers	red pepper flakes	**rosemary**	**CUMIN**
carrots	rice	**salt**	**GARLIC**
cayenne	salsa	**sour cream**	
celery	savory		
chives	scallions		
corn	shallots		
cream	spinach		
fennel	sugar, brown		
ginger	Tabasco		
lime	thyme		
maple syrup	tomatoes		
oranges	tomato, sauce, paste		
orange juice	vinegar		

SIMPLY INCREDIBLE PAIRINGS

black beans + chili powder + cumin

black beans + chipotle + lemon

black beans + cumin + oregano

black beans + sour cream + scallions

BLACK BEAN RECIPES

Simple Black Bean Dip

5 minutes! For an easy appetizer or healthy snack.

Serve with tortilla chips, veggies, or crackers.

Ingredients

2 - 15 oz cans black beans, rinsed and drained

1/2 cup yellow onion, chopped

1/2 cup cilantro

1 garlic clove, chopped

1 jalapeño, seeds removed and chopped

2 Tbsp lime juice

1/4 tsp cumin, ground

1/4 tsp chili powder

1/4 tsp sea salt

1/4 tsp red pepper

Directions

In a food processor, place all ingredients and blend until smooth. Scrape the sides often.

Servings: 6

Prep time: 5 mins

Total time: 5 mins

BLACK BEAN RECIPES

Black Bean Enchilada Stuffed Shells

The combination of sour cream and enchilada sauce is always a winner. But adding it to healthy black beans and vegetables, creates Simply Incredible Flavor.

Ingredients

1 - 12 oz boxes of jumbo pasta shells

1 - 15 oz can black beans, drained

1 cup sweet corn

1 cup diced tomatoes

1 cup salsa, choose your heat

3 cups vegan cheese, shredded, divided

4 cups enchilada sauce

Garnish with 1/4 cup cilantro finely chopped, and vegan sour cream

Directions

1. Pre-heat the oven to 375 degrees.

2. Boil the pasta for only 9 minutes, NOT 12 minutes. Rinse with cold water and drain.

3. Meanwhile, mix together the beans, corn, tomatoes, salsa and 1/2 of the cheese.

4. Take a 9x12 baking sheet and layer the bottom with a thin coating of enchilada sauce, saving the rest for topping.

5. Carefully stuff the shells with the black bean mixture, and place in the 9x12 baking sheet.

6. Carefully pour the remaining enchilada sauce over the shells.

7. Top with the remaining cheese.

8. Cover with foil and bake for 30 minutes.

9. Remove foil and allow to cook for additional 10 minutes.

10. Top with cilantro and serve with sour cream.

Servings: 4

Prep time: 20 min

Cook time: 40 mins

Total time: 1 hour

BLACK BEAN RECIPES

Roasted Vegetable Enchilada Stack

These easy enchiladas are loaded with roasted veggies, black beans, and cheese. They freeze well too!

Ingredients

1 large red pepper, chopped,

1 medium zucchini, chopped

1 medium yellow squash, chopped

1 large onion, chopped

1 Tbsp olive oil

Salt and pepper

1 - 15 oz can black beans, rinsed and drained

1 tsp ground cumin

1 tsp chili powder

2 garlic cloves, minced

1 jalapeño, seeded and minced

1/2 cup chopped fresh cilantro

Salt and pepper, to taste

2 cups red enchilada sauce

12 small corn tortillas

2 cups vegan cheese, shredded

Directions

1. Preheat the oven to 400 degrees. Grease an 8x8 square baking pan and set aside.

2. On a large baking sheet, place red pepper, zucchini, yellow squash, and onion. Drizzle with olive oil and toss until vegetables are coated. Season with salt and pepper.

3. Roast vegetables for 30-40 minutes, or until tender, stirring occasionally. Remove vegetables from oven and let cool to room temperature.

4. Reduce oven temperature to 350 degrees.

5. In a medium bowl, combine roasted vegetables, black beans, cumin, chili powder, garlic, jalapeño, and cilantro. Stir and season with salt and pepper.

6. Spread 1/4 cup of enchilada sauce into the bottom of the baking pan. Add a layer of tortillas, to completely cover the bottom of the pan. You might have to cut the tortillas to make them fit. Top with 1/3 of the vegetable/bean mixture and 1/3 of the cheese. Make a second layer of tortilla, enchilada sauce, vegetables/beans, and cheese. Top with a layer of tortillas, enchilada sauce, vegetables/beans, and cheese.

7. Cover pan with oven safe saran wrap and foil.

8. Bake enchiladas for 20 minutes. Remove the foil/saran wrap and bake for another 10 minutes, until cheese is melted and the enchiladas are bubbling.

9. Remove enchiladas from the oven and let cool for 10 minutes. Cut into squares and serve warm.

Servings: 4 to 6

Prep time: 20 min

Cook time: 1 hour

Total time: 1.3 hour

BLACK BEAN RECIPES

Smothered Black Bean Burrito
WITH AVOCADO SAUCE

There is easy, and then there is really easy! This concept of using multiple complimenting sauces is the easiest way to get Simply Incredible Flavor.

Ingredients

1 cup enchilada sauce

1 - 15 oz can black beans, rinsed and drained

1 - 15 oz can black refried beans

2 cups salsa, choose your heat

2 cups tomatoes, diced

4 cups shredded vegan cheese

2 Tbsp lime juice

4 large flour tortillas (12 to 16 inch tortillas)

Avocado Sauce (Recipe Below)

fresh chopped cilantro for garnish

Directions

1. Heat the oven to 375 degrees.

2. Take a 9x12 inch baking pan and cover the bottom with the enchilada sauce.

3. In a bowl, mix the remaining ingredients together.

4. Equally divide the mixture and roll into the 4 tortillas.

5. Place the 4 jumbo burritos in the 9x12 baking dish.

6. Drizzle 1/2 the avocado sauce over the tops of the burritos.

7. Cover and bake for 30 minutes. It should be steaming hot.

8. Transfer to plates. And drizzle remaining avocado sauce over burritos.

9. Sprinkle with cilantro.

Avocado Sauce

Ingredients

2 avocados

1 cup vegan sour cream

1/2 cup cilantro

1/2 jalapeno pepper, seeded

1/8 tsp salt to taste

Directions

1. In a food processor, mix ingredients together.

2. Add water until it is thick, but pourable.

Servings: 4 » Prep time: 20 min.

Cook time: 30 min. » Total time: 50 min.

BLACK BEAN RECIPES

Black Bean Brownies

This is one of those fun recipes to share with people who don't think vegan can taste great. And it's gluten free too!

Ingredients

2 -15 oz cans black beans, rinsed and drained

1/4 cup cocoa powder, or carob powder

1 cup quick oats

1/2 tsp salt

1 cup maple syrup

1/2 cup coconut oil

2 Tbsp vanilla extract

1 1/2 tsp baking powder

1 cup chocolate chips, dark vegan

Directions

1. Preheat oven to 350 degrees.

2. In a food processor, combine all ingredients except chips.

3. Blend really well until completely smooth.

4. Stir in the chips, and pour into a greased 9x12 pan.

5. Bake the brownies for 20 minutes.

6. Then let cool at least 10 minutes before cutting. If they seem undercooked, place them in the fridge overnight and they will firm up.

Chef's Notes:

Serve them first, and then reveal the secret ingredient. You can also sprinkle the top with more chips and or chopped nuts.

Servings: 12-16

Prep time: 10 min.

Cook time: 20 min.

Total time: 30 min.

BLACK BEAN RECIPES

Easy Black Bean and Zucchini Burgers

This has got to be the easiest veggie burger recipe ever.

High in protein and fiber, and you can always add your own little twists to it.

Ingredients

2 cups black beans, rinsed and drained

2 cups shredded zucchini

3/4 cup ground flax seed

1 Tbsp steak seasoning

Directions

1. Mix all the ingredients together and mash well with a fork.

2. Let it sit for 10 minutes for the flax to gel everything together.

3. Shape into 6 patties, placing them on parchment paper and let set again for 10 minutes or refrigerate overnight.

4. Grill on medium-high heat until crispy golden on each side. A little vegetable oil is recommended, but not too much. It helps sear them together.

Chef's Notes:

These burgers are a challenge to hold together, so be careful. And I generally serve them right on the bun, so they don't need to be handled by the consumers.

Servings: 4 to 6
Prep time: 10 min.
Cook time: 10 min.
Total time: 20 min.

BLACK BEAN RECIPES

Simple Black Bean Salads

This is a great recipe that you can flip into any regional flavor.

Ingredients

2 - 15 oz cans black beans, rinsed and drained

4 cups corn, fresh or frozen

2 tomatoes, chopped

1 cup red onion, chopped

1 scallion, chopped

Juice of 2 limes

1/4 cup chopped, fresh cilantro

1/4 tsp salt

1/4 tsp pepper

Southwest Add:

1 avocado, diced

1 diced jalapeno

1/2 cup salsa

Italian Add:

1/4 cup tomato sauce

2 Tbsp Italian seasoning

Asian Add:

2 Tbsp soy sauce

1/2 cup water chestnuts

1/2 cup bamboo shoots

Directions

1. Combine all ingredients together and allow the salad to rest 30 minutes.

2. Stir and add salt as needed.

BLACK BEAN RECIPES

Black Beans and Rice

Simple and completely versatile.

This recipe can be converted literally into any culture.

Ingredients

kosher salt

4 cups water

1 tsp salt

2 cups long-grain rice

2 Tbsp olive oil or water sauté

1 onion, chopped

1 large green or red pepper, chopped

2 medium cloves garlic, minced

2 - 15 oz cans black beans, undrained

1 cup vegetable stock

2 Tbsp red wine vinegar

2 bay leaves

1 Tbsp chili powder

1/4 tsp ground cumin

1/2 cup sliced scallions to garnish

Directions

1. In a medium saucepan, combine 4 cups of water with 1 teaspoon salt. Bring to a boil.

2. Stir in the rice and educe heat. Cook covered for 20 minutes or until the rice is tender.

3. Remove from heat, and allow to rest for another 20 minutes covered.

4. Meanwhile, in a saucepan, sauté the onion and green pepper until softened, about 5 minutes.

5. Add the garlic and cook for another minute, stirring well.

6. Add the beans, stock, vinegar, bay leaves, chili pepper and cumin. Bring to a boil.

7. Reduce heat to low and let simmer for 10 minutes.

8. Remove the bay leaves.

9. Spoon the beans over the rice and sprinkle with the scallions.

Servings: 6

Prep time: 10 min.

Cook time: 50 min.

Total time: 60 min.

BLACK BEAN RECIPES

Quick Black Bean Chili

This is a great recipe for when you're in a hurry.

Ingredients

2 Tbsp olive oil or water sauté

1 yellow onion, chopped

2 red or green bell peppers, chopped

4 garlic cloves, minced

3 - 15 oz cans black beans, drained

1 - 16 oz can tomato sauce

1/2 cup water

2 Tbsp chili powder

2 tsp oregano, dried

2 tsp cumin, ground

1/2 tsp pepper

salt to taste

Chopped fresh cilantro

Vegan sour cream

Chopped green onions

Directions

1. In a large heavy bottom sauce pot, sauté onions and bell peppers until softened, about 10 minutes.

2. Add the garlic, chili powder, oregano, cumin, and pepper. Stir in for a minute.

3. Mix in beans, water, and tomato sauce. Bring chili to boil, stirring occasionally.

4. Reduce heat to medium-low and simmer until flavors blend and chili thickens, stirring occasionally, about 20 minutes.

5. Season to taste with salt.

6. Ladle chili into bowls. Top with vegan sour cream, cilantro and green onions.

Servings: 4

Prep time: 5 min.

Cook time: 30 min.

Total time: 35 min.

Beans, pinto

The pinto bean is the most popular bean in the United States and northwestern Mexico. It is often eaten whole in broth or mashed and refried. with 44 grams of carbs, it is a healthy food that you can eat every day. One cup of pinto beans has 30 grams of dietary fiber.

Beans, pinto

GOOD These items go well with this food.		BETTER Even better pairing.	BEST The WOW factor!
bell peppers	mint	**chili powder**	**CHILI PEPPERS**
carrots	mustard	**chilies**	**RICE**
cardamon	onions	**cumin**	**SALT**
cayenne	oregano	**jalapeno**	
cheeses	paprika	**parsley**	
chili	savory	**salsa**	
chipotle	scallions		
cilantro	sour cream		
epazote	tomatoes		
garlic			

SIMPLY INCREDIBLE PAIRINGS

pinto beans + cheeses + salsa

pinto beans + chili powder + cumin

pinto beans + poblano chilies + tomatoes

pinto beans + garlic + onions + salt

PINTO BEAN RECIPES

Homemade Refried Beans

Traditionally made with lard, I have tweaked the concept to give you a vegan version that will give you Simply Incredible Flavor without all the fat. And it is soooooo easy!

Ingredients

2 lbs dried pinto beans

5 cloves garlic minced

plenty of water

2 tsp salt

Directions

1. Add the beans and the minced garlic to a large pot. Pour the water in. You should have at least 3 parts water to 1 part beans.

2. Bring to a boil, then turn the heat to low and continue to simmer covered. Allow to cook for about 2 hours, stirring every half hour, until beans are soft. Extra Soft! Careful not to burn.

3. Once the beans are extra soft, drain completely.

4. Mash the beans to desired consistency and add salt. The refried beans should be thick.

5. Use water to thin if necessary. Stir well.

6. Serve warm.

Servings: 10

Prep time: 5 min.

Cook time: 2 hours

Total time: 2 hours

PINTO BEAN RECIPES

Pinto Bean Quesadillas
WITH SWEET POTATO AND KALE

Ingredients

1 Tbsp olive oil

2 cups kale, chopped

2 garlic cloves, minced

1 - 15 oz can pinto beans, rinsed drained

1 sweet potato, medium, cooked, and diced

1/2 tsp chili powder

1/4 tsp cumin

6 flour tortillas, large

3 cups vegan cheese

Directions

1. In a cooking pot, on medium-high heat, sauté the kale for about 5 minutes, until wilted.

2. Add garlic and sauté for another minute.

3. Add remaining ingredients and sauté until hot.

4. In a large skillet, over medium-high heat, place a tortilla.

5. Cover with a generous amount of cheese.

6. Add the pinto bean mixture to only 1/2 of the tortilla.

7. Once the cheese has melted, fold in half. The tortilla should be crisp, but not burning.

8. Cut and serve.

Servings: 6

Prep time: 5 min.

Cook time: 15 min.

Total time: 20 min.

PINTO BEAN RECIPES

Simple Pinto Bean Meatless Meatloaf

Sometimes you need to make something fast. This recipe scores a home run for easy. And this simple glaze will give you that Simply Incredible Flavor that sets your meatless loaf apart.

Ingredients

For the Glaze

1/2 cup ketchup

1/4 cup water

2 Tbsp molasses

2 Tbsp mustard, Dijon

1 tsp chili powder

For the Meatloaf

1 cup oats, old fashioned or quick

1 small onion, chopped

1/2 red bell pepper, chopped

2 garlic cloves, minced

1/2 cup sunflower kernels

1 - 15 oz can pinto beans, rinsed and drained

1 - 15 oz can chickpeas, rinsed and drained

2 Tbsp chili powder

Salt and pepper, to taste

Directions

1. Preheat oven to 375 degrees. lightly grease a loaf pan

2. In a small bowl, whisk together all glaze ingredients. Set aside.

3. In a food processor, add the oats, onion, green pepper, garlic and sunflower kernels and pulse until well combined.

4. Add in chickpeas, pinto beans, chili powder, salt and pepper. Pulse until beans are almost pureed, leaving a bit of texture.

5. Spoon bean mixture into loaf pan and spread out.

6. Pour glaze over bean mixture.

7. Bake for about 35 minutes or until glaze is caramelized and loaf is solid.

Servings: 4 to 6

Prep time: 5 min.

Cook time: 35 min.

Total time: 40 min.

PINTO BEAN RECIPES

Pinto Bean Breakfast Sausage

I love this recipe because I can make big batches and freeze them for future heat and serve use.

Ingredients

2 Tbsp olive oil, or water sauté

1/2 cup onions, finely chopped

1/2 lb. mushrooms, finely chopped

1 Tbsp soy sauce

2 - 15 oz cans pinto beans, rinsed and drained

1/3 cup chickpea flour

2 Tbsp finely chopped fresh sage

1 Tbsp olive oil

2 tsp thyme

1 1/2 tsp maple syrup

1 tsp fennel seeds

1 tsp rosemary

1/2 tsp nutmeg

pinch pepper

pinch red pepper flakes

Directions

1. In a large skillet over medium-high heat, sauté the onions and mushrooms for about 7 minutes. Until very soft.

2. Stir in the soy sauce and remove from the heat. Let cool.

3. In a food processor, add the drained beans, chickpea flour, onion mixture and 1 tablespoon olive oil. Pulse until the beans are finely chopped and hold together. Don't over blend. We want some chunks and bits.

4. Add the remaining ingredients, and pulse until combined.

5. Divide the bean mixture into 12 even portions. Create sausage shaped logs, then roll up tight in plastic wrap and twist the ends like a tootsie roll.

6. Set up a steamer. Place the rolled up sausages in it.

7. Simmer over medium high heat for at least 20 minutes.

8. Remove from heat, and refrigerate for 2 hours or overnight.

9. When ready to serve, unwrap the sausages and cook in a nonstick skillet over medium-high heat.

10. Turning them as needed, until browned and crisp. About 7 minutes.

Chef's Notes:

This recipe can be tweaked in a lot of ways. Any kind of beans will work, plus you can spice it up if you like.

Servings: 12 sausage links » Prep time: 20 min.

Cook time: 20 min. » Total time: 40 min.

Beans, red kidney

73% of the calories in red kidney beans come from carbs. And that's a really good thing. You do not want foods that have high calories from fat. Plus, one serving has a whopping 46 grams of dietary fiber.

Beans, red kidney

GOOD These items go well with this food.		BETTER Even better pairing.	BEST The WOW factor!
bell peppers	pepper	bay leaf	**CHILI POWDER**
cardamom	potatoes	chili	**GARLIC**
carrots	saffron	chili peppers	**SALT**
cayenne	sauerkraut	cilantro	
cinnamon	thyme	cumin	
cloves	tomatoes	parsley	
coriander	turmeric	savory	
curry			
ginger			
onions			

SIMPLY INCREDIBLE PAIRINGS

kidney beans + bell peppers + chili powder + onions

kidney beans + chili powder + cumin + salt

kidney beans + onions + savory + tomatoes

kidney beans + cilantro + garlic + salt

RED KIDNEY BEAN RECIPES

Kidney Bean and Coconut Curry

Ingredients

4 cups dried kidney beans, soaked in water overnight

2 Tbsp vegetable oil or water sauté

2 red onions, chopped

4 tomatoes, large chopped

4 garlic cloves, minced

4 cups coconut milk

2 jalapeño, seeded and chopped

2 Tbsp curry powder

1 Tbsp cardamom, ground

salt to taste

garnish with plenty of fresh chopped cilantro

Directions

1. Drain and rinse the soaked kidney beans.

2. In a large heavy bottom saucepan, cover the kidney beans with water and bring to a boil. Then reduce the heat to low and simmer for about 1 hour, just until tender. Drain and set aside.

3. In the same heavy bottom sauce pot, sauté the onion until softened, about 5 minutes.

4. Add the tomatoes and garlic and cook for 5 minutes.

5. Add the kidney beans, jalapeño, coconut milk, curry, and cardamom.

6. Simmer over low heat for 20 minutes.

7. Season with salt.

8. Garnish with the cilantro and serve with rice.

Chef's Notes:

Serve with cooked basmati or jasmine rice.

Servings: 6 to 8

Prep time: 5 min.

Cook time: 1.5 hours

Total time: 1.5 hours

RED KIDNEY BEAN RECIPES

Kidney Beans and Mushroom Rougaille

This is a Mauritian creole-style tomato-based dish that is quick and easy to make, Despite its simplicity, it brings Simply Incredible Flavor. It can be enjoyed over rice, pasta, noodles, or with a bread or flatbread.

Ingredients

1 tsp vegetable oil or water sauté

1 onion, slivered

1 lb. mushrooms, sliced or quartered

2 green chilies, deseeded and diced

2 garlic cloves, minced

1 Tbsp ginger, minced

1 tsp curry, ground

2 cups red kidney beans, cooked or canned

6 roma tomatoes, chopped

1 cup vegetable stock

1 cup tomato sauce

1 Tbsp thyme, fresh chopped

1/2 cup green peas, frozen

1/2 cup cilantro leaves, chopped

Salt to taste

Directions

1. In a heavy bottom medium size pan, Sauté the onions, mushrooms and chilis for about 5 minutes.

2. Add the ginger, garlic, and curry, and sauté for another minute

3. Add the red kidney beans, tomatoes, vegetable stock, tomato sauce, and thyme, and cook on medium heat for about 10 minutes. Stirring occasionally. The liquid should be reduced to nothing but a sauce.

4. Salt to taste and stir well.

5. Remove from heat, stir in the peas and cilantro right before serving.

Chef's Notes:

This is my savory recipe. But you can also add heat with jalapeño, or pepper.

Servings: 3 to 4

Prep time: 5 min.

Cook time: 15 min.

Total time: 20 min.

RED KIDNEY BEAN RECIPES

Kidney Bean Burgers

Once you have all the ingredients prepped and ready to go, this kidney bean veggie burger can be made in no time at all.

Ingredients

2 - 15 oz cans kidney beans, rinsed and drained

1/4 cup onions, chopped

3 garlic cloves, chopped

1 ginger piece, 1/2 inch, chopped

1 Tbsp curry powder

1 Tbsp chili sauce

2 Tbsp cilantro, chopped

1 tsp thyme

2 Tbsp nutritional yeast flakes

1/2 tsp salt to taste

To tighten up burgers:

quick oats

1/4 cup walnuts, chopped

Directions

1. In a food processor pulse together all the ingredients except the chopped walnuts. It should be coarsely ground, not a fine paste.

2. Transfer to a bowl. The bean mixture should be able to roll into balls and flatten into patties. If it's sticky add some quick oats to get the right consistency. If its dry, add a tablespoon of water.

3. Mix in the chopped walnuts.

4. Spray a sauté pan with non-stick oil and cook burgers on medium heat for about 8 minutes on each side. Don't be in a hurry to flip them, because they will lose shape.

Chef's Notes:

This is a great flavored burger patty, but can fall apart if not cooked, and handled right so take your time. And I suggest serving them on the bun, not leaving them for the consumers to handle. And once the batch is made, you can refrigerate them for later cooking.

Servings: 8 burgers

Prep time: 15 min.

Cook time: 15 min.

Total time: 20 min.

RED KIDNEY BEAN RECIPES

Kidney Bean Salad
WITH DIJON CILANTRO VINAIGRETTE

Ingredients

2 - 15-oz cans kidney beans, rinsed and drained

1 English cucumber, diced

1 medium-sized heirloom tomato, chopped

1 red onion, diced

1 yellow bell pepper, diced

Directions

1. In a medium sized bowl, combine the kidney beans with the chopped vegetables. Mix in the vinaigrette. Allow to rest or chill. Mix prior to serving.

For the Dijon Cilantro Vinaigrette

2 lemons, juiced

1 Tbsp Dijon mustard

1 Tbsp red wine vinegar

1 garlic clove, minced

1 Tbsp honey

3 Tbsp extra virgin olive oil

1/2 cup fresh, chopped cilantro

pinch salt and pepper to taste

Directions

1. To make the vinaigrette - in a small bowl, whisk together the lemon juice, mustard, vinegar, garlic, and honey.

2. Then slowly drizzle the olive oil in while whipping.

3. Add the cilantro and salt and pepper as desired.

Servings: 6 to 8

Prep time: 15 min.

Total time: 15 min.

RED KIDNEY BEAN RECIPES

Kidney Bean and Zucchini Cutlets

Ingredients

2 - 15 oz cans kidney beans, rinsed and drained

2 onions, diced extra fine

1 zucchini, shredded

3/4 cup whole-wheat flour

1 tsp curry powder

1 tsp onion powder

1/2 tsp granulated garlic

1 tsp salt to taste

oil spray for cooking

Directions

1. Drain and rinse the beans, put them into a large bowl and mash them with a fork. Don't over mash them, leave them lumpy.

2. Add the remaining ingredients.

3. Mix well, carefully with your hands or with a fork.

4. Spray a sauté pan with non-stick cooking spray, then form cutlets with your hands and cook on medium-high heat. Cook them until crispy for about 7 minutes on each side.

Servings: 4 to 6

Prep time: 10 min.

Cook time: 15 min.

Total time: 25 min.

Beans, white

White beans certainly have the greatest range of flavor of any bean. You can go sweet or heat. Salty or savory. They also have the highest amount of carbs of any bean, and they have the most fiber of any bean. Definitely one of the beans that you should have on your menu every week.

Beans, white

GOOD These items go well with this food.		BETTER Even better pairing.	BEST The WOW factor!
ancho	mustard, Dijon	**bay leaf**	**MOLASSES**
chili powder	mustard, yellow	**cayenne**	**ONIONS**
apricots, dried	pepper	**chives**	**PARSLEY**
basil	red pepper flakes	**garlic**	**SALT**
broccoli rabe	sage	**mushrooms**	**SAVORY**
carrots	shallots	**rosemary**	
celery	sour cream	**sugar, brown**	
cheese	soy sauce	**vinegar: balsamic**	
chili powder	squash		
cloves	tarragon		
cream	thyme		
fennel	tomato, sauce, paste		
ginger	tomatoes		
ketchup	truffles		
lemon juice	vegetable stock		
maple syrup	vinegar, cider		
mustard, dry			

SIMPLY INCREDIBLE PAIRINGS

white beans + rosemary + balsamic vinegar

white beans + broccoli rabe + mushrooms

white beans + brown sugar + cloves + Dijon + molasses

white beans + cajun + lemon + sour cream + tomato

white beans + garlic + leeks + sage

WHITE BEAN RECIPES

White Bean Hummus

Ingredients

1/2 cup olive oil and or water for blending

1 garlic bulb, roasted

2 - 15-oz cans northern beans, rinsed and drained

Juice of one lemon, or about 1 Tbsp

1 tsp ground cumin

2 Tbsp chopped parsley or cilantro

1/2 Tbsp salt to taste

1/8 tsp white pepper to taste

Directions

1. For the Garlic: Preheat the oven to 400 degrees. Cut the top off of a head of garlic, so the top of each garlic clove is visible. Drizzle a little olive oil on the garlic. Wrap in foil and bake for about 50 minutes, until golden.

2. Place the white beans, and peeled, roasted garlic in a food processor. Add the lemon juice and cumin. Process until smooth by slowly adding water and or oil. Be careful not to add too much. We want this thick. You may need to scrape the sides.

3. Add sea salt to taste and white pepper. Blend until very smooth.

4. Add the chopped parsley or cilantro and pulse a couple times.

5. Serve cool with tortilla chips, pita bread, bagels or any array of fresh chopped vegetables.

Chef's Notes:

This particular hummus is great cold, but you can also warm it up for an additional dimension of Simply Incredible Flavor.

Servings: about 3 cups

Prep time: 5 min.

Cook time: 50 min.

Total time: 1 hour

WHITE BEAN RECIPES

Creamy Roasted Garlic White Bean Soup

This recipe has Simply Incredible Flavor written all over it.

ingredients

1 head of garlic

2 Tbsp olive oil or water sauté

1 large leek, sliced thin

3 carrots, sliced

4 celery stalks, sliced

1 tsp sage, rubbed

1 cup dried navy beans, soaked overnight

3 cups vegetable broth

2 cups cashew milk, unsweetened

2 Tbsp vinegar, balsamic

1/4 tsp pepper to taste

1/4 tsp sea salt to taste

Directions

1. For the Garlic: Preheat the oven to 400 degrees. Cut the top off of a head of garlic, so the top of each garlic clove is visible. Drizzle a little olive oil on the garlic. Wrap in foil and bake for about 50 minutes, until golden.

2. For the Soup: In a large heavy bottom stock pot on medium heat, sauté the leeks until softened. (about 3 minutes).

3. Add the carrots, celery and sage, and cook for about 7 minutes, until the vegetables are tender.

4. Add remaining ingredients, and boil over medium heat, uncovered, until beans are softened and soup is thickening. About 45 minutes.

5. Once the beans are tender, transfer just one cup of the soup to a blender along with the peeled roasted garlic, and blend until smooth. Add a little of water if necessary.

6. Stir the blended soup back into the pot.

7. Add salt to taste.

8. Serve hot.

Chef's Notes:

This soup gets thicker when chilled, so you may need to add a splash of water when reheating.

Servings: about 4 cups

Prep time: 15 min.

Cook time: 1 hour

Total time: 1.3 hours

WHITE BEAN RECIPES

Simply Incredible White Bean Chili

This is one of my all time favorite recipes that I have been doing for many years. Because it is….. Simply Incredible.

Ingredients

2 pounds dried navy beans

2 Tbsp olive oil, or water sauté

2 cups diced onion

2 cups red bell peppers, diced

4 garlic cloves, minced

1 gallon water

2 cups green chiles, diced canned

1/4 cup chili powder

2 Tbsp cumin

1 Tbsp dried oregano

1 1/2 Tbsp salt to taste

1 - 8oz package Butler Soy Curls

1 -14 oz can diced tomatoes

1/2 bunch cilantro leaves, chopped

Directions

1. Rinse beans, cover with plenty of water, and soak for 2 hours, or overnight. Drain.

2. In a large heavy bottom stockpot on medium-high heat, sauté the onion and bell peppers until browned.

3. Add the garlic and sauté for another minute.

4. Add water, beans, green chilies, chili powder, cumin, oregano and salt. Bring to a boil, then simmer for 1 hour.

5. Take the dry Butler Soy Curls and crush them inside the package until they're little pieces. Add soy curls and diced tomatoes to the stock pot and simmer for 30 minutes. The soy curls will absorb liquid, so keep an eye on the pot, you may need to add more water.

6. Taste to see if more salt is needed.

7. Add the cilantro right before serving.

WHITE BEAN RECIPES

Garlic Mashed Beans

1. In a medium size sauce pan, sauté 2 minced garlic cloves in olive oil for about a minute.
2. Rinse and drain a can of Cannellini beans and add to cooked garlic.
3. Add 1/4 cup vegetable broth. Bring to a boil, reduce heat, and simmer for 15 minutes.
4. Mash mixture with 1/2 lemon juiced.
5. Garnish with a drizzle of olive oil, some chopped parsley, or pepper.

Creamy Rosemary and White Bean Soup

1. Sauté a chopped onion in olive oil until soft and translucent.
2. Add the leaves from 2 rosemary sprigs and a clove of garlic. Cook until fragrant.
3. Rinse and add a can of Cannellini beans along with 1 bay leaf.
4. Add vegetable broth to just barely cover beans. Bring to a boil, reduce heat, and simmer about 20 minutes.
5. Remove bay leaf and purée soup in a blender or with an immersion blender until smooth.

WHITE BEAN RECIPES

Baked Jalapeño-White Bean Flautas

1. Rinse and mash a 15 oz can of Cannellini beans.

2. Add 1/4 cup finely chopped fresh cilantro, 1 finely chopped jalapeño (seeds removed), 1 cup vegan shredded cheese, and 1 Tbsp. fresh lime juice.

3. Divide filling among 8 - 6 inch tortillas. Roll up tight to form flautas.

4. Bake in a 425 degree oven, seam side down, on a parchment-lined baking sheet. Tortillas should be crisp and just beginning to crack, 15-20 minutes.

Roasted Tomatoes and Cannellini Bean Bake

1. In an 8x8" baking dish, place 6 halved plum tomatoes, cut side up. Splash with a little olive oil, and top with minced garlic cloves and fresh thyme leaves.

2. Season with sea salt and pepper. Roast in a 375 degree oven for 45 minutes.

3. Chop up the tomatoes.

4. Rinse 1 can Cannellini beans, and mix into tomatoes. Returning them to the baking dish.

5. Top with 1 cup breadcrumbs and drizzle with olive oil.

6. Broil until bubbly and just starting to be charred in spots, about 4 minutes.

WHITE BEAN RECIPES

Cannellini Bean and Roasted Red Pepper Dip

1. Rinse a can of Cannellini beans

2. In a food processor, add 1 roasted red bell pepper, 2 garlic cloves, a splash of fresh lemon juice, a couple pinches of smoked paprika, and a pinch of salt.

3. While blending, add about 1/4 cup olive oil or water to reach the desired consistency.

White Bean and Mint Crostini

1. In a food processor, purée fresh mint leaves, fresh lemon juice, and a splash of olive oil to make a loose pesto.

2. Rinsed and mash some canned Cannellini beans. Mix in with mint pesto.

3. Spread on crostini. Top with fine grated lemon zest and fine chopped red onion.

Garbanzo beans
AKA CHICK PEAS OR CHICKPEAS

Garbanzo beans are my absolute favorite bean. I can eat them right out of the can. At home, we cook off big batches, cool them, and freeze them in quart bags. They can be used in everything from hummus to salads, soups to simply roasting them for a healthy snack. And they are healthy carbs that the body needs. It's easy to get Simply Incredible Flavor when you start with such a flavorful ingredient.

Garbanzo beans
AKA CHICK PEAS OR CHICKPEAS

GOOD These items go well with this food.		BETTER Even better pairing.	BEST The WOW factor!
apple cider	paprika	**chili powder**	**GARLIC**
basil	parsley	**cilantro**	**LEMON JUICE**
bay leaf	pasta	**coriander**	**OLIVES, GREEN**
bell pepper	pepper	**cumin**	**ONIONS**
bread	potatoes	**curry**	**SALT**
cardamom	raisins	**olives, black**	
carrots	red pepper flakes	**rosemary**	
cayenne	rice	**tahini**	
chili peppers	saffron	**vinegar, balsamic**	
chives	sage		
cinnamon	scallions		
cloves	spinach		
couscous	squash		
fennel	tamarind		
ginger	thyme		
leeks	tomatoes		
lemon zest	turmeric		
lemon preserves	vegetable stock		
mint	vinegar, red wine		

SIMPLY INCREDIBLE PAIRINGS

chickpeas + cilantro + cumin

chickpeas + garlic + lemon + tahini + salt

chickpeas + garlic + lemon + thyme

chickpeas + garlic + mint

chickpeas + garlic + parsley

GARBANZO BEAN RECIPES

Roasted Garbanzo Beans

Take canned garbanzo beans rinse, drain, and dry. Place on a parchment paper lined sheet pan. Spray with some olive oil and shake around. Season with anything. Onion, garlic, salt and pepper. OR cinnamon and sugar. OR BBQ. OR Cajun seasoning. Bake at 350 for at least 45 minutes, until crispy. So easy to snack healthy.

Chickpea and Edamame Salad with Lemon and Mint Dressing

1. Take one can of rinsed and drained Chickpeas and mix in 1 1/2 cups of cooked edamame, 1/2 cup sliced green onions and 1/2 cup fresh chopped mint.

2. Add a dressing mixture of one lemon, juice and zest, along with 1 clove minced garlic, olive oil and/or red wine vinegar, and salt and pepper.

3. Toss well.

GARBANZO BEAN RECIPES

Chickpeas, Mushrooms, and Caramelized Onion Risotto

This is risotto at it's best. And we have made it simple to achieve Simply Incredible Flavor.

Ingredients

6 cups low sodium veggie broth (hot)

2 Tbsp balsamic vinegar

1 Tbsp olive oil or water sauté

1 cup onion, diced

1 cup mushrooms, sliced

1 clove garlic, minced

1 cup Arborio rice

1 lemon, juiced

1 cup Chickpeas, rinsed

white pepper to taste

fresh herbs

Instructions

1. Heat veggie broth and balsamic vinegar in a sauce pan.

2. In a heavy bottom large skillet, sauté onions and cook for about 10 minutes, until they become caramelized.

3. Add mushrooms and cook about 5 more minutes until the mushrooms are soft.

4. Add garlic and rice, stir for about 1 minute.

5. Start adding broth, 1 cup at a time, stirring each cup until it is absorbed. Continue 1 cup at a time until the rice is creamy but not mushy.

6. Add the lemon juice and chickpeas. Stir until hot and saucy.

7. Add salt, pepper, and any fresh herbs to taste.

Chef's Notes:

Fresh herbs of any sort will create a great wow factor. Whether it be parsley or cilantro, basil or oregano, fresh thyme and the list goes on. Just add them right at the end with the chickpeas.

GARBANZO BEAN RECIPES

Green Garbanzo Patties with Fresh Herb Tofu Aioli

Ingredients

2 Tbsp olive oil or water sauté

1 cup onion, diced

4 cups shiitake mushrooms, cleaned and stems removed.

2 cups green garbanzo beans

2 garlic cloves, chopped

1 cup brown rice, cooked

1 cup parsley

1 tsp cumin

1 tsp sea salt

1/2 tsp cayenne pepper

Directions

1. In a large skillet on medium-high heat, sauté onions.

2. When onions are translucent add the mushrooms and cook about 5 minutes, until they have cooked down and are tender.

3. Add the garlic and sauté for another minute.

4. Place all the ingredients in a food processor and pulse until incorporated, but not completely pureed.

5. Form into burger patties. Pan fry with a little vegetable oil on medium heat for about 5 minutes on each side, or until golden brown.

Chef's Notes:

If you can't find the green garbanzos, regular ones will do. You can also bake in the oven on a sheet pan for a low oil version.

Fresh Herb Tofu Aioli

Ingredients

6 oz silken tofu

1 Tbsp nutritional yeast flakes

1 Tbsp miso

1 lemon, juiced

1/2 tsp lemon, zest

1 clove garlic, minced

1 tsp mustard, Dijon

1/4 tsp pepper

1 Tbsp olive oil

1 Tbsp parsley, chopped

1 Tbsp dill, fresh chopped

salt to taste

Directions

In a blender or food processor puree all of the ingredients except for the herbs and olive oil. With the machine still running, slowly add the oil until smooth and creamy. Add the herbs and pulse a few times to incorporate. Add salt to taste.

(Makes 1 cup)

Servings: 6 to 8 patties

Prep time: 10 min.

Cook time: 25 min.

Total time: 40 min.

GARBANZO BEAN RECIPES

Smashing Chickpea Avocado Salad

Ingredients

1 - 15 oz can of Chickpeas, rinsed and drained

1 avocado pitted and removed from shell

2 stalks of celery - diced

2 scallions roughly chopped

1 cup parsley

1 Tbsp nutritional yeast flakes

1 small lemon juiced - about 2 Tbsp

pinch of salt to taste

Directions

1. Place all ingredients into a food processor and pulse. Don't over process. We want this to be chunky. Just process enough to hold together. I call this 'smashing' because that's how the chickpeas should look.

Servings: 4

Prep time: 10 min.

Total time: 10 min.

GARBANZO BEAN RECIPES

Coconut Chickpea Truffles

Ingredients

1 cup rolled oats

1/2 cup chickpeas, rinsed, drained and dried

1/2 cup coconut flakes

1/2 cup cashew butter

1/4 cup maple syrup

1/4 tsp salt

stevia powder if needed

1 cup bittersweet/dark chocolate chips

Directions

1. In a food processor, combine the oats and chickpeas, and pulse until they are in small pieces.

2. Add the cashew butter, maple syrup, and salt. Process until it forms a smooth ball. Scrape the sides a few times. Taste to see if it's sweet enough. If not, you may want to add stevia. Process until smooth.

3. Roll the filling into balls and place on a parchment paper lined baking sheet.

4. Place the baking sheet of balls into the freezer and freeze for 20-30 minutes.

5. Melt the chocolate chips in a small pot on low heat.

6. When the balls are firm, drop one by one into the chocolate, cover completely with chocolate. Remove with a spoon and place back on the baking sheet.

7. While the chocolate is still wet, sprinkle a tiny bit of coconut flakes on top of each truffle.

8. Once they are all done, refrigerate until ready to eat. Enjoy!

Servings: 15 - 20 truffles

Prep time: 10 min.

Freezer time: 30 min.

Total time: 40 min.

Yield: 18-20 truffles

GARBANZO BEAN RECIPES

Chickpea Pumpkin Granola Bars

Ingredients

1 Tbsp ground flax

1/4 cup warm water

2 cups canned chickpeas, rinsed and drained

1 Tbsp brown sugar

1 tsp cinnamon

1 1/2 cup rolled oats

1 cup puffed rice cereal

1/2 cup dried cranberries, chopped

1/2 cup dried raisins, chopped

1 Tbsp pumpkin pie spice

1/4 cup pumpkin seeds

Pinch of salt

1/2 cup canned pumpkin puree

1/4 cup pure maple syrup

3 Tbsp melted coconut oil

Directions

1. Preheat oven to 375 degrees.

2. In a measuring cup mix the flax with water and set aside.

3. Combine the chickpeas with brown sugar and cinnamon in a baking dish. Bake for 10 minutes, mash rough and stir, and then bake for another 10 minutes. Let cool.

4. In a large mixing bowl, combine the oats, puffed rice, pumpkin seeds and dried fruit, pumpkin pie spice salt. Then add the cooled mashed chickpeas and mix together.

5. In a separate bowl, mix together the pumpkin puree, maple syrup, and coconut oil. Then mix in the flax mixture.

6. Add wet ingredients to dry and stir to incorporate.

7. Pour mixture into a lightly greased 9x12 inch pan, and press down evenly.

8. Refrigerate for at least 2 hours before cutting.

9. Store in the fridge or freezer.

Servings: Makes 12 bars

Prep time: 10 min.

Cook time: 25 min.

Total time: 40 min.

GARBANZO BEAN RECIPES

Chickpea Blondies
WITH CHOCOLATE CHIPS AND SEA SALT

Ingredients

1 - 15 oz can chickpeas, rinsed and drained

1/2 cup peanut butter

1/3 cup maple syrup

2 tsp vanilla extract

1/2 tsp kosher salt

1/4 tsp baking powder

1/4 tsp baking soda

1/2 cup dark chocolate chips

Sea salt, extra course for sprinkling

Directions

1. Preheat oven to 350 degrees.
2. Lightly grease an 8×8 inch pan.
3. In a food processor, add all the ingredients, except for the chocolate chips. Process until batter is smooth.
4. Mix in 1/2 of the chocolate chips and spread batter evenly in prepared pan.
5. Sprinkle remaining chocolate chips over top.
6. Bake for about 25 minutes, or until a toothpick comes out clean and edges are very light brown.
7. Let cool.
8. Sprinkle with sea salt and cut into 16 squares.

Enjoy!

Chef's Notes:

Get creative. And add nuts, dried fruits, or anything else you like.

Servings: Makes 8 bars

Prep time: 5 min.

Cook time: 25 min.

Total time: 40 min.

GARBANZO BEAN RECIPES

Chocolate Chickpea Cookie Dough

Ingredients

1 1/2 cups chick peas (or 1 can, drained and rinsed very well)

2/3 cup brown sugar

2 tsp vanilla extract

1/4 cup almond nut butter of choice

1/4 cup oats, quick or rolled

1/8 tsp sea salt

1/8 tsp baking soda

if needed thin with up to 1/4 cup almond milk

1/2 cup chocolate chips

Directions

1. Add all ingredients, except for chocolate chips, to a food processor, and process until very smooth. Scrape sides occasionally.

2. Thin with almond milk if needed.

3. Then hand mix in the chocolate chips. This should have the exact texture of real cookie dough!

4. Serve as cookie dough with small forks or spoons.

Corn

Every one of the tastebuds can be highlighted with corn. Sweet or Salty, Savory even Sour and Bitter go great with corn. And the two new tastebuds of Heat and Fat also work great with corn. 82% of the calories in corn come from carbs, and that's a really good thing. Healthy and versatile, and so easy to achieve Simply Incredible Flavor.

Corn

GOOD
These items go well with this food.

- bay leaf
- beans
- bechamel sauce
- caraway seed
- cayenne
- celery
- cheese
- chili powder
- chili sauce
- cornmeal
- cumin
- curry powder
- fennel
- ginger
- leeks
- lemon
- lemon juice
- maple syrup
- marjoram
- mirepoix
- mustard
- nutmeg
- olive oil
- oregano
- paprika
- parsley
- pasta
- polenta
- risotto
- rosemary
- sage
- shallots
- squash
- sugar
- tortillas
- vinaigrette
- vinegars

BETTER
Even better pairing.

- all beans
- black pepper
- butter substitutes
- carrots
- chipotle peppers
- chives
- cilantro
- dill
- fava beans
- jalapeno peppers
- lima beans
- lime juice
- scallions
- serrano peppers
- tarragon
- thyme
- tomatoes
- white pepper

BEST
The WOW factor!

- **BASIL**
- **BELL PEPPERS**
- **CHILI PEPPERS**
- **CREAM**
- **GARLIC**
- **MUSHROOMS**
- **ONIONS**
- **PEPPER**
- **POTATOES**
- **SALT**

SIMPLY INCREDIBLE PAIRINGS

corn + black beans + chipotle

corn + bell pepper + jalapeño + chili + cilantro + tarragon

corn + butter substitute + salt

corn + cayenne + lime + salt

corn + cilantro + salt

CORN RECIPES

Vegan Cornbread

Most cornbreads I have tasted are bland and dry. That's when I decided to go to work and create a cornbread that actually has moisture and Simply Incredible Flavor.

Ingredients

1 cup soy milk

1/2 cup creamed corn

1 1/2 Tbsp vinegar

1 cup cornmeal

1 cup unbleached all-purpose flour*

3/4 tsp salt

1 tsp baking powder

1/2 tsp baking soda

1/8 tsp crushed red pepper flakes (optional)

1/8 tsp parsley (optional)

1/2 cup applesauce

vegetable oil spray

Directions

1. Preheat oven to 350 degrees.

2. Combine soy milk, creamed corn and vinegar, and set aside.

3. In a large bowl, mix cornmeal, flour, salt, baking powder, baking soda, red pepper flakes and parsley.

4. Add soy milk mixture and applesauce to the dry ingredients and stir just until blended.

5. Spread batter into a lightly sprayed 9×9 baking dish.

6. Bake for 25 to 30 minutes, just until a toothpick inserted in the center comes out clean. Serve warm.

Chef's Notes:

*Whole wheat pastry flour works great too.

Servings: 9

Prep time: 5 min.

Cook time: 25 min.

Total time: 30 min.

CORN RECIPES

Corn Chowder

Ingredients

1 Tbsp olive oil or water sauté

1 yellow onion, diced

1 red bell pepper, diced

2 sticks of celery, diced

2 garlic cloves

3 Tbsp flour

1 cup almond milk

2 cups vegetable broth

1 large potato, peeled and diced

1 tsp celery salt

1 tsp parsley

4 ears of corn, shucked (or 4 cups frozen cereal corn)

1 tsp apple cider vinegar

salt and white pepper, to taste

garnish with green onions and cilantro

Directions

1. In a large heavy bottomed pot over medium heat, sauté onion, red bell pepper and celery for 5 minutes or until soft.

2. Add garlic and sauté for 1 minute.

3. Add in flour and cook for 2 more minutes.

4. Add almond milk and vegetable broth.

5. Add potatoes, celery salt, and parsley. Stir well and then bring to a boil. Then simmer covered for 20 minutes. Stirring occasionally so it doesn't burn.

6. Add corn kernels and stir to combine. Let cook for another 10 minutes.

7. Take 1/4 of the soup to a blender and blend till smooth. Pour back into the pot and stir well.

8. Stir in apple cider vinegar and taste. Add salt and pepper to taste.

9. Garnish with chopped green onions, cilantro.

Servings: 4 to 6

Prep time: 10 min.

Cook time: 30 min.

Total time: 40 min.

CORN RECIPES

Corn Fritters

Ingredients

1/3 cup cornmeal, fine ground

1/3 cup flour, any flour

1/2 tsp salt

1/4 tsp pepper

1/2 tsp baking powder

1/2 tsp onion powder

1/4 tsp garlic powder to taste

1/4 cup parsley, chopped

1 cup of Corn + 2 Tbsp almond milk (for creamed corn)

2 Tbsp canned Green Chiles with juices

2 cups corn, frozen kernel, or fresh

Vegetable Oil for frying OR bake for oil free version

FOR THE DIPPING SAUCE

1/4 cup vegenaise

4 tsp Dijon mustard

2 tsp BBQ sauce, smoky

Mix well

Directions

1. Combine the dry ingredients with a whisk.

2. In a food processor, pulse together the 1 cup of corn with almond milk, into creamed corn.

3. Add the green chilies and pulse.

4. Add the corn mixture to the flour mixture until well blended.

5. Add the 2 cups of corn kernels, folding to combine. Once incorporated well, let rest and it will tighten up.

6. Preheat a skillet over medium high heat. Add 1 Tbsp of oil.

7. Using an ice-cream scoop, firmly pack the batter and place into the pan, quickly flatten to form a patty shape.

8. Allow to cook until golden and then flip, cooking the other side.

9. Remove to paper towels to remove any excess oil. Season with salt.

Servings: 8 fritters

Prep time: 5 min.

Cook time: 15 min.

Total time: 20 min.

Lentils

Hold on to your lentils! The facts are in. One cup of lentils has 16 grams of fiber. They are also loaded with potassium and Iron. And the carbs are among the highest too, at 115 grams per serving.

Lentils

GOOD These items go well with this food.		BETTER Even better pairing.	BEST The WOW factor!
apple cider	leeks	**bay leaf**	**CARROTS**
bell pepper	lime juice	**chili powder**	**CELERY**
bread	mint	**cumin**	**GARLIC**
cardamom	mustard	**lemon juice**	**ONIONS**
cayenne	oregano	**parsley**	**SALT**
chillies	pepper	**soy sauce**	
chili peppers	pineapple	**thyme**	
chives	scallions	**vinegar, balsamic**	
cinnamon	shallots		
cloves	spinach		
croutons	squash		
coconut	tomatoes		
cream	turmeric		
curry	turnips		
dill	vegetable stock		
eggplant	walnuts		
ginger	zucchini		
honey			

SIMPLY INCREDIBLE PAIRINGS

lentils + bay leaf + onion + thyme

lentils + bell peppers + cumin + garlic

lentils + carrots + celery + onions + salt

lentils + cumin + turmeric

lentils + leeks + thyme

lentils + tomatoes + salt

LENTIL RECIPES

Simple Lentil Burgers

Ingredients

3 cups cooked lentils, drained dry.

1 cup walnuts, toasted

8 slices whole-wheat sandwich bread, torn into pieces

2 tsp marjoram, dried

2 garlic cloves, chopped

1/2 tsp kosher salt

1/4 tsp pepper

2 Tbsp soy sauce

vegetable oil for grilling, or bake for oil free version.

Directions

1. In a food processor, coarsely chop walnuts.

2. Add bread, marjoram, garlic, salt and pepper, process until coarse crumbly.

3. Add lentils and soy sauce, process just until the mixture just comes together in a mass. If too wet, add more bread, the tighter will hold together better.

4. Form into eight 3-inch patties.

5. In a large nonstick skillet over medium heat, cook the patties until browned on the bottom, 4 minutes. carefully turn over, and cook until browned on the other side for another couple minutes.

Chef's Note's

These burgers can be delicate, be careful handling.

To toast nuts: Toast chopped nuts in a small dry skillet over medium heat, stirring constantly, until fragrant and lightly browned, 2 to 4 minutes.

To cook lentils: Place lentils in a saucepan, cover with at least 1 inch of water, bring to a simmer and cook until just tender, about 20 minutes, depending on the type of lentil. Drain and rinse with cold water.

Servings: 8 patties

Prep time: 10 min.

Cook time: 30 min.

Total time: 40 min.

LENTIL RECIPES

Lentil and Quinoa Chili

Who needs the meat when you have this protein packed bowl of Simply Incredible Flavor?

Ingredients

1 tsp olive oil or water sauté

1 cup onion, diced

1 bell pepper, diced

3 garlic cloves, minced

2 lbs tomatoes, chopped

1/2 cup green chilis, diced

1/2 Tbsp sea salt

1 Tbsp chili powder

1 tsp cumin

1/4 tsp curry powder

1/8 tsp cinnamon

4 cups vegetable broth

1 cup lentils, rinsed

1/2 cup quinoa, rinsed

1 -15 oz can kidney beans, rinsed and drained

1 -15 oz can black beans, rinsed and drained

tomato paste to thicken

1 cup cilantro, chopped

Directions

1. In a large heavy bottom stock pot on medium-high heat, sauté onions and pepper until onions are translucent. About 5 minutes.

2. Add garlic and stir for another minute.

3. Add in tomatoes, green chilis, cumin, chili powder, cinnamon, curry, and salt, bring to a boil. Then lower the heat and simmer for 5 minutes or until tomatoes begin to break down.

4. Add broth, quinoa, and lentils. Bring back to a boil. Cover, and reduce heat to low, and simmer for about 40 minutes or until lentils are tender and quinoa has expanded.

5. Add black beans, kidney beans and some tomato paste, allow to simmer for ten minutes.

6. Taste and adjust seasonings if needed.

7. Add cilantro right before serving.

Chef's Notes:

To thicken chili, the best solution is to add a tablespoon or two of tomato paste. Now it is better to brown the paste in a sauté pan, but it is not necessary. Vegan sour cream goes great with this dish also.

Servings: 6

Prep time: 5 min.

Cook time: 55 min.

Total time: 60 min.

LENTIL RECIPES

Amazing Lentil Sloppy Joe's

The easiest way to make lentil Sloppy Joe's is to simply cook some lentils, drain well and mix in some BBQ sauce, and they're great. But if you want to go to the extreme for some Simply Incredible Flavor, try my Amazing Lentil Sloppy Joe's.

Ingredients

1 Tbsp olive oil or water sauté

1 small onion, diced fine

1 bell pepper, red or yellow, diced fine

2 sticks of celery, chopped fine

1 garlic clove, minced

1 tsp chili powder

1/2 tsp ground cumin

1 cup French lentils

3 cups water

1 - 28 oz can tomato sauce

3 Tbsp tomato paste

2 tsp balsamic vinegar

1 tsp Sriracha sauce

1 tsp salt

Directions

1. In a medium size heavy bottom pan, over medium heat. sauté the diced onions, peppers and celery. Cook for about 5 minutes, until softened.

2. Add the garlic, chili powder, and cumin, cook for an additional minute.

3. Add the lentils, 3 cups of water, tomato sauce, tomato paste, Sriracha and balsamic. Bring the lentils to a boil, then simmer uncovered on medium-low for about 30 minutes, stirring occasionally. Add more water if necessary, but try not to because you want this thick, not watery. When you get down to the last ten minutes, and it's thick, simply cover the lentils and let rest for the next ten minutes off the heat.

4. Add the salt to taste, mix well, and you're ready to serve.

Chef's Notes:

French lentils take less time to cook than regular lentils. They also retain their shape better than ordinary lentils. There's also a subtle flavor difference, where French lentils have an earthy edge.

Servings: 6

Prep time: 5 min.

Cook time: 55 min.

Total time: 60 min.

LENTIL RECIPES

Lentil Cookies

Just for the fun of it. Sometimes I like to create a recipe just as a conversation piece. And this is one of them. Not exactly the healthiest recipe I have, with the sugar and oil. But they taste great, and non-vegan people will become more open to learning about vegan foods because of these. It is still healthier than most cookies out there.

Ingredients

1 cup mixed lentils

1 cup vegan margarine

1 cup brown sugar

1 tsp vanilla

2 Tbsp ground flax seed mixed with 1/4 cup hot water

1 cup whole wheat flour

1 tsp baking soda

1 cup oats, quick

1 cup almonds, slivered

1 cup pumpkin seeds

1 cup chocolate chips, dark

Directions

1. Cook the lentils in boiling water for 35 minutes.

2. Drain well, cool, and crush well with a fork.

3. Preheat oven to 375 degrees. Grease a cookie sheet or line with parchment paper.

4. In a bowl, cream the crushed cooked lentils with margarine, vanilla and brown sugar.

5. Then add the egg replacer of ground flax seed and water.

6. Mix the baking soda in with the flour. And then add to the wet mixture.

7. Stir in the oats, slivered almonds, pumpkin seeds, and chocolate chips and mix well.

8. Drop the cookies by the tablespoon full onto the prepared baking sheet and flatten. Bake the cookies for 15 minutes and allow to cool on a baking rack.

Servings: about 15 cookies

Prep time: 5 min.

Cook time: 55 min.

Total time: 60 min.

LENTIL RECIPES

Lentil Pâté

When the French word pâté has an accent over the "e" it means "paste." When there is no accent over the "e" it means pie. That's a big difference. Usually pâté is an appetizer or spread for breads or crackers.

Ingredients

1 cup dry lentils, pre-cooked in 2 cups of water

1 sweet onion, chopped

4 garlic cloves, minced

4 tsp margarine, vegan margarine

1/2 tsp vinegar, balsamic

1/2 tsp pepper

Water if necessary

Directions

1. In a heavy bottom saucepan, sauté onions and garlic in the margarine over low heat until soft, but not browned.

2. Add lentils and heat until warmed through.

3. Place mixture into a food processor. Add vinegar and pepper. Process until smooth. Add water if necessary, but it's better to keep as thick as possible and scrape the sides a couple times.

Chef's Notes:

Serve lentil pâté at room temperature with toasted bread rounds or crackers. Can be refrigerated and used as a spread.

LENTIL RECIPES

Lentil, Leek, and Sweet Potato Soup

Ingredients

1 Tbsp olive oil or water sauté

4 leeks (white and light green parts), cut into 1/4-inch half-moons

1 garlic clove, minced

6 cups low sodium vegetable broth

1 - 28 oz can diced tomatoes,

2 sweet potatoes, peeled and cut into 1/2-inch pieces

1/2 cup brown lentils

1 bunch kale, spines removed, cut into 1/2-inch pieces

1 Tbsp thyme

1/2 tsp brown sugar

pepper to taste

Directions

1. In a large heavy bottom pan sauté the leeks until softened.

2. Add the garlic and sauté for one minute.

3. Add the tomatoes and cook for 5 minutes.

4. Add remaining ingredients and simmer for 40 minutes, until potatoes are cooked and lentils are tender.

Servings: 6

Prep time: 5 min.

Cook time: 50 min.

Total time: 55 min.

Oats

There is nothing I love better than oats. And they're extremely healthy for you. Oats have 27 grams of carbs and 4 grams of fiber in a one cup serving.

Plus it is easy to jazz up into some Simply Incredible Flavor.

Oats

GOOD These items go well with this food.		BETTER Even better pairing.	BEST The WOW factor!
almonds	orange	**apples**	**MAPLE SYRUP**
apple pie spice	peanuts	**bananas**	**SUGAR**
apricots	pears	**chocolate, dark, white**	**SUGAR, BROWN**
blueberries	pecans	**coconut**	
cherries	persimmons	**cream**	
cinnamon	plums	**dates**	
cranberries	prunes	**peaches**	
currants	pumpkin	**raisins**	
figs, dried	pumpkin pie spice	**salt**	
hazelnuts	raspberries	**vanilla**	
honey	rhubarb		
lemon	strawberries		
milks	walnuts		
nectarines			
nuts			

SIMPLY INCREDIBLE PAIRINGS

oats + almonds + dates

oats + blueberries + lemon

oats + brown sugar + raisins

oats + cinnamon + sugar + vanilla

oats + coconut + maple syrup

oats + cream + peaches

OAT RECIPES

Overnight Oats in a Jar

The principle is simple: Add your oats and all your favorite ingredients into a mason jar. And the night before you want them, add some kind of milk, give it a shake, and put in the fridge. The milk gets soaked up by the oats, and the next morning, you have a delicious ready to eat breakfast.

Ingredients

1 cup rolled oats

2 cups vegan milk

1/4 cup nuts and/or seeds

1 tsp cinnamon

1/2 tsp vanilla

1 Tbsp your favorite sweetener

Chef's Notes:

Options are Endless: Chia Seeds, coconut, flax, fresh or frozen fruits, spices, cocoa, sweeteners, and milks or even juices.

OAT RECIPES

Simple Oat Granola Recipe

Granolas are so easy to make. Once you get the hang of it, you can run with a thousand variations. This is a simple simple recipe.

Ingredients

6 cups rolled oats

6 Tbsp brown sugar, lightly packed

1 tsp cinnamon, ground

1/2 tsp sea salt

2/3 cup honey

1/2 cup vegetable oil (optional)

1 tsp vanilla extract

1 cup dried fruit, small-diced

1 cup nuts or seeds, coarsely chopped

Directions

1. Preheat the oven to 300 degrees.

2. In a large bowl mix the oats, brown sugar, cinnamon, and salt, set aside.

3. In a small bowl, mix honey, oil, and vanilla and stir to combine. Pour over the oat mixture and mix well until the oats are thoroughly coated.

4. On a rimmed baking sheet. place the oats.

5. Bake for 20 minutes, then stir and continue baking another 20 minutes more. Oats should start getting browned, without burning.

6. Cool. It will harden as it cools too.

7. Add the dried fruits and or nuts and seeds to the baking sheet and toss together.

Servings: about 8 cups

Prep time: 5 min.

Cook time: 40 min.

Total time: 45 min.

OAT RECIPES

Easy Homemade Oat Bread

With only 8 ingredients, this simple oat bread is sure to please.

Ingredients

2 1/2 cups warm water (105-115F)

4 Tbsp active dry yeast (two packets)

2 Tbsp honey

2 cups all-purpose flour

2 cups whole wheat flour

2 cups rolled oats

1 Tbsp tsp sea salt

3 Tbsp Margarine, Vegan margarine, melted, for brushing

Directions

1. In a small bowl, mix the yeast, warm water and honey. Stir until the yeast dissolves. Set aside and let rest for 5 to 10 minutes until foamy.

2. In a larger bowl, mix the flours, oats, and salt.

3. Add the wet mixture to the dry and mix very well.

4. Brush two loaf pans with some melted vegan margarine.

5. Turn the dough into the pans, cover with a clean, slightly damp cloth, and set in a warm place for 30 minutes, to rise.

6. Preheat the oven to 350 degrees.

7. With a rack in the middle, bake the bread for about 40 minutes. It should be golden and pulling away from the sides of the pan.

8. You can also leave the bread under the broiler for just a minute, to give the top a bit deeper color.

9. Remove from oven, and turn the bread onto a cooling rack.

Servings: 2 loaves

Prep time: 5 min.

Cook time: 40 min.

Total time: 45 min.

OAT RECIPES

No Bake Oat Balls

These easy no bake oat balls have a taste that will blow you away. They're the perfect tasty snack when you're craving a Simply Incredible Flavored sweet treat!

Ingredients

1 cup rolled oats

1/2 cup almond flour

1/2 cup mini dark chocolate chips

1/2 cup coconut, unsweetened shredded

1/2 cup peanut butter

1/4 cup maple syrup

1/4 cup flaxseed, ground

1 tsp vanilla extract

Directions

1. In a food processor, take oats and pulse a few times until finely chopped.

2. In a medium bowl, and all the ingredients together and mix extremely well.

3. Refrigerate for 30 minutes.

4. Roll the mixture into half dollar size balls. Wetting your hands will help from sticking. If the dough is crumbly and not sticking together, add a few drops of water, and remix until it stays together well when rolled.

5. Place balls in an air tight storage container and keep refrigerated.

Servings: about 30

Prep time: 30 min.

Cook time: 50 min.

Total time: 55 min.

OAT RECIPES

Oatmeal Carrot Cookies

Ingredients

1 cup whole wheat pastry flour

1 cup rolled oats

1 tsp baking powder

1/2 tsp sea salt

1 cup walnuts, chopped fine

1 cup carrots, shredded fine

1/2 cup maple syrup, room temperature

1/2 cup coconut oil, warmed just until it's melted

1 tsp ginger, fresh grated

Directions

1. Preheat oven to 375 degrees and line two baking sheets with parchment paper.

2. In a large bowl whisk together the flour, baking powder, salt, and oats. Add the nuts and carrots.

3. In a separate smaller bowl use a whisk to combine the maple syrup, coconut oil, and ginger.

4. Add the wet to the dry mixture and stir until combined.

5. Drop onto prepared baking sheets, one level tablespoonful at a time. Leave about 2 inches between each cookie.

6. Bake in the top 1/3 of the oven for 10 to 12 minutes. The cookies should be golden on top and bottom.

Servings: 30 cookies

Prep time: 10 min.

Cook time: 15 min.

Total time: 25 min.

OAT RECIPES

Oat & Lentil Pie

Ingredients:

Egg Replacer:

3 Tbsp flax seed, ground with 1/4 cup hot water

Loaf

1 cup of dried lentils - soak about 4 hours

2 cups vegetable broth

3 garlic cloves, minced

1 onion, diced fine

1 red bell pepper, diced

2 carrots, shredded

1 cup kale, chopped fine

1 1/2 cups quick oats, (maybe more)

1/2 tsp cumin powder

1/2 tsp curry powder

Glaze

3 Tbsp ketchup

1 Tbsp balsamic vinegar

1 Tbsp maple syrup

Directions

1. Soak your lentils for at least 4 hours, until doubled in size.

2. Preheat your oven to 350 degrees.

3. In a stock pot on medium heat, cook the drained lentils in 2 cups broth for 20 minutes.

4. Let cool for ten minutes so that it will absorb and thicken.

5. Blend half of your lentils with half a cup of water until smooth.

6. In a small bowl, mix the ground flax seeds and hot water. Set aside.

7. Sauté the onion and peppers for about 10 minutes, until onions are translucent.

8. Add the remaining ingredients and mix well. If it is too dry feel free to add a little water. It should be a little wiggly. If too wet, add more oats.

9. Scoop the mixture into a greased glass pie plate.

10. Whisk the ketchup, balsamic vinegar, and maple syrup together in a small bowl and spread evenly over the top.

11. Place it in the oven for about 40 minutes.

12. Cool for a few minutes to tighten, & serve.

Servings: 6

Prep time: 10 min.

Cook time: 1 hour.

Total time: 1.25 hours

OAT RECIPES

No Bake Oat and Almond Bars

These no-bake bars are an excellent healthy snack. They're chewy and just sweet enough with a hint of peanut butter and almonds.

Ingredients

2 cups pitted dates

1 cup almonds

1 1/2 cups quick oats

1/2 cup hemp seeds

1/2 cup peanut butter

2 Tbsp maple syrup

Directions

1. Place the almonds and dates in a food processor. Mix until it forms a dough and the almonds are broken down.

2. Place all the ingredients into a bowl and mix extremely well.

3. Place the mixture on some wax paper and press into a square. Wrap up in the wax paper.

4. Place in the fridge for at least a few hours.

5. Cut into squares and store in the fridge in an air-tight container.

Servings: 12 to 16 bars

Prep time: 10 min.

Total time: 10 min.

Potatoes

The Amazing Potatoes. We just can't say enough about potatoes. Definitely one of the healthiest, most inexpensive foods in the world that we should be eating all the time. And it has the highest satiety rating of any food. It's a good carb. It's a complex carb.

Eat the potato, not the potato chip!

Whether it be Baked Potatoes, Mashed Potatoes, Potato Wedges, or Potato Casserole, these are the complimenting foods and spices that go best with white, yellow, and red potatoes in order to create Simply incredible flavor.

Potatoes

GOOD
These items go well with this food.

- apples
- basil
- bell peppers
- caraway seeds
- cardamom
- cauliflower
- cayenne
- celery
- celery root
- chickpeas
- chicory
- chile peppers
- chili oil
- cilantro
- cinnamon
- cloves
- coriander
- cumin
- dill
- ginger
- kale
- lemon juice
- marjoram
- mint
- mushrooms
- mustard
- nutmeg
- olive oil
- olives
- paprika
- parsley
- parsnips
- peas
- saffron
- sage
- savory
- scallions
- shallots
- savory
- scallions
- shallots
- spinach
- squash
- sweet potatoes
- tarragon
- tomatoes
- truffles
- turmeric
- turnips
- vegetable stock
- vinegars

BETTER
Even better pairing.

- **bay leaf**
- **cheese**
- **curry**
- **herbs**
- **mayonnaise**
- **sour cream**

BEST
The WOW factor!

- **CARROTS**
- **CHIVES**
- **CREAM**
- **GARLIC**
- **LEEKS**
- **ONIONS**
- **PEPPER**
- **ROSEMARY**
- **SALT**
- **THYME**

SIMPLY INCREDIBLE PAIRINGS

new potatoes + garlic + shallots + tarragon + vinegar

potatoes + carrots + herbs + onions + salt

potatoes + chives + sour cream

potatoes + cream + leeks

potatoes + leeks + nutmeg

potatoes + lemon juice + rosemary + salt

SIMPLY INCREDIBLE
Baked Potatoes

These are the three concepts for cooking baked potatoes.

The standard concept is to preheat an oven to 425 degrees. Prick the potatoes with a fork a few times, rub with olive oil, and sprinkle them with salt and pepper. You can lay them directly on the oven rack or place them on a baking sheet. You will need to cook the potatoes for 45 to 60 minutes, depending on size. The skin will be crispy and poking them with a knife will have no resistance.

The second way is to simply wrap the potato with foil and cook for the same amount of time at the same temperature. This will result in a softer skin and no added oil is needed.

The third way I learned in my younger years when I was blessed to work with some of the worlds greatest chefs. The secret is to place the potatoes on a sheet pan lined with rock salt. That's right, a nice 1/2 inch bed of rock salt, in a baking pan, with the potatoes on top. This process allows the moisture from the potato to circulate into the salt and back into the potato, thus leaving a fluffier interior instead of a dense and crumbly inside. It also creates a more palatable tender skin, rather than a hard crispy skin like normal baking. Pre-heat to 425 degrees. Use a 13x9 inch baking dish with about 3 cups of rock salt on the bottom. Prick the potatoes all the way around, and place on the salt. Also, if you cover the entire pan for the first 30 minutes, then uncover for the last 15 minutes, that seems to provide the best result. I also reuse the same salt over and over for this exact purpose.

SIMPLY INCREDIBLE
Stuffed Spuds

Oh show me the ways...

There are basically two different ways you can do Stuffed Spuds. There is the simple way of stuffing them with everything under the sun. You would simply take a baked potato, cut and open producing a pocket to fill, and then 'stuff' the center with whatever filling you want.

And then there is the 'Twice Baked Potatoes' where you would take a cooked potato, cut in half, scoop out the insides, leaving the skins intact. And then you would mix the inside of the potato with an array of items, stuffing the mixture back into the potato skins and baking them for an additional amount of time.

Then there are the famous potato skins. Which would be where the potatoes are cut in half, the insides are removed, but you do not re-stuff the skins. You would coat the insides with anything and everything and bake until crispy.

21 Ideas
FOR STUFFING POTATOES

Try these concepts to give your stuffed spuds Simply Incredible Flavor.

Each concept begins with pre-baked potatoes.

They may all be served as stuffed or twice baked.

ARTICHOKE: Sauté 1 - 15 oz jar of quartered artichoke hearts, 4 chopped scallions and 1 teaspoon fresh thyme. Scoop the flesh out of 4 baked potatoes, mash with the artichokes and 1 cup vegan sour cream. Stuff into the baked potatoes.

BROCCOLI STUFFED POTATOES: Steam some broccoli flowerets and then sauté in some garlic with vegan margarine or water and salt. Top with vegan sour cream or cheese.

BRUSCHETTA: Toss 1 cup diced tomato, 1/2 cup diced red onions, 1/2 cup vegan shredded mozzarella, 1 tablespoon balsamic vinegar, some fresh chopped basil, and salt to taste. Stuff into baked potatoes and top with some bread crumbs and broil till browned.

CARAMELIZED ONION: In a skillet, sauté 1 onion slivered with 1/2 teaspoon of salt until caramelized. Stuff into a baked potatoes. Top with vegan sour cream.

CHEDDAR N CHIVE: Scoop the flesh out of 4 baked potatoes, mash with 1/4 cup vegan sour cream, chopped chives, and 1 cup grated vegan cheddar. Stuff into the skins and top with more cheese, broil to melted.

CHICKEN POT PIE: Simply take your favorite vegan chicken pot pie recipe, and stuff it into a potato. I like using the Butler Soy Curls as the chicken substitute.

CHILI-CHEESE: Stuff baked potatoes with chili, vegan shredded cheddar cheese and vegan sour cream.

CHIPOTLE, QUINOA, AND BLACK BEAN-STUFFED: Take two cups of cooked quinoa and 2 cups of black beans, and heat with a 1/2 cup of water, and a shot of adobo sauce. Season with salt, and top with diced tomatoes and cilantro.

CILANTRO-LIME: Mix 1/2 cup sour cream, the zest and juice of 1 lime, 1/2 cup chopped cilantro, and salt and pepper. Stuff into baked potatoes, top with salsa.

COLLARD GREEN SWEET POTATOES: Sauté 1 minced garlic clove and 1/2 chopped onion. Add 1 bunch chopped collard greens, 4 cups water, and salt. Simmer until tender and liquid is gone. Add 1 tablespoon apple cider vinegar and a pinch of red pepper. Stuff into baked sweet potatoes. Top with vegan shredded pepper jack cheese and broil to melt.

FAJITA STUFFED: Sauté some slivered bell peppers and onions with your favorite vegan meat substitute. I use Butler Soy Curls. Add some fajita seasoning, and stuff into a potato.

FRENCH ONION: Caramelize 1 diced onion. Scoop the flesh out of 4 baked potatoes and mash with the onion, add 1/4 cup beef-less broth and stuff into the skins, top with vegan white cheese and broil to melt.

GARLIC HERB: Sauté 8 garlic cloves in 1/2 cup vegan margarine with 1/2 tsp salt for only a minute. Add fresh chopped parsley, basil, thyme, oregano, and cilantro. Stuff into potatoes.

GUACAMOLE STUFFED: Mash 3 avocados, 2 tablespoons diced red onions, 1 tablespoon each lime juice, minced garlic, and chopped cilantro, 1/2 teaspoon minced jalapeño, and salt to taste. Stuff into baked potatoes. Top with chopped tomato.

IRISH STUFFED: Boil 4 sliced leeks, 2 cups shredded cabbage, and 2 cups shredded carrots in lightly salted water until soft. Drain water and add 1 cup plain almond milk. Simmer for 10 minutes. Scoop out the flesh of 4 baked potatoes, mash in with the cabbage mixture and stuff into the skins. Top with grated vegan cheddar cheese and broil to melt.

MANGO BLACK BEAN STUFFED SWEET POTATOES: In a small sauce pot, mix 1 1/2 cups black beans, 1 diced mango, 1/2 cup diced tomato, 1 minced jalapeño, 2 tablespoons each chopped cilantro and red onion, and the juice of 2 limes. Bring to a boil then stuff into potatoes.

MAPLE SYRUP AND PECAN: Scoop out baked sweet potatoes and mix with maple syrup and pecans. Stuff into potatoes and top with vegan white cheese or vegan marshmallows.

MUSHROOM ONION: Sauté 2 cups sliced mushrooms with 1/2 onion slivered and salt to taste. Mix in fresh dill and pepper. Stuff into the potatoes. Top with vegan sour cream and more dill.

ROASTED VEGGIE: Bring to boil one can of diced tomatoes with 1 tablespoon of vegan margarine and 1/2 teaspoon salt to taste. Roast your favorite diced veggies, add to the tomatoes along with some fresh herbs. and stir well. Stuff into your baked potatoes.

SLOPPY JOE: Sauté 1 chopped onion and 1 bell pepper. Add 1 pound cooked quinoa. Add 1 cup tomato sauce, 1 tablespoon of each brown sugar and apple cider vinegar, and 1 teaspoon cumin. Simmer until thick. Stuff into baked potatoes.

TACO STUFFED: Take your favorite vegan taco meat and stuff into a baked potato. Top with vegan cheddar cheese, sour cream, cheddar cheese, diced tomatoes, and sliced olives.

SIMPLY INCREDIBLE
Mashed Potatoes

Mashed potatoes can be made dozens of ways.

I would just like to share a couple concepts for you.

TYPES OF POTATOES: The official five types of potatoes are, White Rounds, Red Rounds, Russets, Yellows, and Blues. The most popular known potatoes are simply, Russets, Baby Reds, and Yukon Golds. But there are many more, like Fingerlings, Purple Peruvian, Katahdin, New Potatoes, and Adirondacks, just to name a few.

COUNTRY MASHED: are made with the skin on and have a few lumps in them. You can use any potato.

TO MAKE REGULAR CREAMY MASHED POTATOES: Begin by peeling the potatoes. You can use a potato masher, or use a hand mixer. Avoid using a food processor or blender, because it will make the potatoes a bit 'gluey'. The best creamy mashed potatoes are produced with a potato ricer. There is nothing better. Try mixing in cooked cauliflower for a lighter, creamy dish.

POTATO RECIPES

Apple Mashed Potatoes

Ingredients

4 potatoes, peeled and cubed

2 apples, peeled and quartered

1/2 tsp salt

1 tsp apple cider vinegar

1/8 tsp nutmeg

Soy milk if needed to whip

1/4 cup imitation bacon bits

1/2 cup onion, diced fine

Directions

1. Place the potatoes, apples and salt in a large saucepan. Add enough water to cover. Bring to a boil, cover and cook for 15 minutes, until tender.

2. In a sauté pan, sauté the onions and bacon bits in olive oil, or water sauté. Sauté until golden.

3. Drain the potatoes and apples. Run the potatoes and apples through a ricer. Add, vinegar and nutmeg. Mash, adding some soy milk to whip smooth.

4. Top with grilled onions and bacon bits.

Servings: 4 to 6

Prep time: 10 min.

Cook time: 15 min.

Total time: 25 min.

POTATO RECIPES

Confetti Mashed Potatoes

Ingredients

8 medium red potatoes, cubed

1/4 cup red pepper, chopped fine

1/4 cup yellow pepper, chopped fine

1/4 cup green onion, chopped fine

2 Tbsp vegan margarine

1/8 tsp salt

pinch white pepper

Soy milk for whipping

Directions

1. Place potatoes in a large saucepan and cover with water. Bring to a boil.

2. Add peppers and onions, cook for 15 minutes, until potatoes and vegetables are tender.

3. Drain. And add vegan margarine, salt and pepper. Mash well or whip with hand mixer. Add just a little soy milk until smooth and creamy.

Servings: 6

Prep time: 10 min.

Cook time: 15 min.

Total time: 25 min.

POTATO RECIPES

Potato Pumpkin Mashed

Ingredients

8 cups chopped peeled pumpkin (about 2 pounds)

8 medium Yukon Gold potatoes, peeled and cubed (about 2 pounds)

salt and pepper to taste

soy milk for whipping

Directions

1. Place pumpkin in a large saucepan, add water to cover. Bring to a boil. Reduce heat and cook, uncovered for 25 minutes or until tender.

2. Place potatoes in another saucepan, add water to cover. Bring to a boil. Reduce heat, cook, uncovered, for 15 minutes or until tender.

3. Now you are going to whip the pumpkin just like mashed potatoes. Drain, and whip, adding soy milk and salt until the desired consistency and flavor.

4. Separately do the same for the potatoes.

5. Alternate potatoes and then pumpkin, one large spoonful at a time into a serving bowl. Swirl with a spoon each time. When done use a spatula to press the top. You should have a beautiful two toned presentation that will remain as the dish is served.

Servings: 8

Prep time: 20 min.

Cook time: 25 min.

Total time: 45 min.

POTATO RECIPES

Spanakopita Mashed Potatoes

Ingredients

8 medium potatoes, peeled and chopped

1 - 6 oz pack fresh baby spinach, chopped

2 cloves garlic, minced

1/2 teaspoon salt

1/2 teaspoon pepper

vegan margarine (optional)

soy milk for whipping

Directions

1. Place potatoes in a large saucepan and cover with water. Bring to a boil. Reduce heat, cover and cook for 20 minutes until tender.

2. In another large saucepan, bring 1/2 inch of water to a boil. Add spinach and garlic, cover and steam for 5 minutes or until wilted. Drain, keep warm in pot.

3. Drain potatoes and run through a potato ricer. Add salt and pepper. Add optional margarine, and a little soy milk to whip, if necessary. Fold in spinach and transfer to a serving dish. Garnish with some fresh spinach or basil leaves.

Servings: 6

Prep time: 10 min.

Cook time: 15 min.

Total time: 25 min.

POTATO RECIPES

Caramelized Onion Mashed Potatoes

Ingredients

1 Tbsp olive oil or water sauté

2 large onions, diced small

3 pounds potatoes, peeled and chopped

3 garlic cloves, minced

1/2 cup vegan sour cream

1/4 teaspoon pepper

1 Tbsp butter substitute (optional)

1 cup shredded vegan cheddar cheese

2 Tbsp imitation bacon bits

chopped parsley

Directions

1. Place potatoes in a large saucepan and cover with water. Bring to a boil, and cook for 20 minutes.

2. In a large nonstick skillet over medium heat, sauté onions until soft.

3. Add garlic, sauté for a minute, and set onions aside.

4. Drain potatoes, and run through ricer.

5. Add the sour cream, salt and pepper, whip smooth.

6. Fold in caramelized onions and vegan cheddar cheese.

7. Transfer to a serving bowl.

8. Garnish with vegan butter, bacon bits and parsley.

Yield: 6 servings.

Servings: 6

Prep time: 5 min.

Cook time: 20 min.

Total time: 25 min.

SIMPLY INCREDIBLE
Potato Wedges

THIS COULD BE THE THIRD MOST POPULAR WAY TO EAT POTATOES.

Baked NOT fried.

There are basically two different ways you can make potato wedges. And then there is the Mark Anthony signature way that nobody in the world knows about… except you.

The first is to cut the potato into wedges and bake. You can always season them a hundred different ways. And some people will coat the wedges first with oil so that the spices stick to the potato.

The second way to make potato wedges, is to cook the potatoes first by either baking or boiling the whole potatoes. Then you will want to chill in the fridge overnight. And from there, you would cut them into wedges, season, and bake. This takes a fraction of the time baking, and has a far better crispness to the potatoes.

And for the most amazing potato wedges, try my hybrid creation. This is where you get them 1/2 cooked in water, allowing the starches to surface, and this will enable the spices to stick to the potatoes without the need for oil. This is one of my signature concepts, and it is GOLDEN.

Mark Anthony's Signature Hybrid Potato Wedges

1. Preheat oven to 425 degrees.
2. Line a sheet pan with parchment paper.
3. Wedge the potatoes into fairly thick wedges. Place in cooking pot.
4. Add enough water to cover, and bring to boil.
5. Boil for 5 minutes.
6. After boiling, drain the potatoes and place back into the pot.
7. To coat potatoes, add seasonings of any sort, shake or mix in.
8. Spread evenly on sheet pan, preferably skin side down and bake for 20-25 minutes.
9. Potatoes, should be crispy browned.

Simple Seasonings for Wedges

- A-1 steak seasoning
- bbq spice or sauce
- chicken style seasoning + nutritional yeast flakes
- chili powder + salt
- fajita seasoning
- fresh herbs + salt
- garlic + Parmesan
- garlic + salt + lime zest
- lemon + pepper
- paprika + salt
- pesto
- spicy + sweet
- steak seasoning
- 57 steak sauce

SIMPLY INCREDIBLE
Potato Salads

These potato salad concepts and recipes can be created with 2 to 5 pounds of cooked, chilled, and then diced potatoes. Use any type of potato for any of these recipes.

21 Ideas
FOR POTATO SALAD

CLASSIC FAVORITE: Mix in Vegenaise, chopped scallions, chopped celery stalk, Dijon mustard and vinegar, sugar, and salt.

WALDORF: Double the diced celery and add plenty of chopped apple and chopped walnuts. Don't use mustard in this one.

SWEET RELISH: Use a tablespoon of lemon juice and pinch of salt. Mix in salad dressing, pickle relish, yellow mustard and chopped scallion.

CURRY: Sauté golden raisins in a skillet. Add curry powder and green beans, allow to cool. Then add to the potatoes, diced celery, onions, and red bell peppers. Add vegenaise. Season with salt and red pepper flakes.

GARDEN: Add shredded carrots, sliced radishes, chopped cucumber, chopped scallions and chopped parsley and chives. Mix in vegenaise, lemon juice, and salt and pepper.

GREEN GODDESS: Blend mayonnaise with parsley, tarragon and basil. Add to the chopped potatoes with scallion, cucumbers, lemon juice and salt.

SLAW: Add chopped cabbage, shredded carrots, diced red onions and parsley. Mix in vegenaise, sugar, vinegar, and salt.

DILL: Mix in sour cream and vegenaise with chopped dill and scallions. Also add sugar, cider vinegar, and salt.

HERB-VINEGAR: Mix chopped mixed parsley, with dill chives and chopped shallots. Add vegenaise with lemon juice, olive oil, and salt and pepper.

FRENCH: Use sliced fingerling potatoes. Add chopped mixed parsley, chives, tarragon, and shallot. Mix with olive oil, lemon juice and Dijon mustard. And salt and pepper to taste.

PROVENÇAL: Use sliced fingerlings. Add chopped mixed parsley, chives and tarragon, and shallot. Mix with olive oil, lemon juice and Dijon mustard. Then add shaved fennel bulbs, kalamata olives, and grape tomatoes.

PESTO: Add sliced green olives, and diced red onions. Mix in lemon juice, pesto, vegenaise, and pine nuts.

POTATO PEA: Add frozen peas, chopped celery, onions, and peppers. Mix in vegenaise with diced vegan cheeses.

PICO DE GALLO: Use Yukon gold potatoes and mix in onions, diced tomatoes and celery. Add fresh salsa, salt to taste, garnish with fresh chopped cilantro.

SALSA VERDE: Best with Yukon Gold potatoes. Mix in chopped red onion and bell peppers. Add vegenaise, with diced green chilies (canned). Salt to taste.

THAI: Mix vegenaise with coconut milk, curry paste and lime juice. Toss with potatoes, diced onions, bell pepper, and some shredded basil and mint.

INDIAN: Sauté diced onions, garam masala, and grated ginger, cool. Mix with sour cream, and vegenaise, Add to the potatoes, chickpeas and cilantro.

TOMATO ALFREDO: Add chopped sun-dried tomatoes, and celery. Mix in vegenaise with vegan parmesan cheese and nutmeg.

HONEY MUSTARD: Add celery, raisins, and walnuts. Mix in vegenaise with honey and dijon mustard.

ARTICHOKE: Add quartered artichokes with sliced black and green olives, and chopped green onions. Mix in vegenaise, salt and pepper.

GREEN APPLE: Add chopped green apples, skin on. With chopped walnuts, golden raisins, and parsley. Mix in sour cream and vegenaise, salt pepper, and a shot of sweetener.

SIMPLY INCREDIBLE POTATO CREATIONS

Mashed Potato Bake

Ingredients

2 lbs potatoes, peeled chopped

2 tsp salt

2 Tbsp onion, finely diced

2 Tbsp red pepper, finely diced

2 cloves garlic minced

2 Tbsp chives, chopped

2 Tbsp vegan margarine(optional)

soy milk for whipping

1/2 cup breadcrumbs or Panko

Directions

1. Boil potatoes in salted water for 20 minutes until cooked through.

2. Preheat oven to 400 degrees. Line a baking sheet with parchment paper.

3. Meanwhile sauté the onion, peppers and garlic until translucent and set aside.

4. In a bowl, mash the potatoes, onions, peppers, margarine and chives. Season with salt and pepper to taste. Adjust the texture with a bit of soy milk if necessary.

5. On the baking sheet, using a ring mold, first spray the inside of the ring mold with oil or water. This will help the potato slide out of the ring mold.

6. Sprinkle a layer of breadcrumbs on the bottom, then scoop the potato mixture into the mold, about 1 1/2 inch thick. Press down with a spoon and then finish with another thin layer of breadcrumbs on top.

7. Remove the ring mold, clean, and repeat the process. Should make 4 to 5 cakes

8. Bake in the oven for 15 minutes, until golden. Carefully remove and serve.

Servings: 4

Prep time: 10 min.

Cook time: 40 min.

Total time: 50 min.

SIMPLY INCREDIBLE POTATO CREATIONS

Creamy Vegan Potato Leek Soup

This is what potato leek soup should taste like. Unbelievably creamy, and oh so satisfying! The perfect choice for those chilly days. And it's a healthy vegan creation too.

Ingredients

2 Tbsp olive oil

1 small onion, diced

3 large leeks, thinly sliced (white & light green part only)

5 medium russet potatoes, peeled and chopped

3 cloves garlic, minced

6 cups vegetable broth

1 tsp salt, more to taste

1 tsp dried thyme

1/2 tsp dried rosemary

1/2 tsp coriander, ground

2 bay leaves

1 1/2 Tbsp fresh lemon juice

1 cup coconut milk, canned

salt and pepper, to taste

Garnish: Green onion, chopped

Directions

1. Wash the leeks well.

2. In a large pot, heat oil over medium heat. Add the leeks & onion, sauté in water until softened, about 5 minutes.

3. Add the remaining ingredients, except for the lemon juice and coconut milk. Bring to a boil, and then reduce heat to low and simmer for about 20 minutes, or until the potatoes are tender.

4. Remove from heat and remove bay leaves. Stir in the coconut milk and lemon juice.

5. Add salt and pepper to taste.

6. Using an immersion blender, or a regular blender, carefully blend all the soup well.

7. Serve in soup bowls and top with chopped green onion, and fresh ground pepper.

Chef's Notes:

Leeks can be quite dirty inside the layers because they grow in sandy soil. To clean thoroughly: Cut off the roots, slice the entire leek into pieces. Place in a small bowl of water and swish around to release the dirt, and drain well.

Servings: 6

Prep time: 10 min.

Cook time: 20 min.

Total time: 30 min.

SIMPLY INCREDIBLE POTATO CREATIONS

Smashed Potatoes

Ingredients

15 - 20 small red potatoes

1 tsp salt

olive oil or butter substitute (optional)

your favorite seasonings or salt and pepper

Directions

1. Place potatoes in a large saucepan and cover with water. Add 1 teaspoon of salt to the water.

2. Bring to boiling, reduce heat. Cover and simmer for 30 until potatoes are very tender.

3. Drain potatoes.

4. Preheat oven to 450 degrees.

5. Transfer potatoes to a parchment paper lined sheet pan. Cool for 10 minutes.

6. Smash each potato to about 1/2-inch thickness, keeping each potato in one piece. I use a coffee cup. You can use a potato masher, or a vegetable can.

7. Brush potatoes with optional olive oil.

8. Sprinkle with your favorite seasonings.

9. Bake, uncovered, 20 to 30 minutes or until potatoes are browned and crispy. Flipping half way through cooking can help the uniformity of the crisp, but isn't necessary.

Servings: 4 to 6

Prep time: 5 min.

Cook time: 1 hour

Total time: 1.2 hours

SIMPLY INCREDIBLE POTATO CREATIONS

Leftover Mashed Potato Pancakes

Ingredients

4 cups mashed potatoes

1/4 cup ground flax seed

1/2 cup warm water

1/2 cup flour

oil for frying, or dry fry in a good nonstick skillet.

Optional Ingredients:

salt and pepper, chives, onions, cheeses, imitation bacon bits. Even nutmeg, or garlic, or sweeteners, it all depends on what flavor you're seeking.

Serve With:

vegan sour cream or applesauce.

Directions

1. Mix ground flax seed with warm water and let rest.

2. Mix mashed potatoes, with flour, and ground flax seed.

3. Add any optional ingredients.

4. Preheat skillet on medium heat.

5. Mixture should be very thick.

6. Pour 1/4 cup portions of potato mixture into pan, brown on both sides.

7. Enjoy with sour cream or applesauce.

Servings: 6

Prep time: 5 min.

Cook time: 15 min.

Total time: 20 min.

SIMPLY INCREDIBLE POTATO CREATIONS

Vegan Potatoes Au Gratin

This baked potato casserole dish is covered in a rich and creamy cheese sauce made out of nutritional yeast flakes.

Ingredients

water for boiling

6 potatoes, sliced about 1/3 inch thick

1 onion, chopped

2 Tbsp olive oil or water sauté

2 clove garlic, minced

1/2 cup vegan margarine

1/2 cup flour

1 tsp salt

2 Tbsp soy sauce

1/4 tsp turmeric

3/4 cup nutritional yeast

Garnish with parsley or paprika

Directions

1. Preheat the oven to 350 degrees.

2. Bring a large pot of water to a boil.

3. Add the potatoes, and boil for just 5 minutes.

4. Drain well, saving the potato water for the sauce.

5. Transfer the potatoes to a large baking dish.

6. In a large skillet, sauté onions in olive oil until translucent.

7. Add garlic, and sauté for one minute.

8. Add margarine and flour, stirring continuously until thickened.

9. Gradually add the reserved potato water, salt, soy sauce and turmeric, frequently stirring until thickened into a creamy sauce.

10. Add nutritional yeast, stirring again until well mixed.

11. Pour sauce mixture over the potatoes in the casserole dish. With a spoon, lift potatoes to ensure that some of the sauce will get in-between the potatoes.

12. Cover and bake for 10 minutes.

13. Uncover, and bake for an additional 10 minutes.

14. Remove the casserole from the oven. Sprinkle the top with paprika or parsley, if desired.

15. Allow the potatoes au gratin to cool for 10 minutes before serving, as the sauce will thicken as it cools.

Chef's Notes:

You can actually do this recipe oil free, simply by making a roux/paste out of flour and water and then adding that to the heated liquid ingredients and bringing to a boil. Originally, roux was made with water, not oil. Oil will make it a lot creamier but is not necessary. If you want a whiter sauce, use almond milk instead of potato water.

SIMPLY INCREDIBLE POTATO CREATIONS

Oil Free Scalloped Potatoes
WITH CHICKPEA CHEESE SAUCE

Ingredients

4 pounds potatoes. Yukon gold or red, peeled, sliced 1/4inch thick

Sauce Ingredients

1 - 15 oz can chickpeas with liquid

1 cup almond milk, unsweetened

1/2 cup nutritional yeast flakes

2 large cloves garlic

1 Tbsp onion powder

1 tsp salt

1 tsp turmeric

1/4 tsp ground black pepper

chives for garnish

Directions

1. Pour sauce ingredients into blender. Blend extremely well until smooth and creamy.

2. Preheat oven to 375 degrees.

3. Add some of the sauce to the bottom of a large casserole dish. Shingle the potatoes into the dish. And cover with more sauce. Repeat if necessary, using up all the potatoes and all the sauce.

4. Cover tightly with foil and bake for 50 minutes.

5. Remove foil and bake for another 10 minutes, or until the potatoes are fork tender.

6. Sprinkle with chives and serve hot.

Servings: 6
Prep time: 10 min.
Cook time: 60 min.
Total time: 70 min.

SIMPLY INCREDIBLE POTATO CREATIONS

Crispy Roasted Potatoes
WITH CAPER VINAIGRETTE

Ingredients

2 lb. Yukon gold potatoes, cut into 1 inch chunks

1 lb. sweet potatoes, cut into 1 inch chunks

1 lb baby red potatoes, cut into 1 inch chunks

2 Tbsp salt

2 Tbsp olive oil (optional)

Caper Vinaigrette

1/4 cup parsley leaves, finely chopped

1/4 cup balsamic vinegar

3 Tbsp capers, drained and chopped

1 clove garlic, minced

pinch salt and pepper

2 Tbsp olive oil (optional)

Directions

1. Preheat oven to 450 degrees.

2. In a stock pot, add potatoes and salt and completely cover with water.

3. Bring to a boil and boil for only 5 minutes.

4. Drain well. Return to pot.

5. Toss potatoes well with olive oil.

6. Place on a parchment paper lined baking sheets.

7. Roast for 20 minutes or until crispy golden brown, stir potatoes half way through cooking.

8. Meanwhile, in large bowl, whisk parsley, vinegar, capers and garlic. Then slowly whisk in the olive oil.

9. Toss potatoes with vinaigrette until well coated.

10. Serve hot.

Servings: 4 to 6

Prep time: 10 min.

Cook time: 30 min.

Total time: 40 min.

SIMPLY INCREDIBLE POTATO CREATIONS

Oil Free Homemade Potato Rolls

Many of the potato rolls in the grocery store have as much as 50% calories from fat. This is a healthy version that tastes Simply Incredible.

Ingredients

1/2 cup mashed potatoes, warmed

1 cup almond milk, unsweetened, warmed

2 Tbsp Honey

2 1/4 tsp dry active yeast

2 cups bread flour

1 tsp salt

1/4 tsp baking soda

1/4 tsp baking powder

Directions

1. Stir together warmed milk, mashed potatoes, and honey.

2. Add yeast and stir to very well to incorporate.

3. Let rest for 10 minutes for yeast to become active.

4. Add salt, baking soda, and baking powder and stir well.

5. Add 1 cup of flour and mix until well moistened. If using a stand mixer use the hook attachment.

6. Add a 2nd cup of flour and mix until dough ball forms.

7. Seal with plastic wrap and cover with a towel and place somewhere warm to rise for 1 hour.

8. After 1 hour place your dough onto a lightly floured work surface, knead gently. Add more flour if necessary to keep from sticking.

9. Separate into 16 equal dough balls and place into a 9x12 baking dish lined with parchment paper.

10. Let rise for up to an additional 1 hour. I like to use an another pan upside-down on the pan with the dough balls. You want to use something that will not be in contact with the dough when it rises.

11. Dust with a little sprinkle of flour before baking.

12. Bake for 17-20 minutes.

Servings: 16 rolls

Prep time: 10 min.

Cook time: 20 min.

Total time: 30 min.

Sweet potatoes

Sweet Potatoes are certainly one of the healthiest foods on the planet. They are good complex carbs, high in vitamins and minerals. And quite frankly, they have Simply Incredible Flavor all by themselves.

Sweet potatoes

GOOD These items go well with this food.			BETTER Even better pairing.	BEST The WOW factor!
anise	figs, dried	orange juice	**allspice**	MAPLE SYRUP
apple	fruit juices	orange zest	**butter substitutes**	PECANS
apple juice	fruits	paprika	**cilantro**	SUGAR, BROWN
avocado	garlic	parsley	**coconut**	
bananas	ginger	peanuts	**cream**	
basil	havelnuts	pears	**salt**	
bay leaf	honey	pepper		
beans	kale	persimmons		
bell pepper	ketchup	pineapple		
cheese	leeks	pumpkin		
chestnuts	lemon	pumpkin seeds		
chili pepper	lemon juice	raisins		
chives	lemon zest	red pepper flakes		
chocolate, white	lime juice	rosemary		
cinnamon	marshmallows	sage		
cloves	molasses	sour cream		
coriander	mushrooms	tarragon		
cranberries	mustard	thyme		
cumin	nutmeg	tomatoes		
curry	oatmeal	vanilla		
dates	onions	vinegar		
dill	orange	walnuts		

SIMPLY INCREDIBLE PAIRINGS

sweet potatoes + allspice + cinnamon + ginger

sweet potatoes + apples + sage

sweet potatoes + chili peppers + lemon zest

sweet potatoes + cilantro + lime

sweet potatoes + marshmallows + orange

sweet potatoes + maple syrup + pecans

sweet potatoes + orange + nutmeg

SWEET POTATO RECIPES

Sweet Potato Lasagna

Your guests are going to love this twist on an old time favorite.

Ingredients

1 onion, chopped

1 red bell pepper, seeded and chopped

1 lb mushrooms, sliced

4 garlic cloves, minced

1 lb. bag shredded carrots

1 pkg Silken Lite tofu, drained and crumbled well

3 sweet potatoes, cooked, cooled, pealed and chopped fine

16 ounces frozen chopped spinach, thawed and drained

1/2 teaspoon cayenne pepper

2 tsp oregano

2 tsp basil

1 - 64 oz jar pasta sauce

2 boxes lasagna noodles.

1 lb. vegan mozzarella cheese, optional

6 roma tomatoes, sliced

Directions

1. Pre-heat oven to 350 degrees.

2. In a skillet, sauté the onion, peppers, and mushrooms on medium heat for 5 minutes. No oil needed, the mushrooms will sweat enough moisture to keep the sauté going.

3. Add the garlic and carrots, and sauté for another minute.

4. Set aside to cool.

5. Add the tofu, potatoes, spinach, and the spices to the vegetable mixture. Mix well.

To assemble the vegetable lasagna:

6. Layer the bottom of a 9-by-13-inch casserole dish with sauce.

7. Add a layer of noodles.

8. Spread the vegetable mixture over the noodles, and add some vegan cheese.

9. Cover with sauce.

10. Add another layer of lasagna, pressing down the filling to tighten.

11. Repeat process for another layer.

12. Top with a final layer of lasagna noodles.

13. Sauce the top. And add a final sprinkle of vegan cheese and the sliced roma tomatoes.

14. This should be very saucy. And if you think you need more sauce go for it. I also like to put about a cup of water around the sides if its not soaked with moisture when you press it. You don't want a dry lasagna, and if it did just so happen to be too wet, cooking for an extra couple minutes uncovered will solve that. It will also tighten up when cooling

15. Saran wrap and then foil. Bake for 1 hour.

16. Remove the foil. Let rest for 15 minutes before cutting.

Chef's Notes:

If you don't have oven safe saran wrap, you can use just foil as long as you don't have contact with the tomato sauce. The acid from the tomatoes will eat the aluminum, and contaminate the food. You can use a sheet of parchment paper sprayed with oil, to keep the food from sticking to the paper.

Servings: 9 to 12 » Prep time: 20 min.

Cook time: 1 hour » Total time: 1.3 hours

SWEET POTATO RECIPES

Sweet Potato Nachos

Sometimes when you want to achieve Simply Incredible Flavor, you have to use an ingredient that would never be used in a traditional dish. And this recipe nails it!

These sweet potato chips work absolutely perfect for a new experience in nachos.

Ingredients

4 medium sized sweet potatoes

2 Tbsp olive oil

Directions

1. Preheat oven to 425 degrees.
2. Slice sweet potatoes 1/8 inch thick, or thinner.
3. Place in a bowl and toss with olive oil.
4. Evenly lay out potato slices on a baking sheets, and roast for 15 minutes.
5. Flip, and roast for another 15 minutes.
6. If desired, broil on high for a couple minutes to get them really crispy and browned well.
7. Once all the potatoes are done, you are ready to assemble the nacho platters just like any other nachos.
8. Place on oven safe plates. Top with toppings. Add vegan cheese.
9. Bake at 350 for 5 minutes or until cheese is melted.
10. Then top with cilantro. Serve with sour cream and salsa.

And here are some suggested toppings.

vegan taco meats

vegan fajita meats

Butler Soy Curls

black beans

refried beans

roasted corn

diced red onions

scallions

black olives

diced tomatoes

salsa

sour cream

cilantro

SWEET POTATO RECIPES

Sweet Potato Pound Cake

This is a simple recipe and it's made without oil!

Ingredients

1 cup all-purpose whole wheat flour

1/2 cup pastry flour

1 tsp cinnamon, ground

1 tsp baking powder

1/2 tsp baking soda

1/2 tsp nutmeg, ground

1/4 cup ground flax seed with 1/4 cup warm water

1 cup apple sauce

1 cup brown sugar

1 tsp vanilla extract

1 cup leftover mashed sweet potatoes

1/8 tsp salt

1/2 cup pecans, chopped

Directions

1. Preheat oven to 325 degrees.

2. In a large bowl, sift flour, baking powder, cinnamon, nutmeg, and baking soda.

3. In a cup, mix warm water with ground flax seed and let rest for a couple minutes.

4. In another bowl mix together the apple sauce, brown sugar, vanilla, salt and mashed sweet potatoes. Mix well.

5. Mix in the ground flax seed mixture.

6. Add the wet mixture to the dry mixture. Mix until incorporated, but do not over blend.

7. Spoon batter into a greased 9-inch loaf pan. Sprinkle pecans on top of batter.

8. Bake for 65 to 75 minutes. Toothpick should come out clean when inserted into the center of the cake.

9. Allow to cool, 15 minutes or more.

Servings: 1 loaf

Prep time: 5 min.

Cook time: 1.2 hour

Total time: 1.3 hours

Quinoa

For perfectly fluffy quinoa, use twice as much water as quinoa, then cook, *uncovered*, until the quinoa has absorbed all the water. Once the water is all absorbed, remove the pot from heat, cover it and let the quinoa steam for 5 minutes. That's when the quinoa pops open into fluffy perfection, and that is how to cook quinoa properly.

Quinoa

GOOD These items go well with this food.		BETTER Even better pairing.	BEST The WOW factor!
almonds	mint	**bell peppers**	SALT
anise	nuts	**herbs**	VEGETABLES
apples	orange	**lemon**	
basil	peas	**lemon zest**	
beans	pecans	**mushrooms**	
cardamom	pistachios	**onions**	
celery	raisins	**parsley**	
chili peppers	saffron	**rice**	
chives	scallions	**spinach**	
cinnamon	shallots	**tomatoes**	
coconut	sugar	**tomato, sun-dried**	
coconut milk	tarragon		
cranberries	thyme		
cream	tomato, sauce		
curry	tomato, paste		
currants	truffles		
fennel	vegetable stock		
garlic	walnuts		
ginger	zucchini		

SIMPLY INCREDIBLE PAIRINGS

quinoa + apples + cranberry + sugar

quinoa + black beans + corn + green chilies

quinoa + coconut + lime

quinoa + cranberries + walnuts

quinoa + garlic + mushrooms + thyme

quinoa + herbs + mushrooms + salt

QUINOA RECIPES

Perfect Quinoa

Learn how to cook perfect quinoa, every time. I've tried all the other quinoa cooking methods and this one works best. It's easy to cook fluffy quinoa when you know the right way to do it!

Ingredients

2 cups uncooked quinoa

4 cups water

1/4 tsp salt

Directions

1. Rinse the quinoa. Use a fine mesh colander and rinse under running water for about 30 seconds. Drain well. This step will remove any bitterness on the outside of the quinoa.

2. In a saucepan with lid, combine the rinsed quinoa and water. Bring the mixture to a boil over medium-high heat. Then reduce the heat to medium low for a gentle simmer.

3. Cook the quinoa until almost all the water is absorbed. about 20 minutes . Don't let it burn.

4. Remove the pot from the heat. Cover with lid. Let the quinoa steam for 5 minutes.

5. Remove the lid and fluff the quinoa with a fork.

6. Season with salt, to taste.

Chef's Notes

Store in the fridge for a week, or place in quart baggies in the freezer for months.

QUINOA RECIPES

Coconut Lime Quinoa

5 ingredients and so easy to make a healthy side dish for any meal.

Ingredients

1 cup quinoa

1 - 13 oz can of coconut milk

1/4 cup water

1/4 tsp salt

2 limes, zest and juice

Directions

1. Rinse quinoa in a fine mesh colander for 30 seconds.

2. Place all of the ingredients in a saucepan. Bring the mixture to a boil. Cover with a lid, and simmer on low for 15 minutes.

3. Remove from heat and let the quinoa rest for about 5 minutes.

4. Fluff and serve.

QUINOA RECIPES

One Pan Mexican Quinoa

Light, healthy and nutritious. And it's so easy to make.

Ingredients

2 cup vegetable broth

1 cup quinoa

1 -15 oz can black beans, drained and rinsed

1 -15 oz can fire-roasted diced tomatoes

1 cup corn, fresh or frozen

2 garlic cloves, minced

1 jalapeno, seeded, minced

1 tsp chili powder

1/2 tsp cumin

1/4 tsp sea salt

1 avocado, halved, seeded, peeled and diced

1 lime, juiced

2 Tbsp cilantro, fresh chopped

Directions

1. In a large skilled with a lid, and all ingredients except the avocado, lime and cilantro. Bring to a boil.

2. Reduce heat and simmer until quinoa is cooked through, about 20 minutes.

3. Once liquid is absorbed, remove from heat, cover and let set for 5 minutes.

4. Stir in avocado, lime juice, and cilantro.

5. Serve immediately.

Servings: 4

Prep time: 10 min.

Cook time: 25 min.

Total time: 35 min.

QUINOA RECIPES

4 Ingredient Quinoa

This is an excellent base recipe that you will be able serve as is, or kick it up a notch for Simply Incredible Flavor. It's easy to have great tasting healthy food.

Ingredients

1 cup quinoa

2 cups low sodium vegetable broth

2 lemons, juice, and zest

2 tsp turmeric powder

Directions

1. Rinse quinoa in a fine mesh colander for 30 seconds.

2. Place all of the ingredients in a saucepan. Bring the mixture to a boil, and simmer on low for 15 minutes.

3. Remove from heat and let the quinoa rest, covered, for about 5 minutes.

4. Fluff and serve.

Chef's Notes:

The add-on for this recipe are endless. Chopped green onions, basil, cashews, spinach, corn, just to name a few.

Servings: 4

Prep time: 5 min.

Cook time: 20 min.

Total time: 25 min.

QUINOA RECIPES

Mediterranean Quinoa Salad

Ingredients

For the Salad

3 cups cooked quinoa, chilled

2 cup black olives, sliced

2 cups tear drop tomatoes, cut in half

1 cup yellow peppers, slivers

1 cup red onion, diced

1 cup cilantro, chopped

For the Dressing

1/4 cup balsamic vinegar

2 Tbsp lemon juice

2 Tbsp honey

1 Tbsp oregano dried

pinch salt to taste

pinch pepper to taste

Directions

1. In a medium bowl, mix quinoa and the rest of the salad ingredients.

2. In another small bowl, whisk all the dressing ingredients together.

3. Add dressing to the quinoa and mix gently.

Servings: 6

Prep time: 10 min.

Cook time: 20 min.

Total time: 30 min.

QUINOA RECIPES

One Pot Mushroom Garlic Quinoa

Ingredients

1 Tbsp olive oil or water sauté

1 pound cremini mushrooms, thinly sliced

1 cup onions, diced

1/4 cup red bell pepper, finely diced

5 cloves garlic, minced

1 tsp dried thyme

2 cups vegetable stock

1 cup quinoa

Directions

1. Rinse quinoa in a fine mesh colander for 30 seconds.

2. In a stock pot, sauté the mushrooms, onions, and peppers for 5 minutes.

3. Add the garlic and thyme, sauté for another minute.

4. Add remaining ingredients. Bring the mixture to a boil, and simmer on low for 15 minutes.

5. Remove from heat and let the quinoa rest, covered, for about 5 minutes.

6. Fluff and serve.

Chef's Notes:

Sprinkle with some vegan Parmesan cheese for Simply Incredible Flavor.

Servings: 6

Prep time: 10 min.

Cook time: 25 min.

Total time: 35 min.

QUINOA RECIPES

Sugar-Free Quinoa Granola Bars

Ingredients

1 1/2 cups whole wheat flour

1 tsp cinnamon

1 tsp salt

1/2 tsp baking powder

1/2 tsp baking soda

1 banana, mashed

1/2 cup applesauce

2 Tbsp molasses

2 tsp vanilla extract

1 1/3 cup cooked and cooled quinoa

1 cup rolled oats

1/2 cup dried cranberries

1/4 cup pumpkin seeds

Directions

1. Preheat oven to 375 degrees. Prepare a 9"x12" baking pan by spraying with cooking spray.

2. In a large bowl, whisk together the flour, cinnamon, salt, baking powder and baking soda.

3. In a separate bowl, mix the bananas, applesauce, molasses, and vanilla.

4. Add the wet mixture to the dry ingredients, stirring until the dry ingredients are all incorporated.

5. Fold in the cooked quinoa, oats, cranberries and pumpkin seeds.

6. Spread evenly into the prepared baking pan.

7. Bake in the preheated oven for 10-14 minutes, until the top feels firm and a toothpick inserted in the center comes out clean

8. Remove from oven and let cool before cutting into bars.

Servings: 12 bars

Prep time: 10 min.

Cook time: 35 min.

Total time: 45 min.

QUINOA RECIPES

Quinoa Enchilada Bake

Ingredients

1 cup quinoa

2 cups vegetable stock

2 cloves garlic, minced

1 - 16 oz can enchilada sauce

1 - 4.5 oz can chopped green chilies

1 1/2 cup corn kernels, frozen, canned or roasted

1 1/2 cup canned black beans, drained and rinsed

2 cups vegan shredded cheese

2 Roma tomatos, diced

1 avocado, halved, seeded, peeled and diced

1/4 cup chopped fresh cilantro leaves

Directions

1. Rinse quinoa in a fine mesh colander for 30 seconds.

2. Place vegetable stock, quinoa and garlic in a saucepan. Bring to a boil, and simmer on low for 15 minutes.

3. Remove from heat and let the quinoa rest, covered, for 5 minutes.

4. Preheat oven to 375 degrees.

5. Add the enchilada sauce, green chilies, beans, and corn to the quinoa, and mix.

6. Transfer to a 9x12 baking dish. Top with the vegan cheese, and diced tomatoes.

7. Bake for about 15 minutes, until bubbly and cheese is melted.

8. Garnish with the avocados and cilantro just before serving.

Servings: 8

Prep time: 10 min.

Cook time: 35 min.

Total time: 45 min.

QUINOA RECIPES

Quinoa Stuffed Bell Peppers

Ingredients

3 cups cooked quinoa

1 -16 oz can tomato sauce

1 -4.5 oz can green chiles

1 cup corn kernels

1 cup black beans, cooked, rinsed, drained

1 cup tomatoes, diced

1 cup shredded vegan pepper jack cheese

1/4 cup chopped fresh cilantro leaves

1 tsp chili powder

1 tsp onion powder

1/2 tsp cumin

1/2 tsp garlic powder

6 bell peppers, tops cut, stemmed and seeded

Directions

1. Preheat oven to 350 degrees. Line a 9"x13" baking dish with parchment paper.

2. In a large bowl, combine all the ingredients and mix very well.

3. Spoon the filling into each bell pepper cavity.

4. Place on prepared baking dish, cavity side up, and bake until the peppers are tender and the filling is heated through, about 25-30 minutes.

5. Serve immediately.

Chef's Notes:

Find those peppers that will stand up straight, without having to trim the bottoms. Also I like to put the pepper tops into the oven on a sheet pan for 15 minutes. This will soften them up but not over cook them. And then you can place the tops back on the peppers for a really good presentation.

Servings: 6

Prep time: 15 min.

Cook time: 30 min.

Total time: 45 min.

QUINOA RECIPES

Spinach and Quinoa Salad
WITH SUN DRIED TOMATOES AND LEMON DRESSING

This simple spinach quinoa salad is full of fresh Mediterranean flavors.

Ingredients

1 cup quinoa

2 cups vegetable stock

2 cloves garlic, minced

1/2 cup sun-dried tomatoes, chopped

4 cups roughly chopped fresh spinach

Lemon dressing

2 Tbsp olive oil or water

2 Tbsp lemon juice

2 cloves garlic, minced

1 tsp Dijon mustard

Pinch of red pepper flakes

Salt to taste

pepper, to taste

Directions

1. Rinse quinoa in a fine mesh colander for 30 seconds.

2. Place vegetable stock, quinoa and garlic in a saucepan. Bring to a boil, and simmer on low for 15 minutes.

3. Remove from heat and let the quinoa rest, covered, for 5 minutes.

4. **Meanwhile, prepare the lemon dressing:** Whisk together the olive oil, lemon juice, garlic, mustard, red pepper flakes. Salt and pepper to taste.

5. Once the quinoa is done cooking, fluff it with a fork and then add the chopped sun-dried tomatoes and spinach.

6. Let the heat from the quinoa wilt the spinach a little bit.

7. Toss with the lemon dressing and transfer to serving bowl.

8. Garnish with almonds.

Servings: 4

Prep time: 10 min.

Cook time: 20 min.

Total time: 30 min.

QUINOA RECIPES

Rainbow Quinoa Salad
WITH BEETS, CARROT, AND SPINACH

I love it when I can get Simply Incredible Flavor, Color, AND Nutrition all in one.

Ingredients

Salad

1 cup uncooked quinoa, rinsed

2 cups water

2 garlic cloves, minced

1 cup edamame, frozen

4 cups packed baby spinach

2 cups, shredded carrots

1 - 15 oz can beets, diced, and rinsed

1 yellow bell pepper, matchstick cuts

Vinaigrette

1/4 cup apple cider vinegar

1/4 cup orange juice

2 Tbsp olive oil (optional)

2 Tbsp chopped fresh mint or cilantro

1/4 cup honey

2 Tbsp Dijon mustard, to taste

¼ tsp salt to taste

pepper to taste

1/2 cup slivered almonds

1/2 cup teardrop tomatoes, sliced in half

2 avocado, diced

Directions

1. Rinse quinoa in a fine mesh colander for 30 seconds.

2. Place water, quinoa, edamame, and garlic in a saucepan. Bring to a boil, and simmer on low for 15 minutes.

3. Remove from heat and let the quinoa rest, covered, for 5 minutes.

4. **To prepare the vinaigrette:** Whisk together all of the ingredients until emulsified.

5. **To assemble the salad:** When quinoa is done, mix together with all the chopped vegetables. Put the lid on so the heat can wilt the spinach a little.

6. After about 5 minutes of wilting, Drizzle dressing over the mixture, and gently toss to combine.

7. Season to taste with salt and pepper.

8. Transfer into serving bowl, and garnish with almonds, avocado, and tomatoes.

Servings: 4

Prep time: 30 min.

Cook time: 15 min.

Total time: 45 min.

QUINOA RECIPES

Broccoli Quinoa Slaw
WITH HONEY-MUSTARD DRESSING

Ingredients

Slaw

1 cup uncooked quinoa

2 cups water

2 lbs. broccoli or shredded broccoli slaw

Oil Free Honey-mustard Dressing

1/4 cup Dijon mustard

1/4 cup honey

1 Tbsp apple cider vinegar

Juice of 1 lemon

1 cloves garlic, minced

salt, to taste

pepper, to taste

1/2 cup slivered almonds

1/2 cup chopped fresh basil

Directions

1. To prepare the Quinoa: Rinse quinoa in a fine mesh colander for 30 seconds.

2. Place water, quinoa and garlic in a saucepan. Bring to a boil, and simmer on low for 15 minutes.

3. Remove from heat and let the quinoa rest covered, for 5 minutes.

4. To prepare the dressing: Whisk together all of the ingredients until emulsified.

5. To assemble the salad: When quinoa is done fluff with a fork, mix together with broccoli. The broccoli should be florets that is sliced very thin.

6. Drizzle dressing over the mixture, and gently toss to combine.

7. Season to taste with salt and pepper.

8. Transfer into serving bowl, and garnish with almonds and fresh chopped basil.

Servings: 4

Prep time: 20 min.

Cook time: 20 min.

Total time: 40 min.

Rice

Rice

GOOD These items go well with this food.		BETTER Even better pairing.	BEST The WOW factor!
almonds	orange	**bell peppers**	**BEANS**
anise	parsley	**celery**	**PEPPER**
basil	pecans	**curry**	**SAFFRON**
butter substitute	pistachios	**garlic**	**SALT**
cardamom	potatoes	**ginger**	**TOFU**
chili peppers	raisins	**mushrooms**	
chili powder	rhubarb	**onions**	
chives	spinach	**peas**	
cinnamon	sugar	**scallions**	
coconut	tarragon	**shallots**	
coconut milk	thyme	**tomato sauce**	
cream	tomatoes	**vegetables**	
cumin	tomato paste		
currants	truffles		
fennel	vegetable stock		
lemon	walnuts		
lemon zest	zucchini		
mint			
nuts			

SIMPLY INCREDIBLE PAIRINGS

brown rice + garlic + mushrooms + salt

rice + beans + chili powder + cumin + salt

rice + butter substitute + saffron + salt

rice + coconut + ginger + salt

rice + garlic + salt + tomatoes

wild rice + apple + cranberry + walnut + salt

3 WAYS TO COOK
perfect rice

BASIC STOVETOP METHOD:

The standard concept for stovetop rice is to bring rice to a boil, then simmer with the lid on the pot for a certain amount of time. And then shut off the heat and allow to rest for another 10 to 30 minutes with the lid on.

Generally you will add 1/2 tsp of salt for every one cup of rice. This is not a requirement, but it does help the flavor. You can avoid the excess salt or just reduce it.

Most people add a tablespoon of oil or butter in with the rice. This too is not a requirement. Oil can help prevent excessive sticking with certain kinds of rice, but in all really it isn't worth the extra calories.

The standard method is to have one part rice to two parts water. While this works for long grain white rice, it is not ideal for other rices. That's why I have created a chart here for you that will help you achieve Simply Incredible Rice.

RICE & GRAIN COOKING CHART:

For all types of rice and grain listed below, bring water to boil, add rice/grain and return to boil, then cover with lid and reduce heat to medium low to let simmer. After simmer time, shut off and let rest with lid on, for another 20 minutes.

TYPE OF RICE/GRAIN	RICE/GRAIN TO WATER RATIO	SIMMER TIME	YIELDS
Brown long-grain	1 cup to 1 3/4 cups	40 to 45 minutes	2 1/2 cups
Brown medium, short-grain	1 cup to 2 cups	50 minutes	3 cups
White long-grain	1 cup to 2 cups	18 to 20 minutes	2 cups
White medium-grain	1 cup to 1 1/2 cups	15 minutes	3 cups
White short-grain	1 cup to 1 1/4 cups	15 minutes	3 cups
Basmati	1 cup to 1 1/2 cups	15 to 20 minutes	3 cups
Jasmine	1 cup to 1 3/4 cups	15 to 20 minutes	3 cups
Converted rice (par-boiled)	1 cup to 2 1/4 cups	20 minutes	3 to 4 cups
Sushi rice (Calrose)	1 cup to 1 1/3 cups	18 to 20 minutes	2 1/2 cups
Black Japonica	1 cup to 2 cups	50 minutes	3 cups
Wild rice	1 cup to 2 cups	45 to 50 minutes	2 1/2 cups
Barley	1 cup to 4 cups	45 to 50 minutes	4 cups
Quinoa	1 cup to 2 cups	15 minutes	3 to 4 cups
Bulgur Wheat	1 cup to 2 cups	15 minutes	3 cups

Chef's Notes:

Many people think it necessary to rinse rice. While this can remove some of the starch and reduce the stickiness, it has a down side too. Rinsing rice removes the starches that we need, along with other nutrients. while there may be some benefit, I personally will keep the nutrients.

BAKING METHOD:

Baking rice is easy and can certainly free up some stovetop room if needed. The concept is to take a baking dish that you can cover with foil, add the rice and water, salt and oil if you prefer, and bake till done.

You can use my rice chart to determine the ratio of rice to liquid. And you can always use vegetable broth. Another great concept is to add all types of vegetables and herbs to the rice.

As far as the cooking temperature, 350 to 375 degrees maximum. Anything hotter will burn the edges of the rice.

Bake white rice for 45 minutes, and brown rice for at least an hour. The bigger the quantities, the longer the cooking time. When I cook in restaurants, I am cooking a whole gallon of rice to two gallons of water, and white rice will take an entire hour. I love to wrap the pan with both oven safe saran wrap and foil, and when the top puffs up like a balloon, I know it's done.

EXCESS WATER BOILING METHOD:

This is an easy foolproof way to cook rice. All you have to do is have two to three times the amount of water than the normal stovetop method. Simply boil the rice off like pasta. Boil the white rices for 20 minutes and the brown rices for 30 minutes. Then after boiling, drain the water off the rice in a strainer. Put the rice right back into the pot and cover with a lid. Let the rice rest for 20 minutes, and you're done. Perfect rice every time.

The plus side is that the starch is removed. The outside of the rice is boiled to perfection, and the inside of the rice gets steamed.

RICE RECIPES

Easy Vegan Fried Rice

Ingredients

Rice + Veggies

1 - 12 oz block water packed tofu, extra firm

1 cup brown rice

4 garlic cloves, minced

1 cup green onion, chopped

1/2 cup peas

1/2 cup carrots, finely diced

Sauce

3 Tbsp soy sauce

1 Tbsp peanut butter

3 Tbsp brown sugar

1 clove garlic, minced

2 tsp chili garlic sauce

Directions

1. Preheat oven to 400 degrees and line a baking sheet with parchment paper.

2. **To Prepare Tofu:** Wrap the tofu in a clean absorbent towel and set something heavy on top for at least 10 minutes. This will 'press' out the liquid, and the towel will help suck the moisture. Then dice the tofu into 1/4 inch cubes.

3. Place on baking sheet and splash with a tablespoon of soy sauce.

4. Bake for 30 minutes. Until golden brown and crispy.

5. **To Prepare Brown Rice:** Boil rice in 6 to 8 cups boiling water uncovered for 30 minutes.

6. Strain the rice and return to pot, removed from heat. Cover with a lid and let steam for 20 minutes.

7. **To Prepare the Sauce:** Add all the sauce ingredients to a medium-size mixing bowl and whisk to combine. Taste and adjust flavor as desired. Add soy sauce for salt, peanut butter for creamy, brown sugar for sweet, or chili garlic sauce for heat.

8. **Final Creation:** In a large skillet over medium heat, sauté the garlic, green onion, peas and carrots for 3-4 minutes, stirring occasionally, and season with 1 Tbsp soy sauce.

9. Add cooked rice, tofu, and sauce. Cook over medium-high heat for 5 minutes, stirring frequently.

Servings: 2 to 4

Prep time: 15 min.

Cook time: 1 hour

Total time: 1.3 hours

RICE RECIPES

Cilantro Lime Rice

Ingredients

1 cup long grain white rice

2 cups vegetable broth

1/2 tsp salt

1/4 tsp ground cumin

2 Tbsp fresh lime juice

1 tsp lime zest

2 Tbsp chopped cilantro

Directions

1. In a large saucepan, bring the vegetable broth, salt and ground cumin to a boil.

2. Add the rice, and reduce heat to medium-low. Let simmer with lid on it, for 20 minutes.

3. Remove from heat, and keep lid on for an additional 20 minutes.

4. Remove lid and stir in lime juice, zest and chopped cilantro. Fluff with a fork and serve warm!

Servings: 4

Prep time: 5 min.

Cook time: 30 min.

Total time: 35 min.

RICE RECIPES

Spanish Rice

Ingredients

2 cups rice long grain white

1/4 cup oil (optional)

4 cups vegetable broth

1 - 8oz can tomato sauce

1 garlic clove, minced

pinch of cumin

pinch of salt

pinch of pepper

Directions

1. Heat oil in large frying pan on medium heat.
2. Add rice and cook until golden brown.
3. Add vegetable broth, tomato sauce, garlic, cumin, salt and pepper.
4. Stir and cover pan. Let simmer for 30 minutes.
5. Remove from heat, cover, and let rest for 10 minutes.

Servings: 8

Prep time: 5 min.

Cook time: 40 min.

Total time: 45 min.

RICE RECIPES

Caribbean Confetti Rice

Ingredients

2 cups long grain white rice

1 - 14 oz can unsweetened coconut milk

1 - 15 oz can pineapple tidbits, with juice

1 - 4.5 oz can chopped green chiles

1/2 cup red bell pepper, diced fine

1/2 cup yellow bell pepper, diced fine

1/2 cup red onion, diced fine

2 garlic cloves, minced

1 jalapeños, seeded and diced fine

1 1/2 tsp sea salt

1/2 tsp allspice

1/4 tsp cayenne pepper

1/2 cup cilantro, chopped

Directions

1. In a large pot, add everything except the cilantro. Bring to a boil.

2. Reduce heat to a simmer and allow to simmer with a lid on, for 20 minutes.

3. Remove from heat, and allow to rest for 10 minutes with the lid on.

4. Fluff the rice, mixing in the cilantro, and serve.

Servings: 8

Prep time: 15 min.

Cook time: 30 min.

Total time: 45 min.

RICE RECIPES

Spicy Thai Rice

Ingredients

1 Tbsp vegetable oil or water sauté

1 onion, diced

2 garlic cloves, minced

1/2 tsp ground ginger

1 Thai chili, dried and chopped, OR toasted and chopped

2 1/2 cups water

1/2 tsp salt

1/4 tsp pepper

1 cup jasmine rice

1 whole lemon, juiced

1/4 cup chopped toasted peanuts

4 basil leafs, cut into thin ribbons

1/4 cup chopped fresh cilantro

Directions

1. In a heavy bottom stock pot, sauté onions until translucent.

2. Stir in garlic and ground ginger, sauté for one minute.

3. Add Thai chili, water, rice, salt and pepper, and bring to a boil.

4. Cover with a lid, reduce heat and simmer for 20 minutes.

5. Remove from heat and let rest for 10 minutes with the lid still on.

6. Remove lid and stir in lemon juice.

7. Garnish with prepared peanuts, basil, and cilantro. Serve.

Servings: 4

Prep time: 10 min.

Cook time: 35 min.

Total time: 45 min.

RICE RECIPES

Buttery Lemon Rice

Ingredients

2 Tbsp vegan margarine

1 cup long grain rice

3 garlic cloves, minced

1 tsp lemon zest

1/4 tsp turmeric powder

1 cup vegetable broth

1 cup rice milk

Juice of 1 lemon (about 3 tablespoons)

garnish with fresh chopped dill and scallions

Directions

1. In a heavy bottom stock pot, sauté garlic in margarine until translucent.

2. Add rice, garlic, lemon zest and turmeric, sauté for one minute.

3. Stir in vegetable broth, milk, and lemon juice.

4. Turn up the heat and bring mixture to a boil.

5. Reduce heat to a simmer, cover the pan and simmer for 15 to 20 minutes, or until liquid has evaporated.

6. Remove from heat.

7. Fluff with a fork and taste for seasonings, adjust accordingly.

8. Garnish with dill and serve.

Servings: 2 to 4

Prep time: 10 min.

Cook time: 20 min.

Total time: 30 min.

RICE RECIPES

Yellow Jasmine Rice

Ingredients

2 Tbsp butter

2 garlic cloves, minced

1 tsp turmeric

1/4 tsp cumin

2 cups uncooked long grain jasmine rice

3 1/2 cups vegetable broth

1 bay leaf

Directions

1. In a medium sauce pot on medium-high heat, sauté the garlic, turmeric, and cumin, for just a minute.

2. Add the dry rice to the pot. Stir and cook over medium heat for about 2 minutes to slightly toast the rice. You may hear a crackling noise as the rice toasts.

3. Add the veggie broth and bay leaf to the pot. Bring to a boil, and reduce heat and simmer on low for 20 minutes with the lid on.

4. Turn the heat off, and let it rest, covered, for an additional 10 minutes.

5. Remove bay leaf, and fluff with a fork and serve.

Servings: 6

Prep time: 5 min.

Cook time: 35 min.

Total time: 40 min.

RICE RECIPES

Turmeric Coconut Basmati Rice

Ingredients

2 Tbsp olive oil or water sauté

1/2 onion, diced fine

1 cup basmati rice, rinsed and drained

3 garlic cloves, minced

1 Tbsp ginger, fresh grated

1 1/2 tsp turmeric

1 cup coconut milk

1 1/2 cup water

1/2 tsp salt

Garnish with fresh chopped basil

Directions

1. In a medium saucepan, over medium heat, sauté diced onion for about 5-7 minutes. Stir occasionally, until onions have become golden.

2. Add the rice, garlic, ginger and turmeric to the saucepan and stir until evenly combined. Let rice cook for 3 minutes, stirring frequently.

3. Add the coconut milk, water and salt. Bring to a boil.

4. Once boiling, reduce the heat to low. Simmer, covered, for 15 minutes.

5. Remove from heat, and allow to rest covered for 10 minutes.

6. Fluff the rice with a fork and stir in fresh chopped basil.

Servings: 2 to 4

Prep time: 5 min.

Cook time: 25 min.

Total time: 30 min.

RICE RECIPES

Wild Rice and Mushrooms

Ingredients

3 Tbsp vegan margarine

1 large onion, chopped

1 pound mixed mushrooms, washed and sliced

2 garlic cloves, chopped

2 cups wild rice blend

4 cups vegetable broth

2 Tbsp Kitchen Bouquet

Garnish with scallions

Directions

1. In a heavy bottom sauce pot over medium heat. Sauté the onion and mushrooms for about 7 minutes.

2. Add the garlic and rice and sauté for another couple minutes.

3. Add the vegetable broth and Kitchen Bouquet, bring to a boil.

4. Cover and turn heat to low. Simmer for 40 minutes.

5. Remove from heat and allow to rest covered for 10 minutes.

6. Garnish with scallions.

Servings: 6 to 8

Prep time: 10 min.

Cook time: 1 hour

Total time: 1.2 hours

RICE RECIPES

Cranberry Apple Pecan Wild Rice

Ingredients

1 1/2 cups vegetable broth

1 1/2 cups apple juice

1 Tbsp dijon mustard

1 Tbsp butter substitute, vegan margarine

1/2 tsp salt

1/2 tsp parsley

1/4 tsp pepper

1/4 tsp oregano

1/4 tsp thyme

1 bay leaf

1 cup wild rice blend, rinsed and drained

2 Tbsp butter substitute, vegan margarine

1/2 large onion, diced

1 apple, chopped

3 garlic cloves, minced

2 tsp apple cider vinegar

1/2 cup dried cranberries

1/2 cup pecans, chopped

Garnish (optional)

fresh thyme

fresh parsley

Directions

1. In a large heavy bottom sauce pot, bring broth, apple juice, dijon, butter, salt, pepper, thyme, oregano, parsley and bay leaf to a boil.

2. Add rice, and simmer 50 minutes, covered, until rice is tender.

3. Remove bay leaf. Drain and leave the rice in the strainer.

4. In the same pan, sauté onions and apples for 5 minutes, until onions and apples are tender.

5. Add garlic and apple cider vinegar and sauté for another minute.

6. Return rice to pot.

7. Add cranberries and pecans. Lightly toss.

8. Salt to taste. And serve.

Servings: 4

Prep time: 10 min.

Cook time: 1 hour

Total time: 1.2 hours

RICE RECIPES

Hawaiian Rice

Ingredients

1 Tbsp coconut oil

1 - 15 oz can artichoke quarters

1 small white onion, chopped

1 red bell pepper, seeded and diced

2 garlic cloves, chopped

1 cup uncooked white rice

1 cup vegetable stock

1 cup coconut milk

1 cup pineapple tidbits

2 Tbsp soy sauce

2 Tbsp chopped green onions

garnish with split macadamia nuts

Directions

1. In a heavy bottom sauce pot over medium heat, sauté the artichokes, onions and peppers for about 7 minutes.

2. Add the garlic and sauté for another minute.

3. Add the rice, vegetable stock, and coconut milk. Bring to a boil, then simmer, covered for 20 minutes.

4. Remove from heat and allow to rest covered for another 10 minutes.

5. Add the pineapple, soy sauce and chopped green onions. Mix well.

6. Garnish with chopped macadamia nuts and serve.

Servings: 2 to 4

Prep time: 10 min.

Cook time: 20 min.

Total time: 30 min.

Tofu

Tofu is one of the most versatile foods out there, and tofu takes on any flavor you want. So when it comes to a list of ingredients that are good parring with tofu… ANYTHING GOES.

Think about the textures too. Firm tofu can be grilled into a crispy substitute for meats, or blended into a smooth and creamy dessert. It can be a sweet treat or a spicy dinner entree. It is easy to transform tofu into Simply Incredible Flavor, because it can be flavored every way you can imagine.

Tofu

This is a very small list because in all reality, every food under the sun can go with tofu. And pairing can be endless too. You can run sweet or sour, bitter or savory. You can create heat, or salty. It is like a blank canvas just waiting for a masterpiece to be created.

GOOD — These items go well with this food.		BETTER — Even better pairing.	BEST — The WOW factor!
almonds	nuts	**garlic**	**FRUITS, ALL**
asparagus	onions	**ginger**	**SOY SAUCE**
bell peppers	rice	**honey**	**VEGETABLES, ALL**
cabbage	salad	**mushrooms**	
chili peppers	scallions	**teriyaki**	
chili powder	sesame, oil		
chives	sesame, seeds		
coconut	soups		
desserts	tamari		
miso	tomatoes		
noodles			

TOFU RECIPES

French Silk Pie

Dairy-free, eggless, gluten-free French Silk Pie. What more can you ask for?

Oh… And it tastes Simply Incredible.

Ingredients

Crust:

1 1/2 cups brazil nuts

8 medjool dates, pitted

1/8 tsp salt

2 Tbsp maple syrup

2 Tbsp cacao powder

Filling:

10.5 oz silken tofu, drained, room temp

1 cup dark chocolate chips, melted (or your favorite chip)

1/3 cup cacao powder

1/3 cup maple syrup

1 tsp vanilla extract

1/4 tsp salt

1/4 tsp instant espresso powder (optional)

Optional Toppings:

coconut, vegan whip cream, shaved chocolate, cacao nibs.

Directions

1. In a food processor, blend the nuts, dates, and salt into a fine crumble. Add syrup and cacao powder and process to combine.

2. Transfer into a pie plate and press into a crust. Place in the freezer while working on the next step.

3. In a blender, blend the tofu to a smooth consistency. Add all remaining filling ingredients and blend well, until smooth.

4. Pour over prepared crust, level the filling and tap the pan on the counter a few times to settle it.

5. Freeze for 1 hour to set. Afterwards keep it refrigerated until serving. Enjoy!

Optional:

Drizzle some vegan yogurt over the cake using a or pipping bag, then create some desired swirl patterns. Sprinkle with any additional toppings.

Chef's Note:

The firmness of this pie is entirely controlled by the pie's temperature. If you keep it frozen, it will be firm. I recommend thawing it out a bit for a creamier, silky texture. I keep it refrigerated, but if it seems like it's a bit too soft, just chill it in the freezer for a few minutes, and it will firm right up.

Servings: 6 or 8 » Prep time: 15 min.

Chill time: 1 hour + » Total time: 1. 3 hours

TOFU RECIPES

Vanilla Lime Cheesecake

This easy no-bake vegan cheesecake is light, creamy and sweet. And has a perfect silky texture. As a base recipe, you can use it to create many variations.

Ingredients

For the crust:

1 1/2 cup dates

1/2 cup sunflower seeds

1/2 cup pumpkin seeds

1/2 cup almonds

2 Tbsp coconut oil, soft

For the filling:

1 lb. soft tofu, drained

2/3 cup raw cashews soaked for at least 4 hours, drained

1/3 cup fresh squeezed lime juice

1/4 cup maple syrup

2 tsp vanilla extract

1/2 cup coconut oil, melted

Directions

For the crust:

1. In a food processor, put all crust ingredients, and pulse until you have crumbs that hold together.

2. Use your hands and the back of a spoon to press the crust mixture evenly into a cheesecake pan.

3. Put in the freezer to firm up.

For the filling:

1. Put everything except the coconut oil into a blender or food processor. Blend until smooth.

2. Pour in the coconut oil, while the blender is running. You'll now have a thick and creamy, but pourable filling mixture.

3. Pour the filling into your prepared crust and evenly spread and smooth it out with a spatula.

4. Place the cheesecake in the refrigerator overnight.

5. Serve chilled. Both the crust and filling will soften at room temperature.

Chef's Notes

This recipe freezes well for later use, but you will want to give it time to thaw before serving. If it gets too warm, it will get too soft.

Servings: 4

Prep time: 10 min.

freeze time: 2 hours +

Total time: 2 hours ++

TOFU RECIPES

Sugar Free Lemon Curd

Ingredients

1 cup soft silken tofu, drained well

½ cup maple syrup

¼ cup coconut oil, melted but cool

4 lemons, juice and zest (keep separate)

1 tsp lemon extract

1 tsp vanilla extract

1 Tbsp agar agar powder, or 2 Tbsp flakes

Optional:

a few drops of yellow food coloring

Directions

1. In a blender, whip the tofu, syrup, coconut oil, lemon zest, vanilla and lemon extract. Blend until smooth, scraping the sides when necessary.

2. In a small sauce pan on medium-low heat, heat the lemon juice and agar agar powder until the agar agar dissolves into the liquid. (it should thicken slightly) When it starts to boil, you're done.

3. Pour agar agar into the blender with the tofu and blend until very smooth.

4. Transfer into a glass jar and cool to room temp.

5. Then refrigerate the mixture. It will thicken as it sets in the fridge.

Chef's Notes:

This base recipe works great for pies, tarts, and lemon squares. If you're leaving the lemon curd in a jar to be used as a spread, you may notice some very slight separation occurring after a few days in the fridge, which is perfectly fine. I just drain off any moisture, and hand mix it a little bit before using.

Servings: 2 cups

Prep time: 5 min.

Cook time: 10 min.

Total time: 15 min.

TOFU RECIPES

Balsamic Tofu

This tofu is crispy, not mushy, full of balsamic flavor and pairs perfectly with your favorite Italian dishes! High in protein and very budget friendly. Balsamic tofu could not be easier to make. This recipe will prove that tofu really can have Simply Incredible Flavor. And for those with sensitivities, this is vegan, gluten-free, dairy-free, and grain-free.

Ingredients

2 lbs. extra firm tofu, pressed and cubed

1/2 cup balsamic vinegar

1 tsp Italian seasoning

1/2 tsp salt

Directions

1. Press the tofu thoroughly. Cut into small cubes.

2. In a plastic baggie, mix the balsamic, Italian seasoning and salt.

3. Add the tofu cubes. Lightly toss to coat all tofu. Let marinate for a couple hours, or overnight in the fridge. Flip the bag a couple times to help marinade.

4. Preheat the oven to 400 degrees.

5. Place drained tofu on a parchment paper lined baking sheet, sprayed with nonstick spray.

6. Bake for 35 minutes, flipping 1/2 way through the cooking - until crispy.

7. Transfer to a serving plate, and splash with a little more balsamic and salt. Enjoy

Chef's Notes:

Technically this would serve 8. But considering the Simply Incredible Flavor, I would have to say that it serves 4.

Servings: 4

Prep time: 5 min.

Cook time: 35 min.

Total time: 40 min.

TOFU RECIPES

Peanut Butter Cup Pie

This is a no-bake pie with a graham cracker crust and chocolate ganache top.
Simple to prepare, and Simply Incredible Flavor. You may need to make two.

Ingredients

Crust

1 sleeve graham crackers

1/4 cup vegan butter or coconut oil, melted

Pie

12 ounces firm silken tofu, slightly drained and patted dry

1/2 cup creamy peanut butter

1/4 cup honey

1 - 14 oz can full fat coconut milk OR coconut cream, chilled overnight (don't shake the can! You want the cream and liquid separated)

Chocolate Ganache Topping

1 1/2 cups chocolate chips, dairy-free

1/2 cup coconut milk.

Chopped peanuts for garnish

Directions

For the crust:

1. Preheat oven to 375 degrees. Lightly oil an 8 inch glass pie pan.

2. In a food processor, add graham crackers and process until a coarse meal, not powder.

3. Add melted butter and pulse to combine.

4. Add to the pie pan and press down with your fingers or a spoon to flatten.

5. Bake for 10 minutes or until golden brown. Remove and set aside to cool.

continued on next page

For the Filling

1. In a blender, add tofu, peanut butter, and honey. Blend until smooth, scraping down sides as needed. Taste to adjust seasonings. Add more sweetener, or salt if needed.

2. Next, scoop out the cream from the coconut milk or cream.

3. In a mixing bowl, whip the cream into whipped cream. If desired, sweeten with a little powdered sugar and vanilla.

4. Gently fold the peanut butter-tofu mixture into the whipped cream.

5. Pour filling onto crust and level out with a spatula. Put in the freezer to chill for about 1 hour.

For the Ganache:

1. In a sauce pan, heat your coconut milk to a low simmer until hot.

2. Remove from heat and add the chocolate chips. Let set for 5 minutes without touching, allowing the chips to melt.

3. Stir gently until a smooth ganache forms. If needed. you can microwave for a couple seconds at a time.

4. Now we need to move quickly and spread the ganache on top of the pie. It will harden fast. Use a spatula and do quick full spreads.

5. Top with crushed peanuts.

6. Freeze for another 30 minutes before serving. Remove from freezer, cut and serve.

Chef's Notes:

It is best to cut while more frozen. And then transfer to plates. keep the plated dessert in the fridge until ready to serve.

Servings: 8

Prep time: 25 min.

Cook time: 15 min.

Total time: 40 min.

TOFU RECIPES

Simple Scrambled Tofu

Once you start making scrambled tofu, you will want it often. And there are hundreds of ways to get Simply Incredible Flavor.

Ingredients

1 Tbsp olive oil or water sauté

2 garlic cloves, minced or 1 t sp garlic powder

2 lbs. extra firm tofu, drained well and patted dry with a towel

1/4 cup nutritional yeast flakes

2 Tbsp McKay's vegan chicken style seasoning

1/4 tsp turmeric

salt to taste

Optional ingredients:

1/2 cup red onion, finely diced

1/4 cup red bell pepper, finely diced

Directions

1. In a large sauté pan, sauté onion, bell pepper if desired, and garlic.

2. Crumble tofu and add to the sauté pan.

3. Mix in your seasonings.

4. Cook on medium-high heat stirring occasionally.

5. You can serve it as soon as it's incorporated and heated, or cook it until it gets very browned. I like it somewhere in-between.

Servings: 4

Prep time: 5 min.

Cook time: 10 min.

Total time: 15 min.

TOFU RECIPES

Energy Packed Blueberry Tofu Smoothie

Ingredients

1 cup almond milk

1 cup blueberries, frozen

1/2 cup strawberries, frozen

1 banana, frozen

1 cup baby spinach

1/2 avocado

1/2 cup silken tofu

1/2 cup raw walnuts

1 Tbsp hemp seeds

3 dates, pitted

Directions

1. Blend all ingredients until smooth and creamy.

TOFU RECIPES

Tofu Pancakes

Ingredients

2 cups pastry flour, (any flour works, but I like pastry flour).

1 Tbsp baking powder

1 tsp cinnamon

1/4 tsp salt

1 lb silken tofu

1 cup almond milk

1/4 cup vegetable oil (optional)

2 Tbsp maple syrup

2 tsp vanilla extract

1/2 cup cacao nibs (or mini dark chocolate chips)

Directions

1. In small bowl, mix flour, baking powder, cinnamon and salt.

2. In a blender blend tofu, milk, oil, maple and vanilla. Blend until smooth.

3. Add dry ingredient mixture in 3 increments. Blend in-between each addition. This batter will be relatively thick.

4. Spray a griddle or skillet with cooking spray or coat with vegan margarine. Heat over medium, and ladle about 1/4 cup portions of batter. Sprinkle a few cacao nibs on top.

5. Allow to cook until batter begins to brown around the edges, about five minutes. Test with spatula to see if it's firm enough to flip. Gently flip and cook until the opposite side is lightly browned, and center is fully cooked.

6. Top with extra cacao nibs and maple syrup.

Chef's Notes:

For low oil version, replace the oil with 1/4 cup apple sauce. This is a great base recipe for any pancakes, i.e. blueberry, walnut.

Servings: 4 to 6

Prep time: 10 min.

Cook time: 15 min.

Total time: 25 min.

TOFU RECIPES

Crispy Baked Garlic Tofu

Ingredients

1 lb. block firm tofu, drained and cut into bite-sized cubes

For the Sauce:

4 garlic cloves, minced

2 Tbsp soy sauce

1 tsp onion powder

1 1/2 Tbsp light brown sugar

1 tsp sriracha sauce

Make slurry with 1 Tbsp cornstarch + 1/4 cup water

Directions

1. **For the Tofu:** Preheat oven to 400 degrees. Place tofu pieces on a parchment paper lined baking sheet.

2. Bake tofu for about 35-40 minutes until crisp around the edges, flipping tofu halfway through.

3. **For the Sauce:** In a saucepan over medium heat, mix the sauce ingredients and bring to a boil.

4. Mix cornstarch and water to a small bowl and mix until cornstarch is fully dissolved.

5. Add the cornstarch slurry to the garlic sauce. Stir until everything is completely mixed and sauce has thickened. If sauce is too thick, you can add a little water to thin.

6. **Finishing:** Add tofu to saucepan and coat with sauce.

7. Transfer to serving bowl. Serve while warm.

Chef's Notes:

You can serve with rice if desired. You can also garnish with fresh chopped scallions.

TOFU RECIPES

Easy Tofu Eggless Salad

This is a staple in our dietary menu. And that's because it's extremely healthy and there are always fun unique ways to make it. Simply Incredible Flavor is just one creative idea away.

Ingredients

1 lb. extra firm tofu, squeeze drained, crumbled

1 celery stalk, finely diced

1 tsp turmeric

1 tsp McKay's Chicken Style Seasoning, to taste.

vegan mayonnaise

Directions

1. Drain liquid from the tofu and pat dry with a towel.

2. In a bowl, crumble until finely chunked.

3. Add remaining ingredients and mix well. Put the mayo in last, 1 tablespoon at a time, until you get to the consistency you like.

Chef's Notes:

This is a great base recipe that you can run with in a hundred varieties. One of my favorite ways is to add chopped green olives. Also bell peppers, or artichokes. And for a low fat version, you can also use mustards, or whipped avocado in place of some of the mayo.

Servings: 4

Prep time: 10 min.

Total time: 10 min.

TOFU RECIPES

Almond Crusted Tofu Nuggets

These Almond Crusted Tofu Nuggets have a healthy almond breading and served with a creamy avocado dip. What's not to love with this kind of Simply Incredible Flavor.?

Ingredients

Tofu

2 lb. tofu, firm

1/4 cup soy sauce

2 Tbsp lemon juice

2 Tbsp honey

2 clove garlic minced

Breading

1/2 cup almond flour

2 cup whole almonds

2 Tbsp nutritional yeast flakes

1 tsp paprika

1 tsp salt

1/2 tsp pepper

1/2 cup ground flax seed + 1 cup water, whisk together

Dipping Sauce

2 avocados, peeled and pitted

1 cup dairy-free yogurt

½ cup fresh chopped parsley handful

3 cloves garlic, chopped

Juice of 2 limes

salt and pepper to taste

Directions

1. **For the tofu:** Drain tofu and slice into nugget sizes. About 1" x 1" x 1/2".

2. Lay on clean towel and gently press with another towel to remove excess moisture. Place tofu nuggets in a baking dish.

3. **For the Marinade:** Combine the soy sauce, lemon juice, honey, and minced garlic.

4. Pour over tofu, cover, and let marinate in the fridge for at least 1 hour or even over night. Flip half way through to marinade completely.

5. **For the Breading:** In a food processor, chop almonds until ground. Add the nutritional yeast flakes, paprika, salt and pepper. Then pulse.

6. **Prepare your Breading Station:** Place the flour in one bowl, the ground flax seed and water in another, and then put the breading in a third.

7. **Breading:** Shake off excess marinade from the tofu. Then, one at a time, coat each lightly with flour, then the flax mix, and then the almond breading. Place nuggets on a parchment lined baking sheet.

8. Bake tofu nuggets at 400 degrees for 8 to 10 minutes, flipping halfway through. Cook until golden brown and toasted.

9. **Sauce:** While the nuggets cook, toss all the dipping sauce ingredients into a food processor and blend until smooth and creamy.

10. Serve nuggets warm with dipping sauce!

Chef's Notes

This is again one of my staple concepts that you can tweak to your own liking. Create an Italian herb nugget, or a southwest chili, or a cajun.

Servings: 4 » Prep time: 30 min.
Cook time: 10 min. » Total time: 40 min.

TOFU RECIPES

Dijon Tofu Burgers WITH MAPLE MAYO

This is a burger you are going to love.

Ingredients

Tofu Burger:

1 lb. extra firm tofu

1 onion, small, chopped

1 Tbsp oil or water sauté

2 cups carrots, shredded

1 red bell pepper, roughly cut

1 cup mushrooms, sliced

2 cloves garlic, minced

1/4 tsp salt

1 tsp oregano, dried

1/3 cup basil, chopped fine

1/2 cup walnuts, chopped

1 Tbsp Braggs Liquid Aminos

2 tsp dijon mustard

4 Tbsp tahini

1/2 cup breadcrumbs

salt/pepper, to taste

Maple Dijon Mayonnaise:

1/2 cup vegan mayonnaise

1 Tbsp dijon mustard

1 Tbsp maple syrup

Directions

1. Preheat oven to 375 degrees.

2. In a food processor, start by processing the tofu till it turns into a fine crumble. Put into a large mixing bowl and set aside.

3. Next, process the onions into fine dice pieces.

4. Take the onions and put into a large heated sauté pan and sauté for about 5 minutes, until soft.

5. Meanwhile, in the food processor, add the carrots, red bell peppers, mushrooms and garlic. Pulse until it's a chopped texture, but not mushy.

6. Add the veggies to the onions in the skillet and stir well. Add salt and dried oregano and continue cooking uncovered until all the liquid has evaporated, mushrooms will sweat, and this can take about 10 minutes on medium heat.

7. Combine the entire mixture with the crumbled tofu in your mixing bowl.

8. Add the chopped basil, walnuts, liquid aminos, dijon mustard, and tahini. Mix well.

9. Stir bread crumbs into the mixture. Mix well, adding salt and pepper to taste.

10. Form mixture into 8 burger patties.

11. Place burgers on a parchment paper lined baking sheet. Bake for 30 minutes on one side. Flip, and bake for another 15 minutes on the other side.

12. **Prepare Maple Mayo:** Combine ingredients together and mix well.

13. Once the burgers are done, assemble the burgers with condiments, and serve with maple mayo.

Servings: 4 » Prep time: 30 min.
Cook time: 45 min. » Total time: 1.4 hours

Whole grain

While we have already looked at oats, barley, rice, and quinoa because they are the most popular when it comes to recipes, I didn't want to miss out on the other whole grains that are critical to proper nutrition. Here are just a few:

Wheat, Maize, Rye, Millet, Amaranth, Triticale, Teff, and Buckwheat.

Whole grain

The consumption of whole grains has been proven to reduce heart disease and cancer. It also lowers your LDL and triglycerides. And here is the kicker: Whole grain consumption reduces hypertension, diabetes, and obesity, while refined grains have been shown to increase these health related problems.

So what we need to know is the difference between whole and processed grains. A grain is considered to be a Whole Grain as long as all three parts - bran, germ, and endosperm, are still present in the same proportions as when the grain was grown.

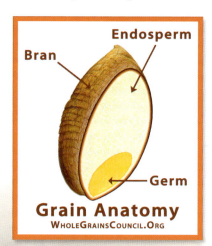

THE BRAN
The bran is the multi-layered outer skin of the edible kernel. It contains important antioxidants, B vitamins and fiber.

THE GERM
The germ is the embryo which has the potential to sprout into a new plant. It contains many B vitamins, some protein, minerals, and healthy fats.

THE ENDOSPERM
The endosperm is the germ's food supply, which provides essential energy to the young plant so it can send roots down for water and nutrients, and send sprouts up for sunlight's photosynthesizing power. The endosperm is by far the largest portion of the kernel. It contains starchy carbohydrates, proteins and small amounts of vitamins and minerals.

Refined and Enriched Grain: are the terms used to refer to grains that are not whole, because they are missing one or more of their three key parts (bran, germ, or endosperm). White flour and white rice are refined grains, for instance, because both have had their bran and germ removed, leaving only the endosperm. Refining a grain removes about a quarter of the protein, and half to two thirds or more of a score of nutrients, leaving the grain a mere shadow of its original self.

Since the late 1800s, when new milling technology allowed the bran and germ to be easily and cheaply separated from the endosperm, most of the grains around the world have been eaten as refined grains. This quickly led to disastrous and widespread nutrition problems, like the deficiency diseases pelagra and beri-beri.

In response, many governments recommended or required that refined grains be "enriched." Enrichment adds back fewer than a half dozen of the many missing nutrients, and does so in proportions different than they originally existed. The better solution is simply to eat whole grains, now that we more fully understand their huge health advantages.

The chart below compares whole wheat flour to refined wheat flour and enriched wheat flour. You can see the vast difference in essential nutrients.

Source: wholegrainscouncil.org

Refining wheat flour removes the bran and germ, decreasing essential nutrients to levels ranging from 8% (vitamin E) to 59% (folate) of the level naturally occurring in whole wheat. Only the calories increase!

Enriching wheat flour adds back five of these nutrients, in amounts different from their original levels in whole wheat flour. All other nutrients stay at the levels shown for refined flour above.

The Gluten Fear: There are a lot of people on a gluten free diet. And according to Dr. McDougall: Out of every 200 people who are eating gluten free, only one is a celiac or gluten intolerant. The other 199 out of 200 people have simply been sucked into this big lie that you should avoid gluten.

Gluten free is now a 7 Billion dollar industry. And according to the British Medical Journal's newest studies: The number of people eating gluten free has tripled since 2014, yet the actual celiac-disease rates have remained the same.

Bottom Line: Eat more whole grains, including wheat. These grains are a staple to living a healthy life.

COOKING BULGUR WHEAT

The standard way to cook bulgur wheat is a ratio of 1 cup bulgur wheat to 2 cups water with 1/2 tsp salt. Bring this to a boil, and then simmer 15 minutes. Drain off any excess liquid.

The better way: The way I like to cook bulgur wheat is a little different. I like to use a large stock pot and bring one gallon of water to a boil. And 1/2 gallon of bulgur wheat to the pot. Return to a full boil, and then remove from heat allowing to rest covered with lid for 30 minutes to one hour. PERFECT Bulgur wheat every time.

When the bulgur wheat is cool, I press it into quart baggies and stack them in the freezer. Then I can grab them any time for fast and healthy meals.

I also love to put a shot soy sauce into the boiling water. This will give it the WOW flavor you have been looking for.

Bulgur Wheat

GOOD These items go well with this food.		BETTER Even better pairing.	BEST The WOW factor!
almonds	pistachios	**bell peppers**	**CUCUMBERS**
anise	pomegranate arils	**celery**	**PEPPER**
basil	potatoes	**chickpeas**	**SALT**
beans	raisins	**cranberries**	
cardamom	spinach	**curry**	
chili peppers	sugar	**garlic**	
chives	tarragon	**ginger**	
cilantro	thyme	**lemon**	
coconut	tomatoes	**lime**	
coconut milk	tomato sauce	**mushrooms**	
cream	tomato paste	**onions**	
currants	truffles	**scallions**	
fennel	vegetable stock	**shallots**	
lemon zest	walnuts	**vegetables**	
mint		**vegetables, roasted**	
nuts			
orange			
parsley			
peas			
pecans			

SIMPLY INCREDIBLE PAIRINGS

bulgur + chickpeas + dill
bulgur + cilantro + lime
bulgur + cucumber + lemon + red pepper
bulgur + dried cranberries + cilantro + walnuts
bulgur + dried cherries + chipotle
bulgur + garlic + roasted eggplant + roasted tomatoes
bulgur + grilled vegetables, any mixed
bulgur + olives + pomegranate arils + cilantro

BULGUR WHEAT RECIPES

Bulgur Chili

This is a chili that is sure to please even the most diehard of meat lovers.

Ingredients

2 Tbsp vegetable oil or water sauté

1 medium onion, diced

1 red bell pepper, seeded and diced

1 jalapeños, seeded and diced fine

4 cloves garlic, minced

3 Tbsp chili powder

2 tsp cumin

1 tsp dried oregano

3/4 cup bulgur

1 - 28 oz can crushed tomatoes

1 - 15 oz can diced tomatoes

2 cups water

1 1/2 tsp kosher salt

2 - 15 oz cans black beans, rinsed and drained

Directions

1. In a large heavy-bottomed pot over medium-high heat, sauté the onion, bell pepper, and jalapeño. Cook about 5 minutes.

2. Add the garlic, chili powder, cumin, and oregano, and cook until fragrant, about 1 minute.

3. Add the bulgur, crushed tomatoes, diced tomatoes, salt, and 2 cups of water.

4. Bring to a boil, then reduce the heat, cover, and simmer for 25 minutes.

5. Add the black beans and you're ready to serve.

6. Serve with toppings of choice.

Chef's Notes:

Topping suggestions: Vegan shredded cheddar cheese, vegan sour cream, diced avocado, cilantro. This is a great chili to make big batches and freeze.

Servings: 8

Prep time: 10 min

Cook time: 30 min

Total time: 40 min

BULGUR WHEAT RECIPES

Tabbouleh

Tabbouleh is a Levantine vegetarian dish, sometimes considered a salad. It is traditionally made with tomatoes, finely chopped parsley, mint, bulgur, and onion, and seasoned with olive oil, lemon juice, and salt. This recipe is an old favorite of mine, where I don't use the oil, but add extra flavor in the vegetables.

Ingredients

4 cups cooked bulgur wheat, cooled

1 cup parsley, fresh chopped

1/2 cup fresh mint, chopped

2 tomatoes, chopped

1 cucumber, peeled and diced small

1/2 red onion, diced small

1/2 yellow bell pepper, diced small

1/4 cup lemon juice, fresh

1/2 tsp salt

1/4 tsp pepper

Directions

In a large bowl, mix all the ingredients together.

My oh my…. that was a real challenge.

Servings 8 to 10

Prep time: 20 min

Cook time: 30 min

Total time: 50 min

Millet

Millet is an ancient grain seed originally from Africa and northern China. It remains a staple in the diets of about a third of the world's population. Rich in iron, B vitamins and calcium, millet has a mild corn flavor and is naturally gluten-free.

MILLET RECIPE

Cooking Millet

Ingredients

1 cup raw millet

2 cups water (or broth, for certain flavors)

¼ tsp salt

1 Tbsp vegan butter or olive oil

Directions

1. Optional Toasting Millet: In a large, dry saucepan, toast the raw millet over medium heat for 4-5 minutes or until it turns a rich golden brown and the grains become fragrant. Be careful not to let them burn.

2. Add the water and salt to the pan.

3. Bring the liquid to a boil.

4. Reduce the heat to low and simmer covered for 15 minutes.

5. Remove from heat, and allow to rest covered for another 10 minutes.

6. Fluff and Serve!

Chef's Notes:

Toasting the millet will enhance the nutty flavor of the grain. Then, there are two ways you can cook it. The first (as shown) will result in a fluffy, whole-grain side dish much like quinoa.

The second way is to use more water: 3 cups instead of 2 cups. This will result in a creamy porridge, with a polenta-like consistency, great for breakfasts. If you're going this route, stir often. This creamy version is also great because you can pour it into a pan to cool, slice it as you would polenta, and fry it.

Winter squash

Winter squash

GOOD These items go well with this food.		BETTER Even better pairing.	BEST The WOW factor!
apple juice	lemon	**allspice**	**PEPPER**
basil	lemon juice	**apples**	**SALT**
bay leaf	lime	**cinnamon**	
bell peppers	maple syrup	**corn**	
bread crumbs	marjoram	**garlic**	
carrots	mint	**pecans**	
cayenne	mushrooms	**potatoes**	
celery	nutmeg	**sour cream**	
chestnuts	nuts	**tomatoes**	
chickpeas	olives, black, green	**vegetable stock**	
chili peppers	onions		
cloves	orange		
coconut	oregano		
coconut milk	parsley		
coriander	pumpkin		
couscous	pumpkin seeds		
cream	red pepper flakes		
cumin	rosemary		
curry	sage		
dill	shallots		
eggplant	spinach		
fenugreek	sugar, brown		
ginger	tarragon		
honey	thyme		
jalapeno	vanilla		
leeks	walnuts		

SIMPLY INCREDIBLE PAIRINGS

acorn squash + ginger + maple syrup

butternut squash + bay leaf + nutmeg

butternut squash + cilantro + coconut + ginger

winter squash + garlic + sage

winter squash + garlic + parsley

winter squash + onions + vegetable stock

WINTER SQUASH RECIPES

Black-eyed Pea and Acorn Squash Stew

Ingredients

2 Tbsp olive oil

1 yellow onions, large, diced

1 Tbsp ginger, fresh grated

1 green Serrano chili, chopped fine

3 cloves garlic, minced

2 tsp sea salt

1 tsp ground cumin

4 cups vegetable broth

1 - 28 oz can tomato puree

1/2 cup peanut butter, smooth

1 acorn squash, peeled, seeded, and cut into 1-inch-thick diced.

2 Tbsp brown sugar

2 - 16 oz cans black-eyed peas, rinsed

2 Tbsp chopped roasted peanuts

3 cups cooked brown rice

Directions

1. In a large skillet, sauté the onions for about 10 minutes.

2. Add the ginger, chili, garlic, salt, and cumin. Cook 5 minutes more, stirring occasionally.

3. Add the broth, tomato puree, peanut butter, acorn squash, and sugar.

4. Cook over medium heat, covered, until the squash is tender, about 30 minutes.

5. Add the black-eyed peas and heat through. And you're ready to serve.

6. Serve over brown rice and the garnish with peanuts.

Chef's Notes:

Acorn squash can be hard to peel You can always cook in the oven first. Or even microwave for 5 minutes, and that makes it easier to peel and chop up.

Servings: 8 » Prep time: 15 min.

Cook time: 45 min. » Total time: 1 hour

WINTER SQUASH RECIPES

Squash Harvest Loaf

Ingredients

2 cups roasted butternut squash purée

1 cup walnut halves and/or pecans

1 cup pumpkin seeds

2 tsp baking soda

2 tsp baking powder

1/2 tsp nutmeg

1 1/2 tsp cinnamon

1 1/2 tsp salt

1 1/2 cups light brown sugar

1 cup apple sauce

3 ripe bananas

3/4 cup warm water mixed with 1/2 cup ground flax seed

3/4 cup almond milk

3 1/2 cups all-purpose flour

Directions

1. **Roasting the butternut squash:** Cut the squash in half. Remove the seeds and place the halves in a rimmed baking sheet, face up. Add 1 cup water into the pan. Cook in a preheated oven at 375 degrees for 1 hour minimum, until the squash is very tender.

2. Let cool, before scooping the squash out.

3. It's easy to take roasted butternut squash and turn it in to puree, by simply putting it into a food processor and blending well.

4. Let cool and use 2 cups of the puree for 2 loaves.

5. **Toast the nuts and seeds:** Place the nuts and seeds on a rimmed baking sheet and toast for 15 minutes at 375 degrees. Remove from the oven and let cool.

6. Keep about 1/2 cup of the nuts for later. The rest are going to get ground up and put into the bread mix.

7. **Making the breads:** Turn the oven temperature down to 325 degrees.

8. Sift the flour, baking powder, baking soda, cinnamon, nutmeg and salt in a bowl.

9. Add the ground seeds and nuts, and mix with a spoon.

10. In the bowl of a stand mixer, combine the apple sauce, sugar, and bananas, use the paddle attachment to mix on medium speed, for 5 minutes.

11. Add the roasted butternut squash and continue to mix for another 2 minutes.

12. Then, slowly add the ground flax seed and water mixture.

13. Remove the bowl from the stand mixer and add the flour and the almond milk, hand mix well.

14. Transfer the batter into 2 greased 9x5 loaf pans. Fill about 2/3 to the top.

15. Sprinkle with the reserved nuts and seeds.

16. Bake in the oven for 1 hour, or until a tooth pick comes out dry when inserted into the middle of the loaf.

17. Remove and let cool for 20 minutes before removing from pan.

Servings: 2 loafs » Prep time: 10 min.
Cook time: 2.5 hours » Total time: 2.7 hours

WINTER SQUASH RECIPES

Tuscan Spaghetti Squash

Ingredients

1 large spaghetti squash

2 Tbsp olive oil, or water sauté

1 cup red onions, diced

1 cup red bell peppers, diced

1 cup mushrooms, sliced

2 cloves garlic, minced

4 cups baby spinach

1/2 cup nutritional yeast flakes

1 /4 cup McKay's Chicken Style Seasoning

1 1/2 c. cherry tomatoes, halved

1 cup basil, fresh chopped

salt to taste

pepper to taste

Directions

1. Preheat oven to 375 degrees.

2. Take 1 large spaghetti squash and stab some slits in it with a knife. Place on a sheet pan in the oven for about one hour. It should be soft enough on the inside for a knife to go through easily.

3. Meanwhile, in a large skillet, sauté the onions, peppers, and mushrooms for about 10 minutes.

4. Add the garlic and a pinch of salt and pepper, and sauté for another minute.

5. Transfer to a large bowl and allow to cool.

6. Top with the spinach, nutritional yeast flakes, and McKay's Chicken Style Seasoning.

7. Remove squash from the oven. Let cool for a few minutes. Cut in half, from the stem down. Careful, this is hot. Remove the seeds, then remove the spaghetti flesh from the squash and place it in the bowl with the rest of the ingredients.

8. Toss well while hot, and flake apart with a fork any squash that's still holding together. The spinach should be wilting a bit.

9. Add salt and pepper if needed.

10. Garnish with chopped basil and cherry tomatoes.

Chef's Notes:

Depending on the dryness of the squash, you may want to add a bit of vegan butter, or hot water. It should be extremely moist, but not dripping wet.

Servings: 2 to 4

Prep time: 10 min.

Cook time: 1.1 hours.

Total time: 1.2 hours

WINTER SQUASH RECIPES

Brown Sugar Delicata Squash

What's not to love? Sweet, savory, salty and with a hint of bitter from the molasses in the brown sugar. This is Simply Incredible Flavor.

Ingredients

2 Delicata squash

2 Tbsp olive oil

2 Tbsp maple syrup

2 Tbsp brown sugar

1/8 tsp salt

pinch of red pepper to taste

1/4 tsp ground cinnamon

cooking spray

Directions

1. Preheat the oven to 400 degrees. Wash the squash - we are going to serve these with the skins on. Half the Delicata squash lengthwise from the stem. Remove the seeds. Cut the halves into 3/4 inch thick slices.

2. In an extra large mixing bowl, mix together the remaining ingredients.

3. Toss the squash to give all the pieces an even coat.

4. Place on a parchment lined baking sheet.

5. Bake for 20-30 minutes or until squash is tender and starting to brown. Serve immediately.

Chef's Notes:

You can do this same concept with any squash or pumpkin.

Servings 4 to 6

Prep Time 5 minutes

Cook Time 25 minutes

Total Time 30 minutes

WINTER SQUASH RECIPES

Butternut Squash Pancakes
WITH WHIPPED MAPLE BUTTER

Ingredients

For the Pancakes:

3 cups whole wheat pastry flour (or all purpose)

1 Tbsp pumpkin pie spice

2 tsp baking powder

1 tsp baking soda

1/2 tsp salt

1/2 cup warm water mixed with 1/4 cup ground flax seed

1 cup butternut squash, cooked and pureed

1/4 cup brown sugar

2 Tbsp vegetable oil

2 1/2 cups almond milk

1 tsp vanilla

For the Whipped Maple Butter:

1/2 cup vegan margarine

1/4 cup pure maple syrup

1/8 tsp pumpkin pie spice

pinch of salt

Directions

1. In a large bowl, whisk together the flour, baking powder, baking soda, salt and pumpkin pie spice.
2. In a medium bowl, whisk together the ground flax seed and water with brown sugar, squash, and vegetable oil. Mix well.
3. Add the vanilla and almond milk and whisk again until well combined.
4. Mix the dry ingredients with the wet mixture and mix well. Stir until combined. Batter should be a thicker pancake batter.
5. Allow batter to rest for 5-10 minutes.
6. Preheat griddle or frying pan to medium heat.
7. Lightly spray with vegetable spray.
8. Drop 1/4 cup scoopfuls of batter onto griddle. Cook for about 3 minutes, until sides are set and the bottom is golden. Flip and finish cooking the other side for another 2 to 3 minutes. These pancakes should be golden brown and fully cooked on the inside.
9. **For the whipped butter:** Using an electric mixer, whip up the butter, maple syrup, salt and spices. It's ready to serve, or refrigerate until ready to serve.

Chef's Notes

You can substitute pureed pumpkin for the squash and make pumpkin pancakes instead. These pancakes are good to refrigerate or freeze for later use.

Servings 20 cakes » Prep Time 10 minutes

Cook Time 15 minutes » Total Time 25 minutes

WINTER SQUASH RECIPES

Butternut Squash Taquitos

These are baked vegetarian Taquitos, with a twist. I use butternut squash to make it a little sweet and chipotles to give it a little heat. This combination produces Simply Incredible Flavor.

Ingredients

1 medium butternut squash

4 cloves garlic

1/2 cup vegan cream cheese

1 cup black beans, rinsed and drained

1 cup corn, rinsed and drained

1 cup chopped onions

2 chipotle in adobo sauce, chopped fine

2 cups vegan cheddar cheese

salt to taste

olive oil

24 small flour tortillas

Directions

1. Preheat oven to 375 degrees.

2. Peel and seed the butternut squash.

3. Cut into random 1 inch cubes.

4. Toss with a splash of olive oil. Place on a baking sheet with the garlic cloves.

5. Bake until tender, 25 minutes. stir and toss half way through cooking.

6. Once fully cooked, allow to cool. After cooled, mash up the butternut squash and garlic. With a potato masher, mash in the cream cheese and mix well. Fold in the black beans, corn, onions, chipotle, cheese, and salt.

7. **Assembling the Taquitos:** Add about 1/4 cup of the mix into the middle of a tortilla and roll up. Place on baking sheet with the tortillas edge facing down to help the Taquito hold together. Repeat until all the mix and tortillas are gone.

8. Place in the oven and bake for about 20 minutes flipping halfway through. Cook them crispy and crunchy.

Active Time: 5 minutes

Inactive Time: 45 minutes

Total Time: 50 minutes

Servings 4 to 6

Prep Time 5 minutes

Cook Time 45 minutes

Total Time 50 minutes

WINTER SQUASH RECIPES

Winter Squash Fruit Leathers

This can be made with leftover squash, or simply bake some fresh. It's a great way to warm up the house on a cold winter day. And the scent will certainly let any guests know that there is some Simply Incredible Flavor in the kitchen.

Ingredients

2 cups cooked winter squash, butternut

1/4 cup honey

1/2 tsp cinnamon

1/8 tsp ginger, ground

1/8 tsp allspice

1/8 tsp nutmeg

pinch of salt

Directions

1. Place the cooked, cooled winter squash into a high-powered blender.

Add the remaining ingredients and blend for about a minute, until the puree is smooth and the ingredients are evenly combined. This should be a pourable thick liquid, if needed, add a little more honey or a splash of water. Blend well.

2. Pour the puree into the center of parchment paper lined baking sheets.

3. Use a spatula to spread the puree out to less than a 1/4 inch thick.

4. Dehydrate between 95 and 145 degrees for about 8 hours, depending on your dehydrator. The leather is done when it is tacky but dry, and no longer wet at all in the center. The leather should be pliable, and not brittle.

Chef's Notes:

You can also do this in the oven on low, and prop the oven door open just a crack for the moisture to be released. Usually takes about 6 hours at 150 degrees.

Pumpkin Leather Recipe

Same concepts, with a little twist

Ingredients

2 cups pumpkin puree

2 cups applesauce

1 cup canned coconut milk

1/4 cup honey

1/4 cup shredded coconut, unsweetened

2 Tbsp dried cranberries, chopped fine

1 tsp ground cinnamon

1/2 tsp ground nutmeg

1/2 tsp ground allspice

pinch of salt

Directions:

Blend all the ingredients well, **except for the coconut and the cranberries**. Put those in last and just pulse a couple times. Then follow directions above.

International Flavor

We have created the simplest ways to achieve any flavor in the world. The trick to creating food from other cultures is to first determine what food is dominant to that culture. So we have comprised a list of all the foods that every major cuisine uses. And we take it one step farther and share with you the most popular pairings.

HOW TO USE THIS SECTION

FIRST: you will find a lists of ingredients for a particular region, or cuisine.

SECOND: you will find Simply Incredible Pairings. When you combine these particular ingredients, you will achieve Simply Incredible Flavor.

Example:

chili peppers + garlic + onions

chili peppers + peanuts + tomatoes

THIRD: you will find some great recipes that capture that particular region or food

GOOD These items go well with this cuisine.	BETTER Even better pairing.	BEST The WOW factor!
allspice	cream sauces	**DILL**
apples	mushrooms	**SOUR CREAM**
bay leaf	**SIMPLY INCREDIBLE PAIRINGS**	
breads	bay leaf + dill + nutmeg + onion	

African

African food has many styles throughout its 54 countries. While each country has its own unique style, we are simply going to give you the broad spectrum of what westerners consider as 'African' food. After all, Egypt and Morocco are in Africa, but we would never consider them to have an 'African' Cuisine. They would be a Middle Eastern Cuisine.

The challenge when it comes to African cuisine is the fact that the country has traditionally never had very many imports. Thus their cooking styles were limited to only the foods available.

We are going to stick to the high carbohydrate elements of African cooking. Countries like Kenya, who maintain the highest percentages of carbs in their diet, actually have the lowest heart disease.

African

GOOD These items go well with this cuisine.		BETTER Even better pairing.	BEST The WOW factor!
avocados	melons	**allspice**	**CHILI PEPPERS**
beans	mint	**bananas**	**CURRY POWDER**
bell peppers	okra	**coconut milk**	**GARLIC**
cassava	papayas	**couscous**	**ONIONS**
carrots	parsley	**curry leaf**	**TAMARIND**
cinnamon	peas	**eggplant**	**YAMS**
cloves	peas, black-eyed	**garam masala**	
coconuts	plantains	**millet, pearl**	
coriander	pumpkin	**peanut butter**	
corn	rice	**peanuts**	
cucumbers	sweet potatoes	**potatoes**	
cumin	teff	**turmeric**	
egusi (bitter melon)	tomatoes		
egusi, seeds	watermelon		
fennel	wheat		
fenugreek seed			
fruits, tropical			
ginger			
maize meal			
mangos			

SIMPLY INCREDIBLE PAIRINGS

chili peppers + garlic + onions

chili peppers + peanuts + tomatoes

coconut + corn + bell peppers

cumin + garlic + mint

potatoes + garlic + fennel

sweet potatoes + peanut butter

AFRICAN RECIPES

Berbere Spice

Berbere is a flavor backbone of Ethiopian Cuisine. You can use this spice blend for soups, stews and casserole. Or use it as a rub for broiled vegetables. It's a great compliment to single component sides like potatoes, beans, rice, or bulgur wheat.

Ingredients

1/2 cup New Mexico chiles, dried ground

1/4 cup paprika

1 Tbsp salt

1 tsp ground ginger

1 tsp onion powder

1/2 tsp fenugreek seed, ground

1/2 tsp garlic powder

1/2 tsp cardamom, ground

1/2 tsp coriander, ground

1/4 tsp nutmeg, ground

1/8 tsp cloves ground

1/8 tsp cinnamon, ground

1/8 tsp allspice, ground

Yield 1 cup

Prep Time 5 minutes

AFRICAN RECIPES

Bo-Kaap Cape Malay Curry Powder

This South African blend is a great curry for many dishes to give you that African flair. Use it for vegetable rubs and even sprinkle it on tomatoes and cucumbers.

Ingredients

1/2 cup coriander seed

1/4 cup fenugreek seeds

1 Tbsp cloves

1 Tbsp fennel seeds

1 Tbsp black mustard seeds

1 Tbsp peppercorns

3 Tbsp cumin seeds

3 dried hot red chilies, small seeds and stems removed

1/4 cup cardamom, ground

1/4 cup turmeric, ground

1 Tbsp ginger, ground

2 curry leaves, fine chopped

Directions

1. Place all the seeds and the red chilies in a frying pan and dry roast for about two minutes, until they release their fragrance.

2. Grind seeds in a food processor, or coffee grinder until finely ground.

3. Add the remaining spices, mixing well.

4. Store airtight, and cool dark areas are best.

Yield: makes about 1 1/2 cups

Prep Time 5 minutes

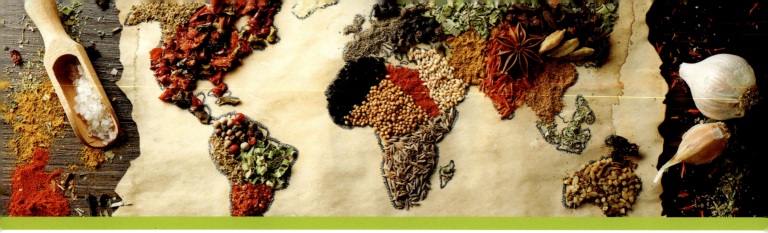

AFRICAN RECIPES

Ethiopian Injera Bread

This is not only the most popular bread in Ethiopia, it is one of the most popular breads throughout all of Africa. This sour flatbread is also used as a utensil to scoop up foods, and even used as a sort of plate liner that soaks up the juices of the meal. And when the 'liner' is gone, the meal is over.

Ingredients

1/4 cup teff flour

3/4 cup all-purpose flour

1 cup water

a pinch of salt

Directions

1. Blend the sifted flours together and mix in the water, stirring well enough to not have any lumping.

2. Cover the bowl with a towel, and set the batter aside for 1 to 3 days. Make sure not to move it.

3. Stir in the salt

4. Heat a nonstick pan until a drop of water dances on the surface. Very lightly oiling the pan is ok. But too much oil will give this bread a unpleasant sogginess.

5. Spread a paddle of batter on the pan. It should be thinner than pancakes, yet thicker than crepes.

6. Holes will appear on the surface. And when the surface is dry to the touch, remove from pan and allow to cool.

Chef's Note:

Black teff is a great flour to bring a unique color

For gluten free: use 3/4 cup teff flour in place of all purpose flour, 1/4 tsp baking powder, 1 cup water, and a pinch of salt to taste. Putting a lid over the batter when cooking will help keep this gluten free version from cracking

Servings 6 to 8

Prep Time 5 minutes

Cook Time 15 minutes

Total Time 20 minutes

AFRICAN RECIPES

Ugali

Ugali is a healthy starch staple found throughout all of Africa. While there are not many known variations to this recipe, it is certainly a neutral enough item that can easily embrace a multitude of flavors. Serve as a side dish with butter substitute, or for an entree, top with a gravy or stew.

Ingredients

2 cups finely ground cornmeal (grind to a flour like consistency)

4 cups water

Directions

1. Heat water to boiling in a saucepan. Slowly pour the corn flour into boiling water. This will avoid lumping.

2. Keep adding more corn flour until it is thicker than mashed potatoes.

3. Cook for three or four minutes, continue to stir. (Continuing to stir the ugali as it thickens is the secret to success)

4. This will be very thick and will hold it's shape when you remove it from the pot.

5. Cover and keep warm. Serve immediately with any meat or vegetable stew, or any dish with a sauce or gravy.

Chef's Note:

Top with a pat of butter or margarine, if desired. Some people like to add salt.

Servings 8

Prep Time 5 minutes

Cook Time 10 minutes

Total Time 15 minutes

AFRICAN RECIPES

Fufu

Ingredients

2 to 4 pounds of yams (use the large, white or yellow yams, not sweet potatoes, and not 'Louisiana yams')

1 tsp butter substitute (optional)

Directions

1. Place whole yams in large pot and cover with water.
2. Bring to a boil and cook until the yams are soft (about 30 min.)
3. Remove pot from heat and cool yams with running water.
4. Drain.
5. Remove peels from yams and put back in the pot
6. Add optional butter.
7. Mash with a potato masher, then beat and stir with a wooden spoon until completely smooth. This can take two people: one to hold the bowl and one to stir.
8. Shape the fufu into balls and serve immediately.

Chef's Notes:

Fufu is great with veggie stew or any dish with a sauce or gravy. You can even tear off pieces, shaping it to use as a scoop for other foods.

Servings 4 or more

Prep Time 10 minutes

Cook Time 30 minutes

Total Time 40 minutes

American

The American diet has become a plethora of processed and prepared foods. It has fallen victim to an over abundance of animal fats, oils, sugars, and salts. This swing of unhealthy lifestyles has resulted in epidemic proportions of heart disease, stroke, cancer and type II diabetes.

But that doesn't have to be so. America has a wonderful variety of flavors that you can adapt into your healthy lifestyle. It's just a matter of knowing how to achieve Simply Incredible Flavor without the high fats, sugars, and salts. Here is where you will discover how easy it is to create a unique flavor in your HEALTHY American Diet.

Barbecue

People always think of 'Barbecue' as an American Cuisine, when in reality the method of cooking over fire has been around for over 5,000 years. However, today's barbecue flavors have nothing to do with cooking over fire, and it is now considered an American created cuisine. Back in the 1800's there were crews of both Chinese and Mexicans working on the railroads being built from coast to coast. Limited resources and a search for a single suitable food supply for both cultures brought forth the mother of invention, and BBQ Sauce was created.

That is why you will experience both Asian and Mexican flavor in most barbecue sauces. And when people discovered this new 'East' meets 'West' flavor, it exploded into a national treasure.

AMERICAN RECIPES

Classic Southern BBQ

Back in the day, we would make this with southern comfort instead of water. Thank God, those days are behind me. And this BBQ sauce tastes great even without the liquor.

Ingredients

1 1/2 cups ketchup

6 Tbsp apple cider vinegar

1/2 cup water

3 Tbsp olive oil (optional)

1 tsp liquid smoke

2 Tbsp brown sugar

1 tsp paprika

1 tsp garlic, minced

1 bay leaf

1/4 tsp Tabasco

1/4 tsp cayenne pepper

juice of one lemon

Directions

1. Add all ingredients in a medium sauce pot. Simmer sauce over medium-low heat for 10 to 15 minutes, stirring occasionally. Watch for burning, lower temperature if needed.

2. For a real Southern BBQ sauce, you would now add a couple tablespoons of butter to the sauce, and mix it in as it cools. But the recipe is great without all that fat.

Chef's Note:

If you really want to add WOW to the flavor, incorporate the zest of one orange to it!

AMERICAN RECIPES

Memphis BBQ Sauce

True Memphis Barbecue is traditionally served without sauce. It's more of a rub thing. But of recent years, many places do their own secret recipe BBQ sauce that will compliment their dry rubbed foods. This sauce captures and compliments the flavors of Memphis Barbecue dry rubs in a fantastic way that has both sweet, vinegar and a hint of heat.

Ingredients

1 1/4 cups ketchup

1 cup water

1/3 cup apple cider vinegar

1/4 cup dark brown sugar

2 Tbsp molasses

1 Tbsp onion powder

1 Tbsp garlic powder

1 tsp celery salt

1 tsp allspice

1/4 tsp black pepper

1/4 tsp cayenne

Directions

1. In a medium sauce pan, combine all ingredients over a medium heat. Stir constantly for 5 minutes. Reduce heat to low and simmer for 20 minutes, stirring occasionally. The sauce should be good and thick.

2. Remove pot from heat and allow sauce to cool. Sauce can be chilled in airtight container.

Chef's Note:

This sauce is best served warm.

AMERICAN RECIPES

St. Louis BBQ

St. Louis Barbecue Sauces are traditionally thinner and a little bit more on the tangy side than their Kansas City neighbor. This is the simple standard version, and you can give it your own signature personality.

Ingredients

2 cups ketchup

1/2 cup water

1/3 cup apple cider vinegar

1/3 cup brown sugar

2 Tbsp yellow mustard

1 Tbsp onion powder

2 tsp garlic powder

1/2 tsp cayenne

1/4 tsp salt

Directions

1. In a medium sauce pan, combine all ingredients over a medium heat. Stir constantly for 5 minutes. Reduce heat to low and simmer for 20 minutes, stirring occasionally. The sauce should be good and thick.

2. Remove pot from heat and allow sauce to cool. Sauce can be chilled in airtight container.

Chef's Note:

with this simple mild flavor, you can run with dozens of unique additions. Orange peal, jalapeño, black molasses, liquid smokes, fire roasted bell peppers, cinnamon, etc.

AMERICAN RECIPES

Texas BBQ Sauce

Texas BBQ has a buttery savory foundation with the sweet, sour, and heat. And you will also experience warmth from the chili powder. Then there is the liquid smoke - look for hickory or mesquite to really create a woodsy flavor.

Ingredients

1 onions, small minced (about a cup)

1/4 cup vegan margarine, (or water sauté)

1 1/2 cups ketchup

1 cup water

1/2 cup apple cider vinegar or lemon juice

2 Tbsp mustard, dijon

2 Tbsp honey

2 garlic cloves, minced

1 Tbsp paprika

1 tsp chili powder

1/4 tsp liquid smoke

Directions

1. Melt butter in a medium saucepan. Add onion, and sauté until golden brown. Or water sauté with 1/4 cup of water stir till water evaporates, repeat if needed.

2. Add garlic and cook for 30 seconds. Don't burn it.

3. Add remaining ingredients, stir and simmer on low for about 15 minutes, allowing to reduce and thicken. Stir occasionally.

4. Pour into a blender and blend until smooth. Use sauce immediately or store in air tight container.

AMERICAN RECIPES

Kansas City BBQ

Kansas City BBQ is known as the slow smoking type of BBQ. You will find that anything and everything is slow smoked. Brisket, ribs, pork, even smoked cheeses. Health is not really a consideration. They also use more black pepper and dusty earthy flavors. I created this recipe to capture the character of the Kansas City smokehouse.

Ingredients

1 1/4 cups ketchup

1 cup water

1/3 cup apple cider vinegar

1/4 cup brown sugar, dark

2 Tbsp molasses

1 Tbsp onion powder

1 Tbsp garlic powder

1 tsp liquid smoke

1 tsp celery salt

1 tsp allspice

1/2 tsp black pepper

1/4 tsp cayenne

Directions

1. In a medium sauce pan, combine all ingredients over a medium heat. Stir constantly for 5 minutes. Reduce heat to low and simmer for 20 minutes, stirring occasionally. The sauce should not be too thick.

2. Remove pot from heat and allow sauce to cool. Store chilled in an airtight container.

Cajun

Cajun has been here since the 1750s and was at one time the only cuisine of America. Technically, Cajuns are an ethnic group consisting of the descendants of Acadian exiles. While this French speaking culture settled mainly in the Maritimes of Eastern Canada, huge groups settled in Louisiana, and that's where the true Cajun flavors were developed into what we know today as Cajun Cuisine.

Cajun

GOOD
These items go well with this cuisine.

- basil
- bell peppers
- blackberries
- blackened foods
- butter substitutes
- celery
- corn
- chili pepper
- chilies
- chives
- cloves
- cucumbers
- curry
- eggplant
- figs
- grits
- marjoram
- milks
- mint
- melons
- mushrooms
- mustard greens
- limes
- leeks
- lemons
- oats
- onions
- oranges, satsuma
- oregano
- paprika
- parsley
- pepper, black
- potatoes
- red pepper flakes
- rice
- sage
- scallions
- squash, yellow
- strawberries
- sugarcane
- sugar, brown
- sweet potatoes
- thyme
- tomatoes
- turnip greens
- walnuts
- zucchini

BETTER
Even better pairing.

- **bayleaf**
- **black eyed peas**
- **chili peppers**
- **collard greens**
- **garlic**
- **pecans**
- **Tabasco sauce**

BEST
The WOW factor!

- **CAYENNE**
- **GUMBO FILE**
- **OKRA**
- **SASSAFRAS**

SIMPLY INCREDIBLE PAIRINGS

corn + cayenne + cream

garlic + greens + lemon juice + salt

garlic + okra + tomatoes + salt

eggplant + gumbo file + okra + chili pepper + salt

sweet potatoes + brown sugar + butter substitutes

CAJUN RECIPES

Cajun Spice Blend

This is one great blend to sprinkle anywhere you need a cajun flair.

Ingredients

2 1/2 tsp paprika

2 tsp salt

2 tsp onion powder

2 tsp garlic powder

1 tsp black pepper

1 tsp cayenne pepper

1 1/4 tsp dried oregano

1 1/4 tsp dried thyme

1/2 tsp red pepper flakes (optional)

Directions

Mix well and store in airtight container.

CAJUN RECIPES

Jambalaya

Certainly one of the most quintessential Cajun dishes is Jambalaya. Since its a one pot meal, anything goes. Make it spicy or mild. There really is no right or wrong way and I have created for you, the easiest way to achieve a Simply Incredible Flavor.

Ingredients

2 Tbsp olive oil (or water sauté)

1 large onion, chopped

4 cloves garlic, minced

1 cup uncooked brown rice

2 1/2 cups water + more for water sauté

1/4 tsp salt

1 to 2 pounds vegan sausage, sliced

4 celery stalks, diced

1 red bell pepper, diced

1 - 32 oz can diced tomatoes, with liquid

1 - 16 oz can kidney beans, drained

1 tsp paprika, smoked

1 tsp oregano, dried

1 tsp basil, dried

1 teaspoon dried thyme

1 bay leaf

1/4 tsp fennel seeds, crushed

Tabasco (just a couple shakes)

Salt and freshly ground pepper to taste

Directions

1. Sauté the onions with olive oil over medium heat until translucent. Or water sauté by using 1/2 cup water, and sautéing until water is evaporated, then repeat as needed until the onions are caramelized.

2. Add garlic, and sauté for a minute.

3. Add 2½ cups of water, 1/4 tsp salt, and rice, bring to a boil, then simmer covered, until the water is absorbed, about 35 minutes.

4. Add the remaining ingredients except the salt. Bring to a simmer, then cover and simmer gently for 15 to 20 minutes. Careful not to burn.

5. Season to taste with salt.

6. Garish with fresh chopped parsley and red pepper flakes.

Chef's Notes:

Some of the best add ons for Simply Incredible Flavor are: diced green chilis, green bell peppers, mushrooms, okra, jalapeños, and even a little coconut sugar can give you a sweet heat sensation.

Serves: 6 to 8 » Prep time: 20 mins

Cook time: 45 mins » Total time: 1 hour 5 mins

CAJUN RECIPES

Gumbo

Similar to Jambalaya, Gumbo is the official dish of New Orleans. Records show it's origination back to 1802. But interestingly enough, the dish actually combines ingredients and culinary practices of several cultures, including French, German, Spanish, West African, and Choctaw. And with all these cultures converging on Louisiana, a masterpiece is born.

Ingredients

2 Tbsp vegetable oil

1 onion, large, chopped

2 green bell peppers, chopped

8 stalks celery, chopped

6 cloves garlic, minced

1/3 cup canola oil

1/2 cup all-purpose flour

6 cups vegetable broth, divided

3 cups diced tomatoes

1 eggplant, peeled and chopped

6 cups chopped okra

1 -15 oz can red beans, drained

2 tsp salt

2 tsp dried thyme

2 tsp gumbo file powder

1 tsp dried basil

1 tsp cayenne pepper

1 tsp ground black pepper

1/2 tsp paprika

1/4 tsp ground cumin

1/4 tsp liquid smoke flavoring

2 bay leaves

Directions:

1. In a large heavy bottom pot, heat one Tbsp vegetable oil in a skillet over medium high heat. Stir in the onion, bell peppers, and celery. Cook and stir until the onions have softened and are golden in color, about 7 minutes.

2. Add garlic and sauté for one minute.

3. Transfer the vegetable mixture to a large bowl and set aside.

4. Heat the remaining 1/3 cup vegetable oil in the same skillet over medium heat for about 30 seconds.

5. Whisk in the flour, stirring constantly until the roux darkens and has a nutty scent, about 5 minutes.

6. Pour in about 2 cups of vegetable broth, whisking constantly until the mixture is smooth.

7. Stir in the remaining ingredients, and the remaining 4 cups of broth.

8. Cover. Turn to a low heat to simmer for 1 1/2 hours. Stirring occasionally.

Chef's Notes: I don't like to cook the roux too much. The roux is the flour and oil mixture. Traditionally the roux is cooked until it is a much darker brown. I will only cook it until it is a lighter color brown. Most people are not accustomed to the deepness of the dish and for many that deep 'burnt' flavor is not palatable. Cooking it lighter will result in flavors that are more complimenting, not overpowering.

Servings 1 cup » Prep Time 15 min.
Cook Time 2 hours » Total Time 2.3 hours

CAJUN RECIPES

Dirty Rice

Dirty rice was actually made with chicken livers, hearts or what ever leftover meats were available. Then they evolved into using higher end sausages. This is a great simple recipe where you can feel free to add any of your favorite vegan meat substitutes, or simply hit it with your favorite vegetables.

Ingredients

2 Tbsp vegetable oil or water sauté

1 1/2 cups onion, diced

1 cup bell peppers diced

4 cloves garlic, minced

2 cups rice, brown

4 cups vegetable stock

1 Tbsp caramel color (optional)

1 tsp dried thyme

1 tsp oregano, dried

1 bay leaf

Directions

1. Sauté, onions and bell peppers in vegetable oil until soft - for about 15 minutes. Or water sauté with 1/4 cup of water.

2. Add garlic and sauté for another minute.

3. Add remaining ingredients, bring to a boil. Then cover and simmer for 30 minutes. Do not overcook.

4. Shut off heat, and allow to rest covered for another 20 minutes.

5. Garnish with green onions.

Chef Notes:

The caramel color is a great secret to 'dirty' up the rice. Or you can use any vegan meats of a darker color, chop small, and sauté them into the cooked onions to give some darkness to the dish.

Servings 4 to 6

Prep Time 10 min.

Cook Time 50 min

Total Time 1 hour

Hawaiian

Hawaii is the home of fusion cuisine, where you take different cultures and mix them together. Bringing a wide variety of plants and animals to the islands, Polynesian voyagers were the first to arrive, dating back to 300 AD. Over generations these people were eventually titled Native Hawaiians. In the 1770s European and American Missionaries brought their flavors to the state. And in the 1850s the need to harvest sugarcane brought immigrant workers from China, Korea, Japan, the Philippines, and even Portugal and Puerto Rico.

The culture, combined with the local crops and a now accessible international trade, has created a burst of global flavors unlike any other in the world.

It's easy to create a Hawaiian dish, just by using pineapple or coconut. But there are many other food items that identify a Hawaiian theme. When you start parring the native crops with the seasonings from around the world, then you will have a Simply Incredible Hawaiian Flavor.

Hawaiian

GOOD These items go well with this cuisine.		BETTER Even better pairing.	BEST The WOW factor!
apple	panko	**avocados**	**COCONUT**
arrowroot	potatoes	**bananas**	**MACADAMIA NUTS**
beans	rice	**coconut milk**	**PINEAPPLE**
chili pepper	salt	**daikon**	**TOFU**
figs	seaweed	**jicama**	**YAMS, PURPLE**
ginger	starfruit	**papaya**	
grapes	strawberry	**passion fruit**	
kimchi	sugar cane	**potatoes, Okinawa purple**	
lemon	sweet potatoes	**salt, Hawaiian lava**	
Li Hing Mui	tamarind		
lime	taro		
mango	turmeric		
miso	vinegar, rice		
mushrooms	watercress		
onions, maui	watermelon		
orange	yams		

SIMPLY INCREDIBLE PAIRINGS

bananas + coconut + lemon + vanilla

coconut + pineapple

coconut + cranberries + macadamia nuts + mango

butter substitute + coconut milk + garlic + purple potatoes

HAWAIIAN RECIPES

Okinawan Sweet Purple Potatoes

Like any other sweet potatoes, these purple joys have a low glycemic index and high content of fiber. And keep the skin on of the Okinawan sweet potatoes when cooking. The skin has almost ten times the antioxidant potency as the flesh.

Directions

1. Cut the potatoes, skin on

2. Boil the potatoes for about 45 minutes, until extra tender.

3. Drain, and return to the same cooking pot.

4. Add enough coconut milk and your favorite spices, mashing until the result is similar to mash potatoes.

The most popular spices are cinnamon, nutmeg, salt and pepper.

Chef's Notes:

You can also bake in the oven just like baked potatoes. And if you put a baking casserole dish filled with water in the oven, it will keep the skins soft. Then serve just like a baked potato. And even better sprinkle with nutmeg. You can also slice the potatoes, and bake on a sheet pan lined with parchment paper. Season any way you like.

HAWAIIAN RECIPES

Poi

Poi is created by taking the plant stem 'corm' of the taro plant. Traditionally baked or steamed, water is added during mashing until the desired consistency is achieved. The Island lingo is based on how many 'fingers' are needed to eat it. 'one finger' is extra thick. While 'two finger' is thinner and 'three finger' is needed to scoop the thinnest of this Hawaiian favorite.

Directions

1. You can either peel the taro root first, chop and then boil, or cook the taro whole and then drain, let cool, and easily peel it after it's boiled.

2. The easiest way to mix is to put the taro into a blender and add water. Only add a 1/4 cup of water at a time.

3. Blend until the desired consistency is achieved. Many people do this by hand mashing and whipping.

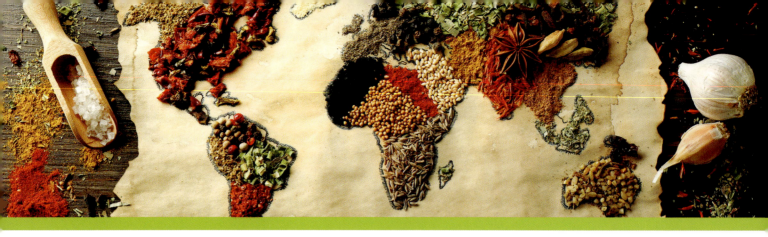

HAWAIIAN RECIPES

Samoan Poi

Unlike regular Poi, this is a popular dessert. Simple. Fast. And you can always add an array of ingredients to create your own signature Samoan Poi.

Ingredients

1 lb ripe bananas

1/2 to 3/4 cup coconut milk

1 tsp vanilla

zest of 1 lemon

sugar, optional

Directions

1. Mash or blend the bananas until smooth.
2. Add the lemon zest
3. Add the coconut milk and vanilla. Mix until well-combined.
4. Taste for sweetness. Add sugar if desired.
5. Chill for at least 30 minutes.

NOTE:

Immediately before serving, stir the discolored top layer into the rest of the poi. Serve over ice in small bowls or wide-mouth glasses. This can be refrigerated for a day, but is best served within hours of making. And for a quick chill, just put in the freezer for 15 minutes.

HAWAIIAN RECIPES

Hawaiian Poke Bowls

Traditionally, a Poke Bowl is a selection of fish over rice, noodles, or greens. With a few adjustments, we can make this a very healthy version. And the best way is to show you, is with a picture!

The picture below features a Vegan poke bowls with tofu, seaweed, watermelon radish, cucumber, edamame beans and rice noodles.

And to really kick it up, drizzle a little sauce over the top. Teriyaki, sweet and sour, pineapple glaze, coconut cream, or avocado sauce…… just to name a few.

Native American

There are over 1,000 Native American tribes, and while there are quite a few differences based on location, here is a basic array of the foods that traditionally encompass Native American cuisine.

Many Native Americans were extremely healthy. They lived an active lifestyle and ate a lot of natural foods and whole grains. But today, the SAD (Standard American Diet) has taken its toll, resulting in epidemic levels of obesity, heart disease and diabetes This is largely due to the adoption of processed and fast food, and an inactive lifestyle.

The most popular Native American Indian staples are known as 'The Three Sisters' - corn, beans, and squash. They were grown all together. The beans would climb up the corn stocks and the squash would cover the ground.

Native American

GOOD These items go well with this cuisine.	BETTER Even better pairing.	BEST The WOW factor!
allspice, potatoes, amaranth, raspberries, barley, rhubarb, beans, green, sage, bell peppers, sagebrush, blueberry, sassafras, breads, tarragon, chestnuts, tomatoes, chili peppers, wild ginger, file powder, wild mint, grains, wild onion, horsemint, juniper berries, loveroot, maple syrup, onions	**apples**, **black berries**, **chili powder**, **cranberry**, **cornmeal**, **pepper**, **quinoa**, **salt**, **sunflowers**, **wheat**	**BEANS**, **CORN**, **HONEY**, **PUMPKIN**, **SQUASH**

SIMPLY INCREDIBLE PAIRINGS

bread + sage + salt

beans + squash + corn + salt

chili pepper + cornmeal + salt

corn + potatoes + sage + salt

honey + squash + wild mint

NATIVE AMERICAN RECIPES

Native Indian Flat Bread

Ingredients

5 cups all-purpose flour (white or whole wheat)

2 Tbsp baking powder

1 1/4 salt

2 cups soy milk

1 1/2 Tbsp butter substitute, melted

3 tsp Herbes de Provence (optional)

1/2 tsp garlic powder (optional)

olive oil, for frying the bread

Directions

1. In a large bowl mix together the flour, baking powder, and salt. mix well.

2. While mixing and kneading, slowly add soy milk and melted butter. You should have a stiff workable dough that is not sticky. If the dough is wet and sticky, you need to add more flour. If the dough will not hold together then you need more soy milk.

3. Add the garlic, herbs. Knead in for a couple minutes.

4. Wrap the dough in plastic wrap and let rest for 8 hours or overnight is best. (Note: The longer the dough rests, the more the added flavors will infuse into the dough).

Now that your dough is made, you're ready to fry some Indian flat bread.

1. First take your dough and divide it into small balls. The size of the balls is up to you.

2. Next take the balls and flatten them out. The should be about 1/8 to a 1/4 inch thick. This will make the bread cook fast and evenly. You can use a rolling pin to get consistency. if there is any sticking, a little flour will sold that.

3. Heat up some oil (very little) in a frying pan and cook them for a few minutes on each side until they turn golden brown and puff up.

Note: Don't fry bread with margarine or butter because it will burn in the frying pan. It you have a good non-stick pan, you can do this with no oil at all.

4. You can top with a butter substitute while still hot, and sprinkle a little kosher salt and garlic powder on top.

Chef's Note: For a dessert type bread, sprinkle with cinnamon and sugar, right after it is cooked.

Variations: You can add the heat, or sweet, and the salt, or add the savory. Nutmeg works great as does hot pepper or chili powder.

Servings 6 to12

Prep Time 5 min.

Rest time 8 hours

Cook Time 30 min

Total Work Time 35 min.

NATIVE AMERICAN RECIPES

Blackfeet Bread

Ingredients

6 cups white flour

3 Tbsp baking powder

1 tsp salt

2 1/2 cups water

Directions

1. Preheat oven to 350 degrees.

2. In a large mixing bowl, mix together flour, baking powder, and salt. Mix well.

3. Gradually stir in water until a thick dough is formed.

4. Knead until the dough is not sticky. It does not need to be perfectly smooth. If sticky, add a little flour at a time.

5. Grease a 9 x 13 baking pan.

6. Flatten dough with a rolling pin, until it is roughly the size of the pan.

7. Place dough in pan and adjust to fit the pan.

8. Bake for 35 minutes. The bread should be slightly browned.

9. Remove from pan onto cutting board or cooling rack. This bread can be cut when warm.

Chef's Notes:

This bread is the standard traditional recipe. And from here you can always add other ingredients. If you use a whole wheat flour, you would need to increase the water by just a 1/4 cup. This will make it just a bit heavier.

Servings 12
Prep Time 10 min.
Cook Time 35 min
Total Time 45 min

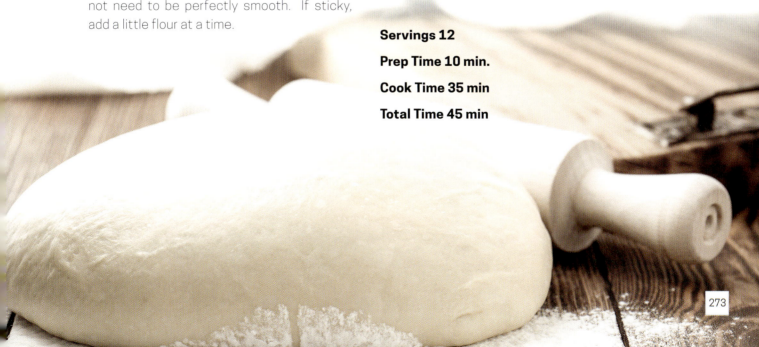

NATIVE AMERICAN RECIPES

Acorn Bread

Ingredients

6 Tbsp cornmeal

1 1/2 cup water

1 tsp salt

1 Tbsp butter substitute

1 pkg active dry yeast

1/4 cup lukewarm water

1 Tbsp honey

2 cups all-purpose flour

2 cups finely ground leached acorn meal

1 cup mashed potatoes, cold or cooled

Directions

1. Preheat oven to 375 degrees.

2. Bring 1 1/2 cups water to a boil. Add cornmeal, stirring constantly. Stir for 2 minutes.

3. Stir in salt and butter. Then cool to lukewarm.

4. Mix yeast, honey, and lukewarm water. let rest for a couple minutes, until bubbly.

5. Add all the ingredients together and knead into a dough. Dough should be a little be sticky.

6. Cover and let rise in warm place until doubled in size.

7. Punch down and shape into two loaves. Place in baking pans. Cover and let rise until doubled in size.

8. Bake at 375 degrees for 45 minutes.

Servings 12

Prep Time 15 min.

Cook Time 45 min

Total Time 1 hour

NATIVE AMERICAN RECIPES

Hopi Corn Stew & Blue Dumplings

Ingredients

For the Stew:

2 Tbsp vegetable oil (or water sauté)

1 medium onion, chopped

1 green bell pepper, chopped

2 garlic cloves, minced

8 cups vegetable stock

4 cups corn kernels

2 cups tomatoes, diced

1 zucchini, chopped

1 yellow squash, chopped

1 Tbsp New Mexico red chili pepper, ground

3 Tbsp whole wheat flour

3 Tbsp vegetable oil

2 tsp salt to taste

1/4 cup cilantro, chopped

For the Blue Dumplings:

3 cups blue cornmeal

1 Tbsp baking powder

2 Tbsp butter substitute

1/2 tsp salt

1 cup soy milk.

Directions

Making the Stew:

1. In an extra large cooking pot, heat oil, and sauté onions and peppers until onions are golden brown. Or water sauté, with 1/4 cup water. Once water has been completely reduced, repeat process.

2. Add garlic and sauté for 30 seconds.

3. Stir in corn, zucchini, squash and tomatoes.

4. Add vegetable stock. Bring to a boil and reduce heat to medium-low and simmer 10 minutes.

5. Make a roux with the 3 tablespoons of flour and 3 tablespoons of oil. Add enough to the stew and mix until thickened. Note: for oil free, use cornstarch and water slurry to thicken.

6. Add the dumplings to the stew and simmer for another 15 minutes.

7. Right before serving, sprinkle with chopped cilantro.

Making the Dumplings:

In a mixing bowl combine cornmeal, baking powder, butter substitute and salt. Stir in enough milk to make a stiff batter. Drop by tablespoons into the stew.

Servings 8 to 10

Prep Time 15 min

Cook Time 30 min

Total Time 45 min

NATIVE AMERICAN RECIPES

Traditional Native American Fried Green Tomatoes

Ingredients

4 large green tomatoes

1 tsp salt

black pepper

2 cups cornmeal, yellow ground

olive oil for sautéing.

Directions

1. Slice tomatoes into 1/2 inch slices and sprinkle generously with salt on both sides. Let stand for 10-15 minutes.

2. Blot dry with paper towels, and sprinkle with pepper.

3. Now dip the tomato slices into the cornmeal.

4. In a large skillet heat the oil, and fry the tomato slices until brown on both sides. Serve immediately.

Chef Notes:

And of course you can really jazz up the flavor by adding your own seasonings to the cornmeal.

Servings 4 to 6

Prep Time 15 min

Cook Time 10 min

Total Time 25 min

Southern

Southern cooking spans the region from Louisiana and Arkansas all the way to the Carolinas. Southern Louisiana terms their style as Creole Cuisine.

Surprising enough, the culture actually has a lot of healthy foods. Throughout my travels, I have found some of the most health conscious people in the southern states.

So when you are preparing traditional southern cuisine, just remember to eliminate all the animal products, and reduce the sugar and fats which have been proven to shorten your life.

Southern

GOOD These items go well with this cuisine.	BETTER Even better pairing.	BEST The WOW factor!
baked goods	**beans**	**BLACK EYED PEAS**
barbecue	**biscuits**	**GREENS**
butter beans	**collard greens**	**PECANS**
butter, substitutes	**cream**	
cheese	**mustard greens**	
corn	**okra**	
eggplant	**sorghum**	
gravy	**sugar**	
grits	**sweet potatoes**	
lima beans	**Tabasco**	
melons	**turnip greens**	
milks	**tomatoes**	
oats		
pies		
potatoes		
rice		
spinach		
squash		

SIMPLY INCREDIBLE PAIRINGS

beans + rice + Tabasco

biscuits + gravy

black eyed peas + butter substitute + garlic + salt

greens + lemon + salt

lima beans + butter substitute + salt

sweet potatoes + pecans

SOUTHERN RECIPES

Easy Crockpot Red Beans and Rice

Ingredients

12 cups boiling water

3 cups long grain brown rice

3 cups dried red kidney beans

2 red onions, chopped

2 red bell peppers, chopped

4 stalks celery, chopped

8 garlic cloves, minced

4 Tbsp Cajun seasoning

2 Tbsp of smoked paprika

1 tsp salt

1/2 cup green onions, chopped

Directions

1. Add everything to the crockpot and stir together.

2. Cook on low for around 6-8 hours. Cooking times may vary slightly depending on your crockpot.

Mix in the fresh chopped green onions right before serving.

Servings 10 - 12

Prep Time 5 min

Cook Time 8 hours

Total Time 8 hours

SOUTHERN RECIPES

Oven Baked Green Tomatoes

Ingredients

4 large green tomatoes

salt and pepper

1 cup almond milk

1 cup almond flour (may use whole wheat)

1 cup nutritional yeast flakes

1 Tbsp garlic powder

1 Tbsp sea salt

1/2 tsp cayenne pepper

Directions

1. Preheat oven to 425 degrees.

2. Slice the green tomatoes into 1/2 inch thick slices.

3. Sprinkle generously with salt. Let stand for 10-15 minutes

4. Pour the almond milk into a small bowl, set aside.

5. In separate contained, mix the almond flour, garlic powder, sea salt, cayenne pepper and nutritional yeast flakes.

6. Blot dry the tomatoes with paper towels, and sprinkle with pepper.

7. Dip the tomato slices into the almond milk, and then into the coating mixture covering both sides.

8. Bake for approximately 15 - 20 minutes or until golden brown.

Chef's Notes:

Serve with your favorite dip and they are best when served hot.

Servings 6 to 8

Prep Time 20 min

Cook Time 15 min

Total Time 35 min

SOUTHERN RECIPES

Smoky Black-eyed Pea & Sweet Potato Soup

This is an traditional New Years Eve soup. Yet it's so good, you will want to make it all the time. I suggest a double batch, and then freeze some for a quick meal.

Ingredients

1 lb. (16 oz bag) dried black-eyed peas, soaked 8 hours (overnight) covered in water

6 cups water

2 bell peppers, chopped

1 large onion, chopped

6 cloves garlic, minced (about 3 Tbsp)

3 cups sweet potato, cut 1/2 inch chunks

1/2 cup salsa, medium heat

1 tsp ground cumin

1 Tbsp smoked paprika

2 tsp salt to taste

pepper if needed

Directions

1. Soak the peas for 8 hours or over night.

2. Drain and rinse them well.

3. In a heavy bottom cooking pot, add peas and the 6 cups water.

4. Bring the beans to a boil and then turn to low simmer, cover with a lid and let cook for 60 minutes.

5. While it is simmering, chop your bell peppers, onion, garlic and sweet potatoes.

6. After 60 minutes, add the remaining ingredients. Stir well and bring it back to a boil.

7. Once boiling, turn down to a low simmer again. But this time, tilt the cover a bit allowing steam to escape. Let it simmer for 20 minutes just until the potatoes are tender.

8. Remove from the heat and serve.

Servings 4 to 6

Prep Time 15 min

Cook Time 1.3 hours

Total Time 1.5 hours

Tex-Mex & Southwest

Southwest and Tex-Mex cooking can overlap in so many ways that we are going to group the two together. There are geographical differences with Texas being Tex-Mex and Southwest cuisine dominating New Mexico, Arizona, and Southern California. But they both have Mexican flair.

Tex-Mex will tend to do the barbecue and Texas chili. Southwest will be heavier on citrus, fresh greens, avocado and Southwest Indian cuisines. Quite often you will see the Tex-Mex related to a hearty working mans appetite, while Southwest has grown into a more sophisticated brand of marketing. Either way, they are both on my favorite flavor in the world list.

Tex-Mex & Southwest

GOOD These items go well with this cuisine.		BETTER Even better pairing.	BEST The WOW factor!
adobo	onions	**beans, refried**	**BEANS**
avocados	onions, red	**chillies**	**CHILI POWDER**
barbecue	parsley	**chipotle**	**CUMIN**
basil	poblano peppers	**corn**	
bell peppers	potatoes	**garlic**	
cheese	quinoa	**jalapeno**	
chilies	rice	**kale**	
chocolate	sour cream	**salsa**	
cilantro	squash	**tortillas**	
cinnamon	tomatoes		
hominy			
oregano			
limes			
nuts			

SIMPLY INCREDIBLE PAIRINGS

beans + cheese

beans + rice

cilantro + garlic + lime + red onion + tomato

corn + bell pepper + onions + tomatoes + salt

corn + chipotle + cilantro + salt

salsa + sour cream

TEX-MEX & SOUTHWEST RECIPES

Stuffed Poblano Peppers in a Chipotle Sauce

Poblano peppers are among the more mild varieties, yet still offer a nice zing. Here, they are stuffed with a hearty mixture of quinoa, mushrooms, corn, and tomatoes.

Ingredients

4 large poblano peppers

2 tsp vegetable oil

1 Tbsp chopped chipotle chile in adobo

1 garlic clove

1 can - 15 ounces diced tomatoes

1/4 tsp salt

1/2 cup fresh cilantro leaves

1/3 cup quinoa

2/3 cup water

1/2 cup onions, fine diced

1/2 cup mushrooms, quartered

1/2 cup corn kernels

1 can - 15 ounces black beans, drained and rinsed

Top with some vegan cheese

Directions

1. Preheat oven to 475 degrees.

2. Rub peppers with oil, and place on a parchment lined sheet pan.

3. Roast the peppers until slightly blackened and softened. About 15 minutes, turning once.

4. When cool enough to handle, remove skins.

5. Make a small slit in each pepper. Start about 1/2 inch from the stem, keeping stem end intact, and slicing downward. Then carefully remove seeds.

6. In a blender, combine chipotle, garlic, and the juice from the diced tomatoes.

7. Add cilantro and pulse once to combine.

8. In a small saucepan, bring 2/3 cup water to a boil. Add quinoa, bring to a boil, cover and reduce heat to medium-low. Cook until tender, about 10 minutes. Remove from heat and let cool 5 minutes with lid on, fluff with a fork.

9. Meanwhile, in a large skillet, sauté or water sauté onions and mushrooms. Cook until mushrooms are tender, about 5 minutes, add corn, beans, and tomatoes, with a pinch of salt.

10. Cook until hot, about 4 minutes. Stir in quinoa.

11. Arrange stuffed peppers with filling in a baking dish. Drizzle sauce over peppers and into the bottom of the dish.

12. Top with a little vegan cheese.

13. Bake until golden, 15 to 20 minutes. Cool in pan 10 minutes.

Servings 4 » Prep Time 15 min

Cook Time 40 min » Total Time 55 min

TEX-MEX & SOUTHWEST RECIPES

Southwest Black Bean Pie

This is fun food with flavor and nutrition.

Ingredients

4 flour tortillas (10 inch size)

1 Tbsp vegetable oil

1 large onion, finely diced

1/4 cup red bell peppers, diced

1 jalapeño pepper, minced (remove seeds for less heat)

1 1/2 cups water

3 cups black beans, drained and rinsed (2 cans)

3 cups corn, kernels

2 garlic cloves, minced

1/2 tsp chili powder

1/4 tsp cumin, ground

1/2 tsp salt

2 1/2 cups shredded vegan cheese

4 scallions, thinly sliced, plus more for garnish

Directions

1. Preheat oven to 350 degrees.

2. With a paring knife, trim tortillas to fit a 9-inch springform pan. Use the bottom of the pan as a guide. Set aside.

3. Sauté or water sauté the onion and jalapeño.

4. Add the remaining ingredients, except the scallion garnish, and cook for about 15 minutes, until the juices are evaporated.

5. Place a trimmed tortilla in bottom of springform pan. And then layer with 1/4 of the beans mixture, and a sprinkle of the vegan cheese. Repeat three more times. Then place the final ingredients on the top with a nice layer of cheese.

6. Bake until cheese melts, and edges are crisping up. About 30 minutes.

7. Remove sides of pan and cut into 6 pie shaped pieces.

8. Sprinkle pie with scallions.

Chef's Notes:

Serve with salsa and sour cream.

Servings 6

Prep Time 25 min

Cook Time 1 hour

Total Time 1.5 hours

TEX-MEX & SOUTHWEST RECIPES

Texas Caviar

Ingredients

Caviar Mixture

1 - 15oz can black eyed peas, drained rinsed

1 - 15oz can black beans, drained rinsed

1 - 15oz can hominy or corn

Sauce:

Cilantro Lime Sauce

1/4 cup lime juice

1 tsp lime zest

1 Tbsp spicy brown mustard

1/2 tsp pepper sauce

1/2 tsp soy sauce

1/4 cup cilantro chopped fine, 1/2 bunch

2 Tbsp olive oil (optional)

Salt and Pepper to taste

Directions

Whip or blend the lime sauce together, and add it to the drained caviar mix. It's that easy to eat healthy.

Servings 8 to 10

Prep Time 10 min

Total Time 10 min

TEX-MEX & SOUTHWEST RECIPES

Tex-Mex Burgers
WITH CHIPOTLE KETCHUP

Ingredients

1 - 15oz can kidney beans, rinsed and drained

1 - 15oz can black beans, rinsed and drained

1/3 cup breadcrumbs

1/4 cup canned whole-kernel yellow corn, drained

1/4 cup onion, fine diced

3 egg replacer. (Whip together 3 Tbsp ground flax seed and 3 Tbsp warm water.)

Directions

1. For the burgers, combine kidney beans and black beans in a large bowl, and partially mash with a fork.

2. Add breadcrumbs, corn, onion, and egg replacer, stir until well blended, and able to form into patties. If needed add a few more breadcrumbs.

3. Form bean mixture into 4 1/2-inch thick patties.

4. Panfry until crispy brown on both sides.

Servings 4
Prep Time 10 min
Cook Time 15 min
Total Time 25 min

Chipotle Ketchup

Ingredients

1 cup ketchup

1 Tbsp chopped chipotle chili in adobo

1 Tbsp honey

1 Tbsp lime juice

1 tsp ground cumin

Directions

Mix all ingredients well

Yield 1 1/4 cups

TEX-MEX & SOUTHWEST RECIPES

Southwest Mayo Spread

Ingredients

1 cup mayonnaise

1 Tbsp Dijon mustard

1 Tbsp chipotle adobo sauce

1/2 lime, juiced

1 clove garlic, minced

Directions

Mix all ingredients together

Yield 1 1/4 cups

Southwest Dip

Ingredients

1 - 16oz container vegan sour cream

1 garlic clove, minced

1 lime, juiced

2 Tbsp finely chopped red onion

2 Tbsp chopped fresh cilantro

1 tsp chili powder

1/2 tsp red pepper flakes

1/4 tsp ground cumin

1/4 tsp salt

Directions

Mix all ingredients together well.

Yield 2 cups

TEX-MEX & SOUTHWEST RECIPES

Texas Spice Blend

Ingredients

2 Tbsp chili powder

2 Tbsp paprika

1 Tbsp garlic powder

1 Tbsp oregano

1 Tbsp coriander, ground

1 Tbsp salt

2 tsp cumin, ground

1 tsp black pepper, ground

1 tsp cayenne pepper

1 tsp crushed red pepper flakes

Directions

Mix all the ingredients together and store in an airtight container.

Yield 1/2 cup

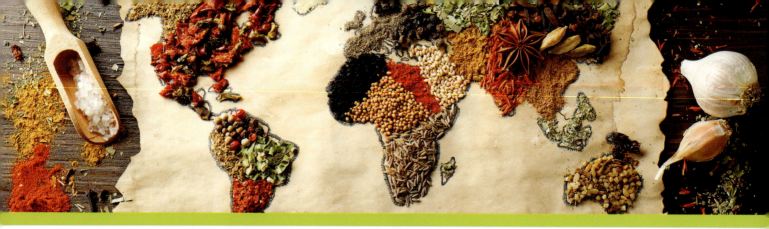

TEX-MEX & SOUTHWEST RECIPES

Southwest Vegetable Broiling Rub

Use as vegetable roasting rub or to flavor chili and soups.

Ingredients

1 Tbsp sea salt

1 Tbsp garlic powder

2 tsp chili powder

1 tsp onion powder

1 tsp cumin, ground

1/2 tsp cocoa powder (optional… but Wow!)

1/4 tsp cayenne pepper

Directions

Mix all ingredients together in a small jar.

Store in a cool, dry place.

Yield 1/4 cup

Salt Free Southwest Seasoning

Ingredients

3 Tbsp chili powder

2 Tbsp paprika, smoked

2 Tbsp garlic powder

2 Tbsp oregano

1 Tbsp onion powder

1 Tbsp cumin, ground

1 Tbsp coriander, ground

2 tsp lime zest, dried

1 tsp black pepper

1/2 tsp cayenne pepper

Directions

Mix all ingredients together in a small jar.

Store in a cool, dry place.

Yield 3/4 cup

Asian

Looking at Asian food, we will stick to the three most popular regions of Chinese, Japanese, and Thai food. There are also other cuisines that have a predominately Asian flair: Vietnamese, Korean, Mongolian, Cambodian, and Filipino.

These regions consume lots of vegetables, lots of rice, noodles, and carbs. And yes, lots of tofu.

Chinese

Chinese chefs favor garlic. You will also find a lot of stir-fry or stewed methods and food is generally served family style. There is a lot more fried food than other Asian cuisines. So be aware of the over use of oil when cooking Chinese. Many recipes can be transformed into low fat versions. The Chinese also tend to use heavier spices than Japanese.

Chinese

GOOD These items go well with this cuisine.		BETTER Even better pairing.	BEST The WOW factor!
bamboo shoots	star anise	**Chinese five spice powder**	**GINGER**
cabbage	sugar - brown sugar	**garlic**	**RICE**
chili paste	tahini	**hoisin sauce**	**SOY SAUCE**
chili pepper	vinegar, rice wine	**plum sauce**	
cinnamon	water chestnuts	**tofu**	
citrus		**vegetable stock**	
curry powder		**vegetables**	
fruit juices			
lemon			
lemongrass			
lime			
noodles			
peanuts			
scallions			
sesame oil			
sesame seeds			
snow peas			
szechuan pepper			

SIMPLY INCREDIBLE PAIRINGS

brown sugar + fruit juices + soy sauce

cabbage + vegetable stock

garlic + ginger

ginger + rice wine + soy sauce

soy sauce + sugar

Szechuan pepper + ginger + star anise

CHINESE RECIPES

Homemade Ginger Sauce

Ingredients

2 carrots, chopped

2 green onions, chopped

2 Tbsp ginger, chopped

2 Tbsp vinegar, balsamic

1 Tbsp olive oil

1 Tbsp sesame oil

1 Tbsp soy sauce

1 tsp sugar

Directions

Combine all ingredients into food processor and blend for 3 minutes until completely smooth.

Keep refrigerated in jar with lid.

Yield 3/4 cup

Simple Sweet and Sour

Ingredients

2 cups pineapple juice

2/3 cup water

1/2 cup vinegar

2 Tbsp soy sauce

1 cup brown sugar

Thicken with 1/4 cup cornstarch and water slurry

Directions

1. Combine all ingredients in a sauce pan.
2. Bring to a boil
3. Thicken with cornstarch slurry

Chef Notes:

You can also add cherry juice to get a more vibrant color. And of course pineapple chunks and cut cherries really add a wow factor.

Yield 4 cups

CHINESE RECIPES

Duck Sauce

Ingredients

1 lb plums, pitted and roughly chopped

2 cups apple juice

1 cup dried apricots, roughly chopped

1/2 cup apple cider vinegar or lemon juice

1/2 cup light brown sugar

2 Tbsp soy sauce

2 tsp fresh ginger, minced

1/2 tsp mustard powder

1/2 tsp crushed red pepper

Directions

1. Put all ingredients into a medium sauce pan, Bring to a boil over medium heat, then reduce and simmer until fruit is completely softened and sauce thickens, about 30 minutes. Stir occasionally.

2. Puree until smooth with a blender.

3. Serve immediately, or place in an airtight container in the refrigerator for up to 4 weeks.

Yield 4 cups

CHINESE RECIPES

Vegetable Lo Mein

Ingredients

8 ounces uncooked lo mein noodles or spaghetti

1 Tbsp vegetable oil

1 red bell pepper, julienned

1 carrot, julienned

½ cup snow peas

3 cloves garlic, minced

sesame seeds and scallions for garnish, if desired

Directions

1. Cook noodles according to package instructions.

2. Sauté or water sauté, red bell pepper, snap peas and carrots for about 5 minutes, until vegetables are tender.

3. Add in garlic and cook for an additional minute.

4. Stir in the sauce and cooked noodles and toss to combine.

5. Serve immediately.

6. Sesame seeds or scallions work great for garnish.

Lo Mein Sauce

3 Tbsp soy sauce

1 tsp sesame oil

1 tsp brown sugar

Directions

Whisk together the soy sauce, sesame oil, and brown sugar. Set aside.

Chef Notes:

The difference between Lo Mein and Chow Mein in that the Chow Mein noodles are crispy fried noodles, where the Lo Mein noodles are served soft. Chow Mein generally uses a flat noodle while Lo Mein noodles are round.

Servings 2 to 4

Prep Time 10 min

Cook Time 10 min

Total Time 20 min

Japanese

Japanese Cuisine generally doesn't have as much garlic as the Chinese dishes. And the Japanese also consume more raw foods. They will tend to be more artistic in their presentations and will serve plated entrees rather than family style. There is less oil in Japanese cooking than Chinese.

Japanese

GOOD These items go well with this cuisine.	BETTER Even better pairing.	BEST The WOW factor!
chili peppers	**ginger**	**RICE**
daikon	**hoisin sauce**	**SOY SAUCE**
garlic	**noodles**	**TOFU**
lemon	**scallions**	
orange	**vegetables**	
pineapple	**wasabi**	
pickles	**yuzu**	
plums		
ponzu sauce		
sake		
sesame oil	**SIMPLY INCREDIBLE PAIRINGS**	
sesame seeds	garlic + ginger + soy sauce	
sweet rice wine	ginger + scallions + soy sauce	
teriyaki sauce	soy sauce + wasabi	
tea		
vinegar, rice wine		

JAPANESE RECIPES

Simple Teriyaki Sauce

Ingredients

1/2 cup water

1/2 cup pineapple juice

1/2 cup soy sauce

1/4 cup brown sugar, packed

1 tsp ginger, ground

1/2 tsp garlic powder

Make slurry by mixing 3 Tbsp cornstarch with 1/4 cup cold water

Directions

1. In medium sauce pan, Mix all ingredients but slurry. Bring to a boil.

2. Add slurry and heat until sauce thickens. If too thick, add a little water to thin.

Yield: 2 cups

JAPANESE RECIPES

Ponzu Sauce

This rather unlikely combination of ingredients leads to an intense soy-like sauce that is simultaneously sweet, tart, bitter, and salty. There are a lot of pre-made Ponzu sauces on the market. Just be aware that many are made with alcohol or fish.

Ingredients

1 cup soy sauce

1/2 cup fresh orange juice

1/4 cup fresh lemon juice

1/4 cup rice vinegar

1/8 tsp crushed red pepper

Directions

Mix all ingredients together and allow to rest for a while before serving.

These are some of my favorite ways for using ponzu:

To finish a dish - A few shakes of Ponzu in the last few minutes of cooking will kick up the flavors in stews or stir-frys.

In a marinade - Ponzu sauce is perfect marinade for vegetables, tofu, and soaking flavor into pastas.

In salad dressing - A Ponzu-based vinaigrette goes particularly well with hearty greens, like kale and radicchio salads.

As a dipping sauce - Ponzu makes a great variation on our standard dipping sauce for steamed vegetables.

In vegan meatloaf, meatballs, and veggie burgers - Much like Worcestershire sauce, Ponzu adds a great flavor.

Yield 2 cups

JAPANESE RECIPES

Yuzu Sauces

Yuzu is to Japan what lime juice is to Mexican cooking. And there are as many Yuzu sauces as there is food to put them on. Here are just a couple simple variations. The actual 'Yuzu Juice' ingredient, is readily available at any Asian food store.

Simple Homemade Yuzu Dressing

Ingredients

1/4 cup of Yuzu juice

1/4 cup of grape seed oil

2 Tbsp of soy sauce

1 Tsp of sugar

pinch fresh ground pepper

Directions

Whip all ingredients together. To really incorporate without separation, you should not mix in the oil until last, and then just drizzle it in while whipping.

Yield 1/2 cup

Creamy Yuzu Sauce
GREAT FOR SALADS

Ingredients

1/2 cup orange juice

1/4 cup vinegar

3 Tbsp mayonnaise

2 Tbsp Yuzu juice

1 tsp Dijon mustard

1 clove garlic, minced

1/2 tsp sea salt

Directions

Whip all ingredients together.

JAPANESE RECIPES

Simple Wasabi Recipe

Outside Japan, it is rare to find real Wasabi plants. Due to its high cost, a common substitute is a mixture of horseradish, mustard, starch and green food coloring or spinach powder. Often packages are labeled as Wasabi while the ingredients do not actually include any part of the Wasabi plant.

This is a S&B Wasabi. A popular Wasabi paste available in every Asian Food store.

Most people would associate Wasabi with Japanese dishes such as sushi or soba noodles. However, Wasabi goes well with many other foods. It can be used just like common Japanese flavorings such as miso and soy sauce.

USES FOR THE WASABI PASTES

Butter Substitutes
Soften butter substitutes then gently fold in wasabi to form a fluffy paste. Use plastic wrap to form the mixture into sticks then chill in a refrigerator. Then you can just slice off pieces for use. Raisins can be also be added to create wasabi raisin butter.

Mayonnaise
Simply mix the wasabi paste with mayonnaise to taste. This slightly pungent dip goes well with fried foods or can be used as a dressing or a spread.

Wasabi bread
Spread wasabi over a slice of bread and toast in an oven.

Wasabi dressing
Wasabi dressing is always a favorite, and so easy to make. Just mix wasabi with vinegar and olive oil. Then add salt and pepper to taste.

Wasabi pasta
Dollop wasabi and butter substitutes on top of cooked pasta. Then splash a dash of soy sauce and mix to create a spectacular Oriental-style pasta.

Wasabi tea
Japanese tea lover will love this: Just add a little bit of wasabi to your Japanese tea and mix well.

Avocado and wasabi soy sauce
Mix the wasabi paste and soy sauce to taste. Then add bite-sized slices of avocado.

JAPANESE RECIPES

Simple Miso Soup

Ingredients

8 cups water

6 Tbsp miso paste

1 - 16oz package tofu, diced

4 green onions, sliced diagonally into 1/2 inch pieces

Directions

1. Bring water to a boil. Reduce heat to medium.
2. Whisk in the miso paste.
3. Stir in tofu.
4. Separate the layers of the green onions, and add them to the soup.
5. Simmer gently for 2 to 3 minutes before serving.

Servings 4 to 6

Prep Time 5 min

Cook Time 10 min

Total Time 15 min

Thai

The most noticeable difference between Thai Cuisine and Chinese is that Thai will be a lot spicier. Thai food often includes sweet, sour, salty, savory, and bitter flavors all at the same time. It is a cultural passion of utmost importance to balance all the taste buds in the same recipe, thus making Thai Cuisine one of the most flavorful cuisines on the planet.

Thai

GOOD These items go well with this cuisine.	BETTER Even better pairing.	BEST The WOW factor!
basil	**coconut**	**CHILI PEPPERS**
bell peppers	**lemongrass**	**GARLIC**
cilantro	**peanuts**	**GINGER**
citrus	**schezwan sauce**	**NOODLES, Pad Thai**
coriander	**teriyaki sauce**	
cumin		
curry		
herbs		
lemon		
lime mint		
noodles		
orange		
rice		
sugar		
turmeric		
vegetables		

SIMPLY INCREDIBLE PAIRINGS

chili peppers + curry

chili peppers + garlic

chili peppers + peanuts

coconut + curry

THAI RECIPES

Thai Coconut Soup

Ingredients

1 can (14 oz.) coconut milk

3 cups vegetable broth

6 quarter-size slices fresh ginger

1 stalk fresh lemongrass, cut in 1-in. pieces

1 lb Tofu, diced

1 cup sliced mushrooms

1 Tbsp fresh lime juice

1 tsp sugar

1 tsp Thai chili paste

1/4 cup basil, chopped

1/4 cup cilantro, chopped

Directions

1. In a medium saucepan, combine coconut milk, broth, ginger, and lemongrass. Bring to boil.

2. Add tofu, mushrooms, lime juice, sugar, and chili paste. Reduce heat and simmer 10 minutes.

3. Discard lemongrass. Garnish servings with basil and cilantro.

Chef's Notes:

This is a great base recipe. And from here, you can run with a multitude of variations.

Servings 4 to 6

Prep Time 10 min

Cook Time 15 min

Total Time 25 min

THAI RECIPES

Drunken Noodles

Ingredients

Vegetable oil

1 lb. firm tofu, cubed and dried

1 cup vegetable stock

2 Tbsp hoisin sauce

1 Tbsp roasted red chile paste

2 tsp soy sauce

1 tsp sugar

1/2 tsp molasses

1 red bell pepper, seeded and sliced

1 large jalapeño, seeded and sliced

2 red Thai bird chile, minced

1 pound pad Thai rice noodles, broke in half and cooked

4 garlic cloves, minced

1/2 cup Thai basil leaves

Lime wedges, for serving

Directions

1. In a nonstick skillet, heat 1/4 inch of oil. Add the tofu and cook over medium high heat. Continue turning until crisp, about 5 minutes. Drain.

2. In a bowl, whisk the vegetable stock, hoisin sauce, chile paste, soy sauce, molasses and sugar.

3. In a large skillet or wok, heat 2 tablespoons of oil. Add the bell pepper, jalapeño, and Thai chile. Stir-fry over high heat until fragrant, about 2 minutes.

4. Add the noodles and garlic and stir-fry until browned, about 4 minutes.

5. Add the sauce and toss over moderately high heat, until absorbed.

6. Fold in the basil and the cooked tofu.

7. Garnish with more basil and serve with lime wedges.

Servings 4 to 6

Prep Time 15 min

Cook Time 10 min

Total Time 25 min

THAI RECIPES

Simple Pad Thai Recipe

Pad Thai, Phat Thai or Phad Thai, is a stir-fried rice noodle dish commonly served as a street food and at casual local eateries in Thailand.

Ingredients

1 - 12oz package rice noodles

1 quart hot water for soaking the noodles

2 Tbsp olive oil

1 - 6oz package extra-firm tofu, drained and cut into chunks

2 cloves garlic, minced

4 Tbsp soy sauce

1 cup water

2 Tbsp peanut butter

2 limes, juiced

3 Tbsp sugar

Sriracha, to taste

1 cup bean sprouts

Sliced green onions, for garnish

Chopped peanuts, for garnish (optional)

Directions

1. Submerge the rice noodles in hot water and let soak for about 15 minutes.

2. In a large frying pan or wok, heat the olive oil over medium heat and add the tofu chunks.

3. Drizzle 1 tablespoon of the soy sauce over the tofu and sauté until golden brown.

4. Add the garlic and sauté for 30 seconds. Remove from heat.

5. In a separate bowl, whisk together the peanut butter, lime juice, sugar, Sriracha, remaining soy sauce, and 1 cup of water.

6. In the wok, combine the soaked noodles, bean sprouts, and peanut butter mixture to the tofu and cook through, about 5 minutes.

7. Garnish with sliced green onions, chopped peanuts and serve. Enjoy!

Chef Notes:

In order to reduce the amount of oil, you can bake the tofu in the oven to crisp up the outside. And then water sauté the vegetables.

Servings 4

Prep Time 15 min

Cook Time 10 min

Total Time 25 min

THAI RECIPES

Thai Peanut Sauce

This peanut sauce is great on noodles, or a salad. Fantastic for coleslaw or 'kale slaw'. And it's even great for breads, or as the sauce for a pizza, instead of the tomato sauce. It is also multi-functional as you can use the same sauce for creativity in Thai, African, and Indian dishes.

Ingredients

1/2 cup crunchy peanut butter

1/4 cup cilantro, cleaned and chopped

4 scallions, white parts, minced

1 garlic clove, minced

4 Tbsp rice wine vinegar

3 Tbsp soy sauce, low sodium

2 Tbsp peanut oil

1 Tbsp chili paste

1 Tbsp toasted sesame oil

2 tsp minced ginger

1 tsp brown sugar

Directions

1. Mix all the ingredients together.

2. Allow flavors to rest in the fridge. Bring to room temperature, and then taste it again. Adjust for seasonings as desired.

Yield: about 1 cup

Chef Notes:

For the peanut oil, I use the oil from the top of fresh peanut butter when it settles. If you are going oil free, add water instead. For chili paste Sambal Olek is readily available. And Asian food stores generally have all you need to create Simply Amazing Asian flavor.

Yield 2 cups

THAI RECIPES

Vegan 'Fish' Sauce

This is the dairy free, gluten-free, wheat free, substitute for fish sauce.

Ingredients

1/2 cups shredded wakame (Asian Seaweed)

2 cups water

3 garlic cloves, minced

1 tsp whole peppercorns

1/3 cup regular soy sauce,

1 teaspoon of genmai miso

Directions

1. In a large sauce pan, combine wakame, garlic, peppercorns and water. Bring to a boil.

2. Lower heat and simmer about 20 minutes.

3. Strain. Return the liquid back to the pot.

4. Add soy sauce, bring back to a boil and cook until mixture is reduced and almost unbearably salty.

5. Remove from heat and stir in miso.

6. Store in a bottle or glass jar and keep in the refrigerator. Use to replace fish sauce in vegan recipes at an even one-to one ratio.

Chef's Notes

Wakame is a seaweed often used in seaweed salad in Asian restaurants. It's shredded into little strips. It's available in most Asian food stores. You can also use mushroom soy sauce, or black soy sauce.

Yield 2 cups

Belgian

Belgian Cuisine has one of the broadest varieties, and is influenced by their neighbors of Germany, France, and the Netherlands. They have been known for having the quality of France, and the quantity of Germany.

Belgian is big on potatoes and of course chocolate, but the most popular would have to be the Belgian waffle. And for a bonus, we are going to share with you the way to make healthy Belgian waffles.

Belgian

GOOD These items go well with this cuisine.		BETTER Even better pairing.	BEST The WOW factor!
Brussels sprouts	shallots	chocolate	**WAFFLES**
leeks	soups		
mustard	stews		
oats	vinegar		
potatoes	white asparagus		

Simply Incredible Waffles

Waffles are so easy to make. I'm going to give you a basic recipe for making Simply Incredible Waffles. This is a base recipe and tastes great just the way it is. But more important here is the concept. Because once you have the concept, you will be able to make dozens of different types of waffles with the same concept.

The Ratio: This recipe calls for 6 cups of soy milk and 6 cups of oats. And as long as you keep this same ratio between liquid and oats, your waffles will turn out great. You can do 1 gallon of liquid and 1 gallon of oats if you like.

The Liquid: You can use any liquid you want, even water. Almond milk works great. And if you want a passion fruit waffle, you can use orange juice or apple, or make a great Hawaiian delight with pineapple.

The Oats: You can use quick oats or regular oats. Steel cut oats do not work well.

The Sweetener: There are a lot of sweeteners you can use. Whether it be sugars, honey, maple syrup, or even stevia, a little sweetener helps a lot. And sugar types of sweeteners will help bring a crispiness and better coloring to the waffle.

The Extra Ingredients: This is where you can go to the extreme to achieve Simply Incredible Flavor. Add fruits, add nuts, even chocolate chips. You can create sweet waffles, or savory waffles. And if you want, make some with basil, oregano and garlic, creating a waffle that can then be used for pizza. This will be an amazing journey of flavor that even the kids will enjoy creating their own signature waffles.

BELGIAN RECIPES

The Simply Incredible Waffle Recipe

Ingredients

6 cups soy milk

6 cups oats, quick

1/4 cup ground flax seed

1/4 cup honey

1 Tbsp vanilla

1 Tbsp salt

1 Tbsp cinnamon

Directions

1. Mix all the ingredients together, and let rest for 1 hour or even overnight.

2. Blend in a blender, small batches at a time.

3. Pour into the waffle iron. Follow the directions for your particular waffle iron. My 'Waring' brand waffle iron must be flipped as soon as it is filled and closed. And then in about 6 minutes, the timer goes off and the waffle is done.

Servings 10 waffles

Prep Time 5 min

Rest Time: 1 hour

Cook Time 6 min per waffle

Total Time 60 min. - with one waffle iron

Chef's Notes:

We have three waffle irons. When we make waffles, we make dozens at a time, and freeze them. To freeze waffles, put 4 waffles flat on a cookie sheet pan. Then after they are frozen, put about 5 to 6 waffles in a gallon freezer bag. This is called IQF - Individual Quick Freeze. It's is the same thing they do with blueberries to keep them from sticking together. If you were to put the waffles into the baggies before they were IQF, they would stick together and also be smashed into an unappealing shape. In the mornings we can remove a couple waffles from the freezer, microwave for 30 seconds and put them in the toaster. Perfect waffles any time we want them.

Caribbean

There are a total of 25 countries in the Caribbean including Jamaica, Cuba, Aruba, and Puerto Rico. And with the estimated 7,000 islands, variations can be next to impossible to keep track of.

While there are countless differences, we are going to stick to the similarities. This will give you the essentials you need to create Caribbean flavors of every sort.

Caribbean

GOOD These items go well with this cuisine.		BETTER Even better pairing.	BEST The WOW factor!
allspice	onions	**avocado**	**JERK SEASONING**
bay leaves	orange	**brown sugar**	**PLANTAINS**
beans	oregano	**cilantro**	
bell peppers	parsley	**citrus**	
chili peppers	pigeon peas	**coconut milk**	
chocolate	pineapple	**fruits**	
cinnamon	rice	**lime**	
cloves	sugar, white	**papaya**	
curry	sweet potatoes	**potatoes**	
cumin	tamarind		
dill	thyme		
garlic	watercress		
ginger			
hot sauce			
molasses			
nutmeg			

SIMPLY INCREDIBLE PAIRINGS

allspice + cumin + garlic

avocado + onions + pineapple + watercress

bay leaf + green bell pepper + garlic + onions + oregano (safrito)

cilantro + garlic + onions (sofrito)

citrus juice + garlic + olive oil (adobo)

CARIBBEAN RECIPES

Zaboca & Channa Bruschetta

Zaboca defined: avocado. Channa defined: Chickpeas, or spiced chickpeas.

Ingredients

3 ripe avocados

2 cups chick peas, drained and rinsed

1 tomato, roma diced

2 garlic cloves, minced

2 scallions, finely chopped

8 sprigs cilantro, finely chopped

8 sprigs parsley, finely chopped

1/2 hot pepper, finely chopped (optional)

1 lime or lemon, juiced

1 tsp salt

Italian or French bread

olive oil (optional)

Directions

1. Preheat oven to 375 degrees.

2. Scoop out the avocado flesh into a bowl, and using a fork, mash well.

3. Add the remaining ingredients and fold until well incorporated. If you want to give a quick chop to the chickpeas, that's fine too.

4. Slice the bread into 1/2 inch diagonal ovals.

5. Place on a baking sheet and toast in oven for 2 minutes on each side. Just until browned.

6. Remove the bread from the oven and brush the tops of the toasts with olive oil and set aside.

7. Spoon a portion of the mixture onto each of the toasts and serve immediately.

Chef's Notes:

You do not really need oil for this particular bruschetta. The reason you would brush the bread with oil is because water and oil don't mix. So if you are going to have these setting for a while before serving, brushing will reduce the amount of moisture from penetrating the bread. When your bruschetta toppings have a lot of moisture, using oil will help.

Servings 12

Prep Time 15 min

Cook Time 5 min

Total Time 20 min

CARIBBEAN RECIPES

Pikliz

Haitian Pikliz is a spicy coleslaw. It is often served with every meal including breakfast.

Ingredients

1 cup vinegar

1/2 cup lime juice, fresh

4 cloves garlic, minced

3 habaneros, minced

1 bell pepper, thinly sliced

1 large carrot, grated

1 medium yellow onion, thinly sliced

1/2 head cabbage, thinly sliced

salt to taste

Directions

In a large bowl, combine all the ingredients and season with salt and pepper. Store in an airtight container for up to 1 week.

Chef's Notes:

The longer the sturdy, crunchy vegetables soak up the vinegar and citrus, the better. You can regulate the spice by adding or reducing the habaneros, or even use jalapeño peppers.

Servings 6 to 8
Prep Time 10 min
Total Time 10 min

CARIBBEAN RECIPES

Wasakaka

Dominican Republic's Wasakaka is similar to Argentina's Chimichurri. With just four ingredients. *Wasakaka* is one of the simplest most popular Caribbean condiments there is.

Ingredients

1/2 cup water

1/2 cup fresh lime juice

1/2 cup parsley, chopped fine

1/4 cup olive oil

2 cloves garlic, minced

sea salt to taste

black pepper, ground to taste

Directions

In a medium bowl, mix all ingredients and season with salt and pepper. Store in an airtight container.

Yield 1 1/2 cups

CARIBBEAN RECIPES

Pique

Puerto Rico's Pique is a spicy, heavily-seasoned vinegar. The goal is to tap into the perfect combination of sweet, salty, sour, and spicy. It will be found on the tables of almost every home and restaurant in Puerto Rico. Traditionally used as an accompaniment for rice, beans and plantains. But like Puerto Ricans, you'll find many uses to splash this delight everywhere.

Ingredients

1 cup apple cider vinegar

1 tsp salt, kosher

1 tsp oregano, dried

10 whole black peppercorns

6 small chili peppers (choose any combination of ajíes caballeros, habaneros, jalapeños, and/or muranga reds) peeled and halved lengthwise

4 cloves garlic, peeled and cut in half, not chopped

1 bay leaf

1 slice pineapple rind

Directions

In a small bowl, whisk together the vinegar, salt, and oregano. Place remaining ingredients in a jar and pour the liquid over the top. Cover with the lid and store at room temperature for up to 2 weeks, or refrigerate for longer shelf life.

Chef's Notes:

This is one of the homemade Caribbean sauces that you need to bottle so it can cure.

Yield 1 cup

CARIBBEAN RECIPES

Cuban Mojo Sauce

Mojo is commonly used as a marinade in Cuban cooking. It is also served as a sauce with the island's root vegetables. The main ingredient is garlic, and a lot of it.

Ingredients

12 cloves garlic, minced

1/4 cup olive oil

1/4 cup fresh orange juice

1/4 cup fresh lime juice

1 tsp salt, kosher or sea salt

1 tsp oregano, fresh chopped

1/4 tsp ground cumin

Directions

In a medium bowl, combine all ingredients, and whisk. Store in an airtight container. Shake before splashing on food.

Chef's Notes:

The amount of oil used varies depending on what you're cooking. You can range from extra heavy oils for brushing and baking concepts. Or you can use very little oil for marinating tofu. It's one of the simpler condiments to make, and a little goes a long way.

Yield 3/4 cup

CARIBBEAN RECIPES

Trinidad Green Seasoning

This is a savory herb-laced salsa from Trinidad and Tobago. It is used as a marinade or to flavor soups, stews, or salads.

Ingredients

1/2 cup cilantro, finely chopped

1/2 cup parsley, finely chopped

1/4 cup lime juice, fresh

2 Tbsp water

1 Tbsp thyme, finely chopped

2 cloves garlic, minced

2 scallions, thinly sliced

1 stalk celery, finely chopped

1/2 small red onion, finely chopped

1/4 red bell pepper, finely chopped

Sea salt to taste

black pepper, ground, to taste

Directions

Mix all the ingredients together and season with salt and pepper. Store in an airtight container.

Yield 3 cups

French

The French are good at creating innovative flavors and showboating elegant plate presentations. As far as the food itself goes, it's not exactly known to be healthy. Lots of oils, meats, cheeses, and cream sauces. This places the typical French Cuisine high on the list of foods to avoid. But on the bright side, their portion control is first rate. Where other countries over eat, the French get an A+. And here is where we are going to share with you the seasoning you can use to get a French flair in your recipes and achieve Simply Incredible Flavor.

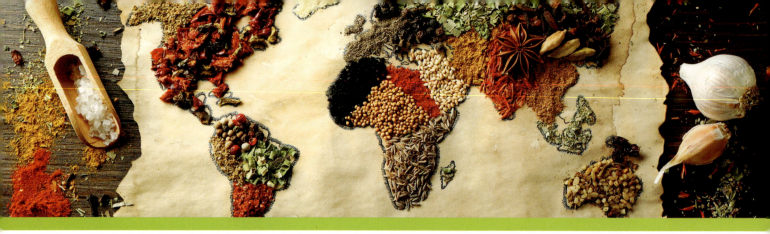

French

GOOD These items go well with this cuisine.		BETTER Even better pairing.	BEST The WOW factor!
anise	potatoes	**butter**	**CREAM**
basil	stock, vegetable	**chocolate**	**SAUCES**
bell peppers	tarragon	**garlic**	
cabbage	thyme	**herbs**	
cheese	tomatoes	**shallots**	
mustard	vegetables	**truffles**	
olive oil	vinegars		
onions			
parsley			
pastries			

SIMPLY INCREDIBLE PAIRINGS

basil + garlic + olive oil

basil + tomatoes

eggplant + garlic + onions + tomatoes

garlic + lemon + saffron

garlic + olives + onions + tomatoes

marjoram + rosemary + sage + thyme (herbes de Provence)

FRENCH RECIPES

Roasted Root Vegetable Bisque

Basically bisque is a smooth, creamy, highly seasoned soup of French origin. Most people think of bisque as a seafood, but any cream soup made from roasted and pureed fruits or vegetables, are also called bisques.

Ingredients

1 large sweet potato, peeled and diced

2 carrots, peeled and diced

1 parsnip, peeled and diced

1 rutabaga, peeled and diced

1 poblano chili, seeded and chopped

4 cups vegetable stock

1 - 14 oz can coconut milk, separate and save the cream

1 Tbsp maple syrup

1 1/2 tsp sea salt

1 tsp thyme fresh minced

1/4 tsp rosemary fresh chopped

1/4 tsp cayenne pepper

Directions

1. Preheat oven to 400 degrees.

2. On two sheet pans lined with parchment paper, place the vegetables. One sheet with carrots, parsnips, poblano chili. On the other sheet, the sweet potatoes and rutabaga.

3. Bake in oven until tender roasted, about 35 minutes. The sheet with the carrots may be done first.

4. After roasting, transfer vegetables to a high-speed blender.

5. Add the remaining ingredients.

6. Make sure lid is tight on top of blender.

7. Process soup until very, very smooth and velvety.

8. Serve immediately or pour into a large pot to keep warm or reheat on the stove.

9. Season with additional salt to taste if necessary.

10. Whip the coconut cream a bit and splash on top of soup before serving.

11. Garnish with parsley.

Servings 4 to 6 » Prep Time 10 min

Cook Time 35 min » Total Time 45 min

FRENCH RECIPES

Raw Vegan Sun-dried Tomato Olive Pate

WHAT IS A PÂTÉ?

When the French word pâté has an accent over the "e" it means "paste." When there is no accent over the "e" it means pie. That's a big difference.

When spelled with the accent, pâté refers to well-seasoned ground meats that can be satiny smooth and spreadable or formed into a loaf shape like a French country pâté.

It can be made with pork, veal, ham, liver, fish, poultry, game or vegetables. Sometimes they are cooked in a crust and at other times they are baked in terrines which have been lined with strips of fat or bacon.

Pâtés can be hot or cold and are usually served as a first course (especially in the case of a warm pâté) or as an appetizer passed on trays with other canapés or on an hors d'oeuvres spread.

Ingredients

1 cup sunflower seeds

5 sun-dried tomatoes

1/4 cup kalamata olives

1/4 red bell pepper

1 Tbsp green onion, or red onion

1 Tbsp fresh basil

1 Tbsp fresh parsley

1 Tbsp nutritional yeast flakes,

1 Tbsp lemon juice

1 clove garlic

Directions

1. Soak the sunflower seeds in water for 2 hours or overnight in the refrigerator.

2. Soak the sun-dried tomatoes in water for 30 minutes.

3. Strain the seeds and tomatoes. Add them to a food processor with the remaining ingredients.

4. Blend until smooth, about 1 minute.

5. Store in an airtight container in the fridge.

Chef's Notes:

This is a great recipe to serve with crackers and fresh cut vegetables. Depending on the salt in the olives, you may or may not need to add additional salt. This recipe is also real easy to make double or triple batches.

**Servings 4 to 6 » Prep Time 10 min
Cook Time 35 min » Total Time 45 min**

FRENCH RECIPES

Vegan French Crepes

Ingredients

1/2 cup soy milk

1/2 cup water

1/4 cup melted soy margarine

1 Tbsp turbinado sugar

2 Tbsp maple syrup

1 cup all-purpose flour, unbleached

1/4 tsp salt

Directions

1. In a large mixing bowl, blend all ingredients until smooth.

2. Cover and chill the mixture for 2 hours.

3. Remix the batter. It should be much thinner than pancake batter.

4. Lightly oil a 6 inch nonstick skillet with some vegan margarine.

5. Heat on medium-high until the skillet is hot.

6. Pour only about 3 tablespoons of batter into the skillet.

7. Shake and tilt the pan to make the batter cover the skillet's bottom.

8. Cook until golden, flip and cook on opposite side.

Chef's Notes:

While this is the 'standard' French crepe, I like to add a couple drops of vanilla, or a pinch of cinnamon or nutmeg. And you will certainly want to stuff these crepes with your favorite fillings. Everything from fresh and preserved fruits to cream cheese and even spinach and sautéd mushrooms. Whether entrees or desserts, the crepe gives you an endless array of Simply Incredible French Flavor.

Servings 6 to 8

Prep Time 10 min

Cook Time 15 min

Total Time 25 min

FRENCH RECIPES

French Toast Bites
WITH A BLACKBERRY GINGER SAUCE

These French toast bites are bursting with Simply Incredible Flavor. They are the perfect size for breakfast on the go!

Ingredients
For the Blackberry Ginger Sauce:

1 cup blackberries

1 Tbsp maple syrup

1 Tbsp lemon juice

1 tsp freshly grated ginger

1 tsp chia seeds

Directions:

Combine all ingredients in a small sauce pot over medium heat. Break up with a spatula as the mixture simmers until a thick sauce forms, about 10 minutes. Remove from heat and set aside to cool.

Ingredients
For the French Toast Bites

1/2 loaf cinnamon raisin bread, cubed

1 - 12 oz box silken tofu, firm

1 cup almond milk

1 Tbsp chia seeds

1 Tbsp maple syrup

1 tsp vanilla

1 tsp cinnamon

1/4 tsp nutmeg

For the French toast bites:

1. Preheat oven to 350 degrees and spray mini-muffin tins with baking spray.

2. Place the cubed raisin bread in a large bowl.

3. In a food processor, blend all the remaining ingredients until smooth. About 30 seconds.

4. Add the almond milk mixture to the cubed bread. Carefully mix until well combined. Let sit for 5 minutes so that the bread can absorb the liquid.

5. Spoon the bread mixture into muffin tin so that each one is about half full.

6. Place a small spoonful of the blackberry sauce on top of each one. And then spoon the remainder of the bread mixture on top of that. You want the bread to be heaping over the level of the muffin tin.

7. Bake for about 25 minutes until puffed and golden brown around the edges, and not soggy in the middle.

8. Remove from oven, let cool a few minutes before carefully removing from the muffin tin.

9. Serve warm with additional maple syrup. Or even enjoy cold.

Chef's Notes:

You can also do these in large muffin tins, or a casserole dish. It will just take a little more time baking. Store extra French toast bites in the refrigerator and toast them before serving as leftovers.

Servings 4 to 6 » Prep Time 20 min
Cook Time 25 min » Total Time 45 min

German

When you think of Germany, you think of bratwurst and sauerkraut. But there are so many more amazing flavors. The foods and parings listed below will definitely help you produce delicious dishes with a German flair.

German

GOOD These items go well with this cuisine.		BETTER Even better pairing.	BEST The WOW factor!
allspice	mace	**apples**	**POTATOES**
anise	nutmeg	**fennel**	**SAUERKRAUT**
asparagus	parsley	**horseradish**	
bay leaf	pepper	**mustard**	
breads	poppy seeds	**paprica**	
caraway seeds	sage	**rye**	
chives	sugar	**sour cream**	
chocolate	white asparagus	**vinegar**	
cinnamon			
cream cheese			
cucumbers			
dill			
ginger			
juniper berries			

SIMPLY INCREDIBLE PAIRINGS

caraway + paprika + sour cream

caraway + sauerkraut

cream cheese + chocolate + sugar

dill + cucumbers

nutmeg + potatoes

sugar + vinegar

GERMAN RECIPES

Hot German Potato Salad

Ingredients

6 cups red potatoes, cooked and diced, skin on

1/2 cup cabbage, chopped

1/2 cup onion, diced

1/2 cup water

1/2 cup apple cider vinegar

3 Tbsp sugar

2 Tbsp parsley

1 tsp salt

1/4 tsp pepper

Directions

1. Preheat over to 350 degrees.

2. In a large cooking pot, add the cabbage, onion, vinegar, water, sugar, salt and pepper.

3. Bring to a boil, and cook for 5 minutes.

4. Then add the diced potatoes and parsley.

5. Heat through, let rest for 5 minutes, allowing the potatoes to absorb any moisture.

6. Drain off any excess moisture, and put potatoes into a baking dish.

7. Bake for 20 minutes.

8. Sprinkle with parsley and serve.

Servings 6 to 10

Prep Time 10 min

Cook Time 25 min

Total Time 35 min

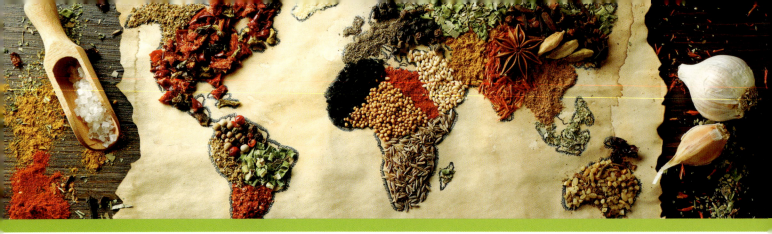

GERMAN RECIPES

Vegan Schnitzel

Schnitzel is a meat dish originating in Austria.

This vegan Schnitzel is as real as it gets without the harmful animal products and fat that typically accompanies the traditional serving.

Ingredients

Cutlet

1 cup vital wheat gluten

2 Tbsp nutritional yeast

1 tsp onion powder

1/2 tsp sage, rubbed

1/2 tsp salt

3/4 cup vegetable broth

2 Tbsp tahini

1 Tbsp Kitchen Bouquet (optional)

3 cups of vegetable broth

1 onion chopped

vegetable oil for frying

Breading Ingredients

Pan #1 - 1 cup all purpose flour mixed with 1/2 tsp pepper

Pan #2 - 1 block tofu blended smooth with soy milk to the consistency of eggs.

Pan #3 - 2 cups breadcrumbs mixed with 2 Tbsp flour.

Directions

Making the Cutlets

1. In a mixing bowl, mix together wheat gluten, nutritional yeast, onion powder and sage.

2. In another bowl, whisk the 3/4 cup broth, tahini and Kitchen Bouquet until smooth.

3. Mix the dry ingredients with the wet and stir until well combined.

4. Knead the dough until it is elastic but not dry. if dough too sticky, add little gluten flour.

5. Let dough rest for 10 minutes.

6. Divide the dough into eight equal pieces.

7. Roll out each piece of dough until it is a ½" thick cutlet and then place in a large casserole dish.

8. Cover them with vegetable broth and slivered onions.

9. Cook for 1 hour at 350 degrees, flipping after 30 minutes

Breading The Cutlets

1. Making sure to cover both sides, dip each cutlet into the flour, then the egg replacer, then the breading.

Frying

1. In a large, heavy-bottomed frying pan, heat 1" of oil on medium-high. There needs to be enough oil to cover the cutlets completely.

2. Fry the cutlets a couple at a time, about 5 minutes or until they are golden brown, flipping when they are half done.

3. Drain off cutlets on paper towels and pat off excess oil.

4. Topping with your favorite mushroom gravy, or sauerkraut.

Chef's Notes:

These Schnitzel cutlets can also be used for sandwiches with the onions from the broth.

Low Oil Version:

For the low oil version, instead of frying, you will want to place them on sheet pans after breading and bake them. When I do it this way, I still spray every one with some veggie spray. It's a fraction of oil, and will still provide a crispy effect.

Servings 8 cutlets

Prep Time 30 min

Cook Time 45 min

Total Time 1.3 hours

GERMAN RECIPES

Simply Amazing Vegan Brats

Nothing says German like German Brats. These are completely fat-free and hold up very well on the grill. Perfect for those summertime BBQs!

Ingredients

Wet Ingredients

1 cup cannelloni beans, rinsed, drained, and mashed

2 Tbsp miso paste, white

1/4 cup soy sauce, low sodium

12 cups veggie broth

1/2 tsp liquid smoke

Dry Ingredients

2 1/2 cups vital wheat gluten

1/2 cup nutritional yeast

2 tsp fennel seeds

2 tsp garlic powder

2 tsp onion powder

2 tsp rubbed sage

1 tsp dry mustard powder

1 tsp smoked paprika

1 tsp salt

1 tsp ground pepper

1/2 tsp allspice

Instructions

1. Whisk all dry ingredients together in a large bowl until thoroughly combined

2. In another bowl, blend all wet ingredients until thoroughly mixed and smooth

3. Add the wet ingredients to the dry and mix to form a loose dough

4. Cover and let rest while preparing foil sheets and steamer.

5. Add 2 inches of water to an extra large steamer and turn it on.

6. Make 10 foil squares about 8in x 8in.

7. Cut the dough into 10 equal pieces and shape into logs 5-6" long

8. Roll each log in foil and twist edges like a tootsie roll to seal

9. Steam for 45 minutes

10. Let rest 30 minutes. Then unravel.

11. Enjoy as is, fry in a pan, or grill for additional browning

Chef's Notes

Garnish with your favorite condiments. Ketchup, Mustard, Pickle Relish, Grilled Onions, Sauerkraut.

Prep time: 20 mins » Cook time: 40 mins

Total time: 1.3 hours » Serves: 10 Brats

Greek

The first cookbook ever written was by the Greek poet Archestratos in 320 B.C. Greek cooking has changed dramatically from it's original ingredients of wheat, olive oil and wine. While these are still dominant, the transportation and preservation of food has expanded Greek foods into an array of delightful flavors.

Over time, Greeks adapted huge amounts of meat and cheeses including lots of lamb, and yogurts which were fermented by wild bacterias in goat skin bags for preserving. But in the last several generations, the Greek Cuisine has shifted towards the healthier foods like potatoes, tomatoes, peppers, okra, and beans. Spices like mint, fennel, dill and cloves are staples in creating Simply Incredible Greek Flavor.

Greek

GOOD These items go well with this cuisine.	BETTER Even better pairing.	BEST The WOW factor!
allspice, pine nuts anise, raisins basil, rice bay leaf, spinach bell peppers, thyme cinnamon, tomatoes cloves, zucchini custard eggplant fennel honey kebobs mint nutmeg nuts olive oil onions oregano parsley phyllo dough	**cheese, feta** **cucumber** **dill** **figs** **grape leaves** **olives, black** **pita bread** **yogurt**	**GARLIC** **LEMON** **OLIVES, GREEN**

SIMPLY INCREDIBLE PAIRINGS

cucumber + dill

cucumber + dill + garlic + yogurt

dill + lemon

eggplant + garlic

garlic + lemon + oregano

grape leaves + rice

lemon + oregano

phyllo dough + honey + nuts

rice + nuts

spinach + feta cheese

tomatoes + cinnamon

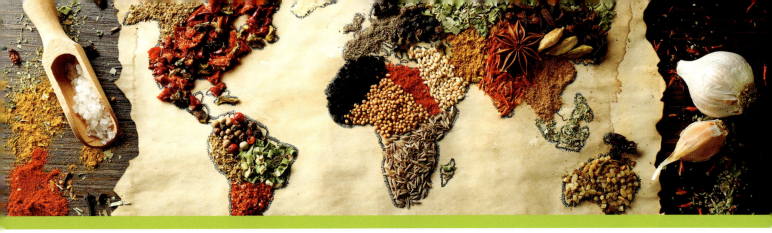

GREEK RECIPES

Greek Dolma

Stuffed Grape Leaves are a fun easy way to incorporate great flavor. And once you get the hang of it, you will be able to create hundreds of varieties.

Ingredients

1 - 16 oz jar grape leaves

Stuffing

3 cups cooked rice

1/3 cup vegetable broth

1/2 cup onions, diced

1/2 cup bell peppers, diced

1/2 cup celery, diced

1/2 cup tomatoes, diced

1/2 cup chopped walnuts

1 Tbsp parsley

1/2 tsp salt

1/4 tsp allspice

1/4 tsp pepper, black ground

1 quart water

1 lemon juiced

Directions

1. These leaves are packed in brine. So it is important to rinse them well in warm water before using.

2. Separate the most perfect leaves from those which are imperfect.

3. Line the bottom of a glass baking dish with the imperfect leaves. It is okay to line several layers. These imperfect leaves act as a cushioning layer for the stuffed rolls and will be discarded after baking.

4. Mix stuffing ingredients thoroughly.

5. Place a grape leaf vein side up and stem end toward you on the counter.

6. Near the base put 1 heaping teaspoon of stuffing.

7. Fold both sides over stuffing and then roll up from the base end to the tip. It is important to roll them tightly so that they don't become unrolled while cooking.

8. Lay the rolls very close to each other in rows. It is okay to make several layers if necessary.

9. Pour in warm water and lemon juice.

10. Cover dish with foil, and poke some holes in the top.

11. Bake in oven at 350 degrees about 45 minutes.

Serves: 30 to 40 rolls » Prep time: 40 min

Cook time: 45 min » Total time: 1.5 hours

GREEK RECIPES

Spanakopita
GREEK SPINACH PIE

This is a classic Greek Spanakopita. But this time we are making it with much less oil. It will be far lighter in the calorie count. The flavor is in the spinach and garlic.

Ingredients

1 cup diced onion

1/4 cup water x 2 plus more for splashing

2 garlic cloves, minced

3 lbs. spinach, fresh

1 bunch kale, remove stems, shredded

1/2 lemon, juiced

1/4 cup vegan mozzarella cheese

2 tsp dill, fresh

1 tsp sea salt

1/2 tsp nutmeg

1/2 of 1 -16 oz package of vegan filo dough, frozen

Directions

1. Preheat oven to 400 degrees.

2. Lightly spray a pie tin or circular pan with vegetable spray.

3. In a large skillet, water sauté the diced onions.

4. Add the garlic.

5. Add the squeeze of lemon

6. Add washed spinach and kale, cook until wilted. Remove from heat and let cool.

7. In a bowl combine spinach mixture with vegan cheese, dill, nutmeg, and salt.

8. To assemble, lay 4 to 6 filo sheets covering every angle on the pan. Spray or splash with the smallest amount of water. Continue to arrange filo sheets in a clockwork fashion. Lightly watering the tops of each new pair of filo dough as you go.

9. Place spinach mixture in the center and spread into an even layer.

10. Carefully fold the excess filo inward and layer 4 or more sheets on top tucking the sheets in around the pan.

11. Precut the Spanakopita into 6 pieces. Spray the top very lightly with vegetable oil.

12. Bake for 30 minutes, until edges are golden and center is set. Allow to cool and tighten up. Recut along the precut lines. And serve.

Serves: 6 » Prep time: 15 min

Cook time: 30 min » Total time: 45 min

GREEK RECIPES

Tzatziki Sauce
GREEK CUCUMBER/YOGURT SAUCE

Ingredients

3 cups vegan yogurt

3 Tbsp lemon juice

1 garlic clove, minced

1 large English cucumber, diced

1 Tbsp salt

1 Tbsp dill, fresh chopped

1 Tbsp mint, fresh

pinch of pepper

salt to taste

Directions

1. Peel cucumbers and dice. Put them in a colander and sprinkle with the tablespoon of salt. This will draw water out of the cucumber. Cover with a plate and sit something heavy on top. Let sit for 30 minutes. Drain well and wipe dry with a paper towel.

2. In a blender, add cucumbers, garlic, lemon juice, dill, mint, and a pinch of pepper. Process until well blended, then stir in yogurt. Taste before adding any extra salt, then salt if needed.

3. Place in refrigerator for at least two hours before serving so flavors can blend.

Chef's Notes:

Try to find the thickest yogurt you can find. And if it is too wet, try using 1/2 yogurt, and 1/2 vegan sour cream.

Serves: 12

Prep time: 40 mins

Cook time: 45 mins

Total time: 1.5 hours

GREEK RECIPES

Greek Cabbage Rolls

Nothing beats the comfort of stuffed cabbage rolls on those cold winter days. But more than just comfort, they're healthy. Extremely healthy. And there are a hundred ways to create Simply Incredible Flavor.

Ingredients

Sauce:

2 Tbsp vegetable oil, or water sauté

1 onion, chopped

4 garlic cloves, minced

2 - 28 oz cans diced fire-roasted tomatoes

1 Tbsp tomato paste

1 tsp salt to taste

pinch pepper

Cabbage and Filling:

1 large cabbage

3 cups cooked lentils

3 cup cooked brown rice or and grains.

1 cup onion, diced

2 garlic cloves, minced

2 Tbsp minced fresh parsley

2 tsp lemon juice

1 tsp paprika, smoked

1/2 tsp salt to taste

1/4 tsp allspice

Garnish with 1/2 cup or raisins, and 1/2 cup pine nuts

Directions

1. **For the Sauce:** In a large skillet, sauté the onions for about 5 minutes.

2. Add the garlic and cook for another minute.

3. Add all remaining sauce ingredients, reduce heat to low, and cover. Cook for at least 30 minutes.

4. **For the Cabbage:** Fill a large deep pan with enough water to cover a whole cabbage and bring it to a boil. Use a paring knife and remove the core. Put the cabbage core-end up into the boiling water and cook until the leaves soften and begin to fall off the cabbage. Remove each leaf and repeat until you have plenty of whole cabbage leaves. Allow to cool

5. In a medium bowl, mix the lentils with all the remaining ingredients, adding salt and pepper to taste.

6. In a large baking dish or a dutch oven, sauce the bottom with 1/2 of your sauce.

7. **Assembling the Cabbage Rolls:** Preheat the oven to 325 degrees.

8. Dry each cabbage leaf gently and trim the thick rib near the stem end of each leaf.

9. Put the cabbage leaf on your work surface with the concave side up, like a cup, with the stem end toward you. Place about 1/3 cup of the lentil mixture near the stem end, and mold it into an oblong shape. Fold the stem up over the filling and then fold each of the sides toward the middle. Continue rolling the filling up the rest of the leaf. You should have a nice, tight package.

10. Place the cabbage roll in your baking dish with the seam side down. Repeat until all the product is gone. Keep the cabbage rolls snug together in a single layer.

11. Spread the remaining sauce over the top of the rolls. Sprinkle with raisins and pine nuts.

12. Cover cabbage rolls and bake for about 40 minutes.

13. Remove from oven and remove cover. Allow to cool a bit, and the cabbage rolls will tighten up, making them easier to handle.

Chef's Notes

Add green olives, or fire roasted red bell pepper.

Throw in some chopped fresh dill or caraway seeds.

Spice it up with red pepper flakes or cayenne.

Create a Louisiana flair by adding some Creole seasoning.

Add chili powder and cumin for a Mexican flair.

Add corn and you have Southwest.

Make them like a Polish golabki by adding sauerkraut to the sauce or filling.

Give it an Italian twist with basil and oregano.

Go in a Middle Eastern direction by increasing the allspice and adding cinnamon and mint.

Choose other grains: bulgur wheat, kasha, brown rice, quinoa, etc.

And try freezing a whole cabbage: Thaw it out and your leaves are ready to roll. You don't have to boil off the cabbage.

Serves: 5

Prep time: 1 hour

Cook time: 1.5 hours

Total time: 2.5 hours

Hungarian

Hungarian or 'Magyar' cuisine is primarily based on meat and potatoes, cheeses, and dairy products. Fortunately they are also heavy on stews, soups, and casserole, which are easily converted into healthier vegan dishes that carry the same Hungarian flavors.

Hungarian

GOOD These items go well with this cuisine.		BETTER Even better pairing.	BEST The WOW factor!
allspice	cream cheese	**apples**	**ONIONS**
anise	dill	**mushrooms**	**PAPRIKA**
asparagus	garlic	**rye**	**POTATOES**
bay leaf	mustard	**sour cream**	
bell peppers	nutmeg		
breads	oats		
caraway seeds	tomatoes		
chili pepper	vinegar		
chocolate	wheat		
cinnamon			
cream			

SIMPLY INCREDIBLE PAIRINGS

allspice + apples + oats + sugar

cream + mustard + onions + potatoes

onions + paprika

onions + paprika + potatoes

onions + paprika + sour cream

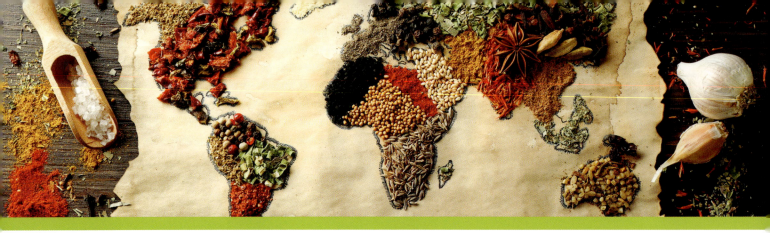

MORE ABOUT PAPRIKA

Paprika in Hungarian also refers to the peppers from which the spice is made. The peppers are native to the Americas and were taken to Hungary by merchants where it flourished. Hungarian paprika is revered the world over because it is said that the soil the peppers are grown in lends a flavor like no other.

The Spanish, however, will argue that their paprika, especially smoked paprika, is superior to Hungarian paprika. It's all a matter of taste.

What the two paprikas have in common is a grading system. This is the grading system for Hungarian paprika:

SPECIAL QUALITY: Mild and sweet with a bright red color

DELICATE: Light to dark red with a mild and rich flavor

EXQUISITE DELICATE: Similar to Delicate but more pungent

PUNGENT EXQUISITE DELICATE: An even more pungent version of Delicate

ROSE: Pale red with strong aroma and mild pungency

NOBLE SWEET: The most common paprika that is bright red and slightly pungent

HALF-SWEET: A blend of mild and pungent paprikas

STRONG: Light brown in color and the hottest paprika

HUNGARIAN RECIPES

Sausage Stuffed Kolache

Sausage Kolache is a classic Czech breakfast pastry. This is the easy, healthy way to make great Stuffed Kolache. And be creative. This recipe is fun to create with different fillings.

Ingredients

1 package active dry yeast (2 1/4 tsp)

1/4 cup water, warmed

1 cup non dairy milk, warmed

1/4 cup vegan margarine, softened

3 tsp egg replacer mixed with 4 Tbsp warm water

1/2 cup sugar

1 tsp salt

4 3/4 cups flour

Filling

vegan cheddar cheese,

vegan sausage, crumbled

sliced jar jalapeños

Directions

1. Mix the yeast in with warm water, and let rest for 5 minutes, until foamy.

2. In a mixer's bowl, on low, using a dough hook, mix the yeast with milk, melted margarine, eggs replacer mix, sugar, and salt. Mix thoroughly.

3. Add the flour one cup at a time, and mix in only until just combined. The dough will be tacky but should be firm enough to crawl up the dough hook. Add additional flour if needed. Remove dough from hook.

4. Cover with plastic wrap and let rest for about 2 hours, until dough has doubled.

5. Punch down and refrigerate for at least 4 hours.

6. Divide dough into 2 1/2 inch balls, and set on parchment paper lined baking sheet.

7. Cover and let rest for 15 minutes.

8. Flatten each dough ball and top with vegan cheese, sausage and jalapeño slice. Then wrap the dough around the fillings, pinching the edges together and placing seam-side down on the baking sheet. Repeat until they are all done.

9. Cover and let rest for 20 minutes.

10. Preheat oven to 375 degrees.

11. Bake for 25-30 minutes, until browned.

12. Let the Kolache cool for 10 minutes and serve.

Chef's Notes:

This is a great base recipe, and you can stuff them with most ANYTHING. Be creative.

Serves: 8 to 10 » Prep time: 20 min

Rest time 6 + hours » Cook time: 30 min

Total work time: 50 min

HUNGARIAN RECIPES

Hungarian Lecso
PEPPER, SAUSAGE AND TOMATO STEW

Ingredients

2 Tbsp olive oil, or water sauté

2 medium onions, large chopped

2 red peppers, large chopped

1 green bell pepper, large chopped

3 garlic cloves, minced

2 lb Hungarian vegan sausage, angle sliced

2 cups water

2 tomatoes, large, chopped

2 - 14 oz can stewed tomatoes

1/4 cup tomato, paste

1 tsp Hungarian paprika, sweet

1 tsp Hungarian paprika, hot

1 tsp sugar, natural

1 tsp salt

1/2 tsp pepper

Directions

1. In a large high wall skillet, on medium-high heat, sauté the onions and peppers for about five minutes.

2. Add the garlic and sauté for another minute.

3. Add remaining ingredients. Reduce heat to medium-low.

4. Simmer for 30 minutes, stirring occasionally, until it has reduced into a saucy consistency.

5. Serve as is, with bread, or over jasmine rice. Mmmm

Serves: 4-6

Prep time: 15 min

Cook time: 30 min

Total time: 45 min

HUNGARIAN RECIPES

Turos Csusza
HUNGARIAN MAC AND CHEESE

Pure comfort food. Hungarian Mac and Cheese is traditionally more cream cheese and sour cream rather than American cheeses. This recipe has the perfect balance to experience Simply Incredible Hungarian Flavor.

Ingredients

12 ounces pasta, rotini, shells, or any kind

8 ounces vegan cream cheese

10 ounces vegan sour cream

1 cup vegan bacon, chopped

sea salt to taste

pepper to taste (Hungarian would use heavy black pepper for this dish)

1/2 cup vegan cheese

Directions

1. Cook the pasta per instructions. Drain and set aside.

2. In a medium sauce pot, mix the cream cheese, sour cream, and 1/2 of the vegan bacon. Mix well and heat over medium heat until warmed through and smooth. Season with salt and pepper.

3. Mix in the pasta, and stir continually until hot.

4. Quickly fold in the vegan cheese, and transfer to serving bowl.

5. Garnish with the remaining bacon.

Chef's Notes:

This is a great base recipe, and you can always add other items like steamed broccoli, artichokes, or vegan meats.

Serves: 4

Prep time: 15 min

Cook time: 20 min

Total time: 35 min

HUNGARIAN RECIPES

Hungarian Tofu and Potato Goulash

Ingredients

2 tsp olive oil or water sauté

1 large white onion, diced large

1 bell pepper, diced large

5 garlic cloves, minced

1- 14 oz can diced tomatoes

1 - 6 oz can tomato paste

1/4 cup paprika, mild or hot

2 tsp oregano, dried

1 tsp basil, dried

1 bay leaf

1/2 tsp salt

1/4 tsp pepper

2 pounds baby red potatoes, quartered

3 cups water

2 - 12 oz packages tofu, extra firm, cubed

1/4 cup fresh parsley, chopped

Directions

1. In a large heavy bottom pot, sauté the onions and peppers for about 5 minutes.

2. Add in the garlic and sauté for another minute.

3. Add in the tomatoes, tomato paste, paprika, oregano, basil, salt, pepper, and bay leaf. Stir these ingredients into the onions and garlic. Allow the spices and the tomato paste to cook for about 3 minutes.

4. Add in the potatoes and the water. Stir well to combine.

5. Place a lid on the pot and bring to a boil for 5 minutes.

6. Reduce heat to low and simmer for 15 minutes.

7. Add the tofu and simmer for another 15 minutes, until the goulash thickens to your desired consistency.

8. Once the potatoes are cooked, stir in the parsley.

9. Remove from heat and allow the goulash to rest for 5 minutes before serving.

Serves: 6

Prep time: 10 min

Cook time: 50 min

Total time: 60 min

Indian

This is Indian food at it's best. India generally doesn't eat any cows for religious restrictions, and generally use a lot of fresh fruits and vegetables. Northern India tends to use more grains and wheat, while the southern India style gravitates to rice.

I'm sure you will love Indian Cuisine. Just remember, sometimes their spices are a bit heavy for American tastebuds. I tone down my Indian recipes for people who aren't accustomed to their flavors. You can always add more spices in the same ratios if more is needed. This way you can control the depth and still get Simply Incredible Indian Flavor.

Indian

GOOD These items go well with this cuisine.		BETTER Even better pairing.		BEST The WOW factor!
allspice	pepper, black & white	cardamom	garlic	**CHICKPEAS**
almonds	pistachios	cauliflower	ginger	**CURRIES**
anise	poppy seeds	cilantro	nutmeg	**LEMON**
breads	saffron	cinnamon	potatoes	**LENTILS**
chili peppers	sage	coconut	rice, basmati	**SPICES**
chili powder	spinach	coriander	tomatoes	**TAHINI**
cloves	tamarind	cumin	vegetables	**TURMERIC**
eggplant		fennel		
fenugreek				
ghee				
herbs				
hummus				
mace				
mint				
paprika				
peas				

SIMPLY INCREDIBLE PAIRINGS

chickpeas + garlic + lemon + tahini + salt

cinnamon + cloves + nutmeg

coriander + cumin + turmeric

cumin + garlic + ginger

garlic + ginger

garlic + ginger + onion

potatoes + chili powder + turmeric

INDIAN RECIPES

Paratha

This is the ultimate whole wheat Indian Flat Bread. One of the most popular staples in all of Indian cooking.

Ingredients

2 cups whole wheat flour

1 tsp oil

½ teaspoon salt

3/4 to 1 cup water as needed

spray oil for cooking, add as required

Directions

For The Dough:

1. In a bowl, take whole wheat flour. add salt, oil and water.

2. Mix and then knead into a smooth soft dough. Add more water if required while kneading. Or add more flour if it is tacky.

3. Cover and set the dough aside for 30 minutes.

Folding Concepts:

Triangular fold:

1. Pinch a medium sized ball from the dough. Flatten and dust with some flour.

2. With a rolling pin, roll into a circle of about 4 inches diameter.

3. Spray lightly on the dough circle. fold in half. Spray on this half and fold again. Now you have a triangle shape.

4. Dust some flour on the folded triangle, and begin to roll the folded triangle.

5. Add some flour if needed and roll into about an 8 inch size triangle.

Square fold:

1. Roll a medium sized ball on a lightly dusted board to a circle of about 4 to 5 inches in diameter.

2. Lightly spray with oil on the rolled dough.

3. Bring one side of rolled dough towards the center and press lightly. Spray the folded part. Fold the opposite side of the rolled dough on top of the folded part, press lightly. And again spray. Repeat this process for the top and bottom and you will end up with a square.

4. Sprinkle some flour on the folded paratha, and begin to roll. Add some more flour if needed while rolling. Roll into about an 8 inch square paratha.

Cooking the Paratha:

1. Heat on medium-high, a large skillet or an electric griddle works well.

2. Place a paratha on the griddle. you will soon see the paratha puffing up from the base at some places.

3. Flip the paratha when the base is about 1/4 cooked. Spray the top lightly.

4. Flip again when the second side is about 1/2 cooked. You will notice some brown spots. Lightly spray this side now.

5. Flip again a couple of times till you see more brown spots and the paratha is cooked evenly. Make all parathas this way. Either serve them hot or stack them in a cloth lined basket.

6. These can be used for many things. Traditionally served with any Indian dal or vegetable curry.

Serves: 8 » Prep time: 15 min
Cook time: 20 min » Total time: 35 min

INDIAN RECIPES

Red Bell Pepper Parathas

Ingredients

1 cup fire roasted red bell pepper

1/2 cup water

1 tomato, chopped

1 tsp onion, powder

1/2 tsp turmeric, powder

1/2 tsp salt

1/4 tsp pepper

2 cups whole wheat flour

Directions

1. Blend all the ingredients except the flour in a blender. I prefer not to blend it until completely smooth. Leave some little visible pieces.

2. In a bowl, mix the flour with the liquid. Knead well, You may need to add water or flour. You are looking for a soft dough that is not tacky.

3. Let dough rest for a minimum of 30 minutes.

4. Divide the dough into 8 portions. Roll into balls and with a little flour and a rolling pin, roll out into 6-8 inch circles.

5. Heat, a large skillet or an electric griddle, on medium-high.

6. Place the parathas on the griddle and spray lightly with oil, flip and spray the other side.

7. Cook for a couple minutes on each side, until slight browning occurs.

8. Serve hot, or place in a cloth lined basket.

Serves: 8

Prep time: 15 min

Cook time: 20 min

Total time: 35 min

INDIAN RECIPES

Indian Dal

Ingredients

2 Tbsp olive oil

1 yellow onion, chopped fine

4 cloves garlic, minced

2 Tbsp ginger, fresh chopped

1 tsp whole cumin seeds

1/4 tsp cardamom, ground

2 cups red lentils, rinsed

4 cups vegetable stock

2 cup chopped tomatoes, with juice

1 tsp turmeric, ground

1/4 tsp sea salt

1 jalapeño, seeded and chopped fine

1/2 cup chopped fresh cilantro

Directions

1. In a large pot over medium high heat, sauté onions and cook until softened, about 5 minutes.

2. Add garlic and ginger, cumin, and cardamom. Sauté until fragrant, about 2 minutes.

3. Add lentils, stock, tomatoes, turmeric, salt and jalapeño and bring to a boil. Reduce heat to medium low, cover and simmer, stirring often, until lentils are soft, about 15 minutes.

4. Remove from heat and stir in cilantro.

5. Ladle into bowls and serve.

Serves: 4 to 6

Prep time: 10 min

Cook time: 25 min

Total time: 35 min

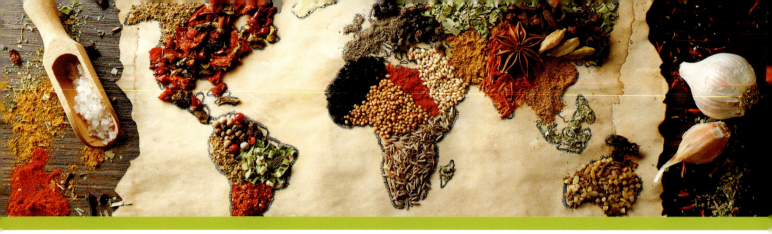

INDIAN RECIPES

Garam Masala Spice Blend

Ingredients

2 small dried red chilies

1 tsp black peppercorns (or 1/2 tsp ground black pepper)

1 tsp cumin seeds (or 1/2 tsp ground cumin)

1 tsp cardamom pods (or 1/2 tsp ground cardamom)

1/2 tsp cloves (or 1/4 tsp ground cloves)

1/8 tsp nutmeg

Directions:

Grind in grinder, and/or mix into a powder with mortar and pestle. Store in airtight container.

Yield: 1/4 cup

INDIAN RECIPES

Chana Masala

Chana Masala is a popular Northern India entree, but also has a huge presence through all of India, and Pakistan. While there are hundreds of variations of Chana Masala, this version with green chili, cilantro, and garam masala, will delight everybody. A healthy, plant-based meal that's easy to make and has Simply Incredible Flavor.

Ingredients

3 Tbsp olive oil (or do a water sauté)

1 onion, large yellow, finely diced

1 Tbsp cumin, ground

1/2 tsp sea salt, divided

4 garlic cloves, minced

1 Tbsp ginger, fresh minced

1/2 cup fresh cilantro, chopped

3 green chilies, fresh sliced with seeds

1 Tbsp coriander, ground

1 tsp chili powder

1 tsp turmeric, ground

1 cup water

1 - 28 oz can diced tomatoes

2 - 15 oz cans chickpeas, drained

1 tsp garam masala (recipe included if needed) *(see previous page)*

2 tsp coconut sugar

2 Tbsp lemon juice, plus more to taste

1/2 cup cilantro, fresh for garnish

Directions

1. In a large pot over medium heat, sauté onion, cumin, and 1/4 tsp salt. OR do a water sauté with 1/4 cup water, stirring till water evaporates. Repeat water sauté, if needed to soften onions.

2. Add garlic, ginger, cilantro, and green chilies.

3. Next add coriander, chili powder, and turmeric. Add a little more oil at this point if the pan is looking dry. OR add another 1/4 cup of water for a sauté. Mix, allowing water to reduce.

4. Add 1 cup water, pureed tomatoes, chickpeas and remaining 1/4 tsp salt. You are looking for a soup consistency at this point, and it will cook down into more of a stew.

5. Simmer uncovered for 15-20 minutes, until thick and stew-like. Stir occasionally.

6. When the Chana Masala is thickened and bubbly, taste and adjust seasonings as needed. Add more salt for saltiness, chili powder for heat, and now is when you can add the coconut sugar for sweetness.

7. Remove from heat and stir in the lemon juice and Garam Masala. Stir to mix, then let cool slightly before serving.

8. Garnish with fresh cilantro and lemon.

Chef's Note:

Chana Masala can be enjoyed as a stew on its own. It's great served with white or brown rice. You can also use this Chana Masala to smother potatoes or sweet potatoes. This is a good dish to make big batches and freeze.

Serves: 6 » Prep time: 5 min
Cook time: 25 min » Total time: 30 min

INDIAN RECIPES

Aloo Gobi

Aloo Gobi is a popular vegetarian dish from India. It is most popular in Indian, Bangladeshi, Pakistani, and Nepali cuisines.

Ingredients

1/4 cup olive oil OR water sauté

1 large onion, diced

1 tsp cumin seed

1 Tbsp ginger, fresh, peeled and grated

2 cloves garlic, chopped

2 tsp turmeric

1 tsp salt

1 bunch cilantro, separate stalks and leaves. roughly chopped

1 small green chili, diced (or one tsp chili powder)

1 - 15 oz can diced tomatoes, with juice

1/2 water

1 large cauliflower, core removed and broken apart

3 large potatoes, peeled and cut into one inch pieces

2 tsp Garam Masala spice blend (page 354)

Directions

1. In a large pot, sauté the chopped onion and one teaspoon of cumin seeds.

2. Add chopped cilantro stalks, turmeric, chilis, ginger, garlic, and salt. Allow to blend ingredients by adding 1/4 cup of water and reduce.

3. Stir in tomatoes and another 1/4 cup water.

4. Add potatoes and cauliflower and mix well to cover completely with the sauce.

5. Cover and simmer for 20 minutes until potatoes are cooked.

6. Add 2 teaspoons of Garam Masala, and stir in well.

7. Turn off the heat, cover, and let rest for 10 minutes.

Serves: 8

Prep time: 10 min

Cook time: 30 min

Total time: 40 min

Irish

Irish corned beef and cabbage would not be the same without the potatoes. Interestingly enough potatoes weren't even introduced to Ireland until the 18th century. To travel back farther, we would need to look at the Celtic culinary history that has evolved into the Irish cuisine that we know today.

Healthy versions of Irish cooking is ample, in large part due to many of the monastic orders of the region who had adapted strict vegetarian diets.

Irish

GOOD These items go well with this cuisine.		BETTER Even better pairing.	BEST The WOW factor!
apples	oats	**beets**	**CABBAGE**
basil	oregano	**carrots**	**POTATOES**
bay leaf	parsley	**garlic**	
breads	peas	**mint**	
broccoli	parsnips	**onions**	
butter substitute	pickling	**rosemary**	
cauliflower	salt	**sage**	
cloves	savory	**tomatoes**	
coriander	squash		
herbs	thyme		
honey	vegetable broth		
lentils	vegetables		
maple syrup	vinegars		
marjoram			

SIMPLY INCREDIBLE PAIRINGS

cabbage + carrots + potatoes

potatoes + rosemary + salt

358

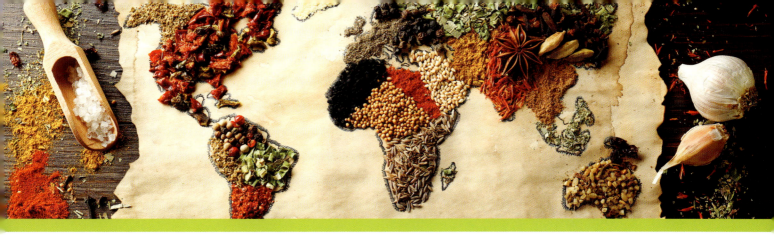

IRISH RECIPES

1 Hour Shepherd's Pie

This is a hearty, 9-ingredient vegan Shepherd's Pie that is loaded with veggies and savory lentils. It's simple to make, but still has Simply Incredible Flavor.

Ingredients

Mashed Potatoes

3 pounds potatoes, thoroughly washed

2 Tbsp vegan butter

Salt and pepper to taste

Filling

1 medium onion, diced

2 cloves garlic, minced

1 1/2 cups uncooked brown or green lentils, rinsed and drained

4 cups vegetable stock

1 Tbsp fresh thyme

1 10-ounce bag frozen mixed veggies: peas, carrots, green beans and corn

Thicken with slurry of: 3 Tbsp cornstarch mixed with 1/4 cup cold water.

Directions

1. Chop potatoes in large cubes, and place in a large pot filled with water until they're covered. Bring to a boil on medium high heat. Cover and cook for 30 minutes, or until fully cooked.

2. Once cooked, drain. Mash until smooth. Add vegan butter and season with salt and pepper to taste. Cover and set aside. You can always use a little soy milk to thin potatoes if needed.

3. Preheat oven to 400 degrees and lightly grease a 9x13 baking dish.

4. In a large saucepan over medium heat, sauté onions until lightly browned, about 5 minutes.

5. Add garlic and sauté for another minute.

6. Add the lentils, vegetable stock, thyme, salt and pepper. Bring to a low boil, then reduce heat to simmer. Continue cooking until lentils are tender, about 30 minutes.

7. Add the frozen veggies, stir, and cover to melt the flavors together.

8. When lentils are boiling again, thicken with the slurry of water and cornstarch.

9. Taste and adjust seasonings as needed. Then transfer to your prepared baking dish.

10. Carefully top with mashed potatoes. Smooth down with a spoon or fork.

11. Place on a baking sheet to catch overflow and bake for 20 minutes, until lightly browned on top.

12. Let cool briefly before serving. The longer it sits, the more it will thicken.

Serves: 6 » Prep time: 15 min

Cook time: 45 min » Total time: 60 min

IRISH RECIPES

Scottish Oatcakes

Ingredients

1 1/2 cups old-fashioned oats

1 cup all purpose flour

1/2 cup sugar

1/2 teaspoon baking soda

1/4 teaspoon salt

1/2 cup chilled vegan margarine, cut into pieces

1/4 cup almond milk, unsweetened

Directions

1. Preheat oven to 350 degrees.

2. Lightly spray with vegetable oil, two parchment lined baking sheets.

3. Place oats in large bowl. Sift flour, and add sugar, baking soda and salt into same bowl.

4. Using a fork and your fingers, rub in vegan butter into mixture until it resembles coarse meal.

5. Add almond milk. Stir until dough forms. Transfer dough to a floured surface.

6. Roll out dough to 1/4-inch thick. Using 2 1/2 inch round cookie cutter, cut out rounds. Arrange on the baking sheets, leaving a little space in-between. Gather the remaining pieces, re-roll and cut out additional rounds.

7. Bake oatcakes until edges are light golden, about 12 minutes. Transfer baking sheets to racks and cool 5 minutes. They are ready to serve.

Serves: 18 cakes

Prep time: 5 min

Cook time: 15 min

Total time: 20 min

IRISH RECIPES

Irish Soda Bread

Ingredients

1 1/2 cups almond milk, unsweetened

1 1/2 Tbsp lemon juice

2 cups white pastry flour

2 cups whole wheat flour

½ cup sugar

2 tsp baking soda

1 tsp salt

4 Tbsp vegan margarine

1 cup currants or raisins

1 tsp caraway seeds, optional

Directions

1. Preheat oven to 350 degrees. Lightly spray a baking sheet with cooking spray.

2. In a small bowl, combine soy milk and lemon juice. Set aside.

3. In a large bowl, sift together flours, with sugar, soda, and salt. Mix well.

4. Use your fingers and a fork to cut butter into dry mixture. It should be crumbly.

5. Pour in soy milk mixture and currants.

6. On a lightly floured surface, gently knead just until the dough comes together, just 8 to 10 turns. Do not overwork or it will become tough.

7. On the baking sheet, shape into an oval disc about 2 inches in height.

8. Cut an "X" into the top with a serrated knife, sprinkle with caraway seeds, and bake for 40-45 minutes.

9. Allow to cool on a wire rack.

Chef's Notes:
This is a base recipe. And you can really add creativity to this. Try adding cinnamon and honey or molasses.

Serves: 8 to 10

Prep time: 10 min

Cook time: 45 min

Total time: 55 min

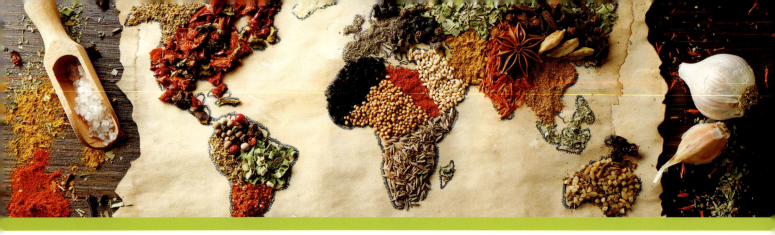

IRISH RECIPES

Irish Stew

Ingredients

2 Tbsp olive oil

2 stalks of celery, chopped

1 yellow onion, chopped

4 garlic cloves, minced

1/4 cup all-purpose flour

6 cups vegetable broth

3 carrots, cut into chunks

2 parsnips, cut into chunks

1/2 lb. mushrooms, quartered

3 cups baby or new potatoes, halved

1/2 cup tomato paste

2 bay leaves

2 tsp brown sugar

1 tsp dried thyme

3/4 tsp salt

1/2 tsp pepper

Directions

1. In a heavy bottom large pot over medium-high heat, sauté onions and celery until the onion becomes translucent.

2. Add garlic and sauté for another minute.

3. Sprinkle in the flour. Stir well and cook for another minute to heat up the flour.

4. Add the remaining ingredients, and stir well.

5. Bring to a boil, turn to medium low and simmer for about 20 minutes. Stirring often, so not to burn on the bottom.

6. This stew should be thick. If too thin, allow to reduce longer. If too thick, add a little water to thin.

Serves: 6

Prep time: 10 min

Cook time: 30 min

Total time: 40 min

Italian

While there are many regions that influence Italian cuisine, we will keep it simple by categorizing them as the north and south. Without writing a whole book on Italian cooking, I would like to just go over the basics.

The bigger differences between the north and the south is based on the history of farming. Northern territories had far more cattle so cheeses and butter were more widely available. In the south it was olive oil. Southern Italy uses far more tomatoes than the north.

Interestingly enough, pasta is predominant in the South while rice dominates in the North. Even in baking, the north produces cakes whereas the south produces pastries. And the most important difference is the spice. Northerners season with pepper while the south runs with chili - a lot of chili.

General Italian

GOOD These items go well with this cuisine.		BETTER Even better pairing.	BEST The WOW factor!
artichokes	saffron	**basil**	**CAPERS**
bell pepper	sage	**oregano**	**GARLIC**

cheese:
  Mozzarella
  Parmesan
  Ricotta
	spinach
	thyme
	zucchini
		pasta
		tomatoes and sauces
			OLIVES

eggplant			
fennel			
greens		### SIMPLY INCREDIBLE PAIRINGS	
honey		basil + garlic + oregano	
lemon		basil + garlic + olive oil	
Marsala		basil + garlic + tomatoes	
mushrooms		bell peppers + olive oil + tomatoes	
nuts		capers + garlic + wine vinegar	
olive oil		capers + lemon juice	
oranges and zest		garlic + olive oil + parsley	
parsley		garlic + oregano + tomato	
red pepper flakes		garlic + saffron	
rosemary		garlic + wine vinegar	
		red pepper flakes + fennel	

Italian, northern

GOOD These items go well with this cuisine.	BETTER Even better pairing.	BEST The WOW factor!
asparagus butter cheeses, rich and creamy hazelnuts Marsala nuts Pastas, egg based and ribbon pastas pine nuts potatoes truffles	basil beans lemon juice polenta rice vinegars	**CREAM SAUCES**

Italian, southern

GOOD These items go well with this cuisine.		BETTER Even better pairing.	BEST The WOW factor!
bell peppers cinnamon fennel marjoram olive oil	pasta - tube shapes pizza raisins red pepper flakes	chili peppers eggplant garlic oregano	**NUTMEG** **TOMATO AND SAUCES**

ITALIAN RECIPES

Ultimate Lasagna

There is good lasagna, and then there is great lasagna. And this is my Simply Incredible Lasagna. This recipe makes a big batch because I freeze portions for later use.

Ingredients

3 boxes dry lasagna noodles (no need to pre-cook)

3 quarts Pomodoro sauce, or spaghetti sauce

2 pounds vegan mozzarella cheese

1 - 24 oz jar vegenaise

2 -12 oz bags frozen spinach

1 -12 oz bag fresh shredded carrots

1 can green olives, grained and diced

1 can black olives, drained and diced

Directions

1. In 2, 9x12 lightly oiled pans we are going to begin layering. Start with a thin layer of sauce to keep the pasta from sticking to the pan.

2. Add a layer of the lasagna noodles. Spread thin layers of spinach, carrots, olives, shredded cheese, sauce and veganaise.

3. Then add another of lasagna and press down on the layer to tighten it up. Repeat the layering again. Top with the final, third layer of pasta, and then cover with sauce and cheese.

4. You will want to cover this with an oven safe saran wrap and foil, cook at 350 for one hour and fifteen minutes.

5. Remove covering and allow to cool for 15 minutes before serving.

Chef's Notes:

After the lasagna cools, we slice and freeze it. After it is frozen, you can actually break apart the pieces where you cut them. Then wrap the individual pieces in saran wrap and foil. Keep frozen then pull out a portion at a time.

ITALIAN RECIPES

Alfredo Sauce

This is my signature Alfredo Sauce. It is very easy to make, and it tastes Simply Incredible.

Ingredients

1 package extra firm tofu

2 cups soy milk, plain

1 cup rice Parmesan cheese

1 tsp onion powder

1 tsp garlic powder

1/2 tsp salt

1/4 tsp red pepper

1/4 tsp nutmeg

Directions:

1. Blend all the ingredients together in a blender until smooth.

2. Heat in a medium heavy bottom sauce pot. Stir constantly.

3. Serve.

Chef's Notes:

The tricky part is to get the right consistency. I will generally add a couple more tablespoons of soy milk when it heats up. And if it is too thin, you can simply cook it a little longer and it will thicken. If you are going to stir into your favorite pasta, I would keep it on the thinner side because the pasta will soak up some moisture.

ITALIAN RECIPES

Vegan Pesto

Ingredients

1/2 cup pine nuts

1/2 cup olive oil

1/2 cup nutritional yeast

5 cloves garlic

1 bunch fresh basil leaves (about 2 cups)

salt and pepper to taste

Directions

1. Lightly toast the pine nuts in a skillet over medium heat, stirring constantly.

2. In a food processor, gradually mix the pine nuts, olive oil, garlic, nutritional yeast, and basil, and process until smooth. Season with salt and pepper.

Chef's Notes:

This is delicious on pasta or spread on French bread then toast in the oven.

Yield 1 cup

Prep time: 5 min

Total time: 5 min

ITALIAN RECIPES

Simple Pasta e Fagioli Recipe

This is an easy base recipe. Ditalini pasta is commonly used for Pasta e Fagioli, but any short pasta will work.

Ingredients

3 Tbsp olive oil or water sauté

1 cup onion, chopped

1 large carrot, peeled and chopped

1 large celery stalk, chopped

2 garlic cloves, minced

1/4 tsp crushed red pepper flakes

2 tsp Italian seasoning

6 cups vegetable stock

2 cups tomatoes, chopped

1/2 pound ditalini pasta

2 - 15oz cans cannellini beans, drained and rinsed (or 4 cups of freshly cooked beans)

1/4 cup chopped parsley

Salt and black pepper to taste

Directions

1. Sauté the onions, carrots and celery until its soft and translucent. Add the garlic, red pepper flakes and Italian seasoning and sauté for another minute.

2. Add the vegetable stock, beans, and tomatoes, and bring to a boil.

3. Add the pasta and keep the soup at a simmer.

4. When the pasta is al dente, turn off the heat and stir in the parsley.

5. Add salt and black pepper to taste.

Chef's Notes:

Traditionally, Pasta e Fagioli is made with cushion meat, a cut of pork. Meat substitutes like Butler Soy Curls work great, just break them up a bit and add to soup. Another twist is to use any type of beans. Pinto beans are actually very popular. And you can also make the soup a thicker type with a little tomato paste.

Serves: 4 to 6

Prep time: 15 min

Cook time: 35 min

Total time: 50 min

ITALIAN RECIPES

Minestrone Soup

Minestrone soup is simply a thick vegetable soup with pasta. You can also use rice or potatoes in place of pasta.

Ingredients

2 Tbsp vegetable oil or water sauté

1 large onion, diced

4 cloves garlic, minced

6 cups vegetable broth

1 - 28 oz can diced tomatoes

3 Tbsp tomato paste

1 - 14 oz can crushed tomatoes

1 - 15 oz can kidney beans, drained and rinsed

2 stalks celery, diced

1 large carrot, diced

2 cups green beans, 1/2 in cut

1 tsp dried oregano

1 tsp dried basil

2 tsp chili powder

1/2 tsp cumin, powder

sea salt to taste

ground pepper to taste

1 cup elbow pasta, dry

Directions

1. Sauté the onion and cook until translucent, about 5 minutes. Add the garlic and cook another 30 seconds.

2. Add the remaining ingredients, except the pasta. Simmer for 30 minutes.

3. Add the pasta and simmer for another 20 minutes, and serve.

Chef's notes:

The difference between a good minestrone and a great minestrone is the chili powder. In the restaurants, we will often make the soup without the pasta for storage and or freezing. And then we simply add cooked pasta to the soup prior to serving. This keeps the pasta from over cooking.

Serves: 6

Prep time: 10 min

Cook time: 55 min

Total time: 65 min

Latin American

Latin American cuisine is a blended mix of unique flavors influenced by the diverse cultures of many Latin American countries. The variety comes in because multiple countries use specific spices, often differing amounts of the same spice.

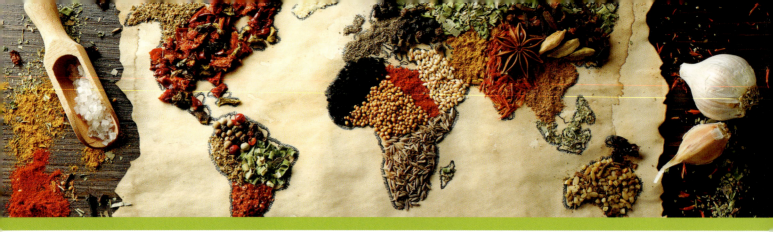

Latin American

GOOD These items go well with this cuisine.		BETTER Even better pairing.	BEST The WOW factor!
beans, black	onions	**cardamom**	**CHOCOLATE**
bell peppers	orange	**chile peppers**	**CILANTRO**
carrots	paprika	**coconut milk**	**CLOVES**
cassava (yuca root)	parsley	**lemons**	**COCONUT**
celery	pepper	**peppers**	**LIME**
chickpeas	potatoes	**saffron**	**POMEGRANATES**
collard greens	pumpkin	**salt**	**RICE**
coffee	rosemary	**tomatoes**	
curry	savory		
garlic	shallots		
ginger	spinach		
honey	sugar		
kale	tarragon		
malanga (yautía root)	thyme		
mint	truffles		
mushrooms	vinegar		
nutmeg	yams		

SIMPLY INCREDIBLE PAIRINGS

cloves + carrots + mushrooms + onions + peppers

cloves + honey + pumpkin

coconut + lime

lemon + mint

lime + mint + onions + tomatoes + salt

rice + saffron + salt

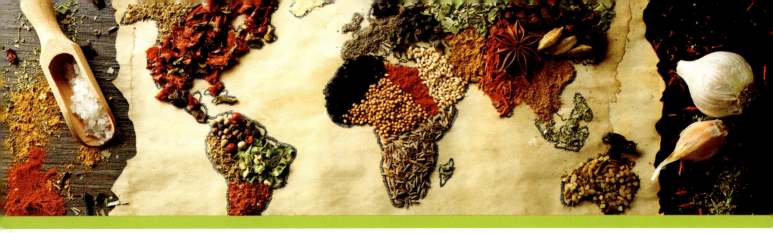

LATIN AMERICAN RECIPES

Vegan Ceviche

This is a fabulous substitute for seafood or fish ceviche, without the risk of food poisoning that the raw marinated seafood ceviche is known for.

These items go well with this cuisine.

Ingredients

2 cans jackfruit, in brine

8 limes, juiced

3 tomatoes, peeled seeded and diced

5 green onions, fine sliced

2 stalks celery, sliced

1/2 yellow bell pepper, diced

1/4 cup fresh parsley, chopped

1/4 cup chopped fresh cilantro

pinch of crushed red chili peppers

pinch of salt

pinch of pepper

Directions

1. Boil jack fruit for 40 minutes. and cool.

2. In a large bowl, break up the jack fruit into pieces to simulate the meat from a white fish ……sort of flakey.

3. Add the remaining ingredients and let rest for a couple hours, allowing the flavors to blend.

4. Mix and serve.

Chef's Notes:

Jack fruit is readily available at Asian food stores. Ceviche is usually accompanied by side dishes that compliment its flavors, such as sweet potato, lettuce, corn, avocado or plantains. Make sure you add some spice to this recipe. I use the crushed red chili pepper, but you can also use jalapeño or hot pepper spices.

Serves: 6 to 8

Prep time: 10 min

Cook time: 40 min

Total time: 50 min

LATIN AMERICAN RECIPES

Sopapillas

Sopapillas is a delicate fried or baked bread generally served with honey or sprinkled with powdered sugar.

Ingredients

1 cup all-purpose flour

1 1/2 tsp baking powder

1/4 tsp salt

1 Tbsp coconut oil (cold)

1/3 cup warm water

Oil for deep-fat frying

Honey and Confectioners sugar

Directions

1. In a large bowl, combine flour, baking powder and salt.

2. Cut in coconut oil until mixture resembles fine crumbs.

3. Gradually add water, tossing with a fork until a loose ball forms (dough will be crumbly).

4. On a lightly floured surface, knead the dough for about 3 minutes, until smooth.

5. Cover and let rest for 15 minutes.

6. Roll out dough to about 1/4 in thick.

7. Using a small round biscuit cutter, cut out circles, Re-roll out scraps and repeat.

8. In a heavy bottom pot, heat 2 inches of oil to 375 degrees.

9. Fry Sopapillas for 1-2 minutes on each side.

10. Drain on paper towels, keep warm in oven or serve immediately.

11. Serve with honey and/or dust with confectioners' sugar if desired.

Chef's Notes:

You can also make square Sopapillas, which is more of a northern Mexican style. And for a simple non-fried concept, you can simply use filo dough, cut squares and bake them in the oven.

Serves: 6 to 8

Prep time: 10 min

Cook time: 55 min

Total time: 65 min

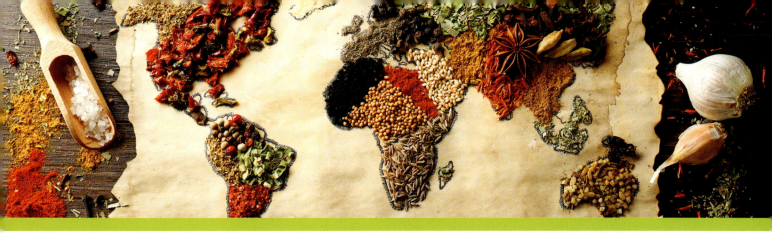

LATIN AMERICAN RECIPES

Sancocho

Sancocho is a traditional Panama root stew in several Latin American cuisines derived from the Spanish dish known as cocido.

Ingredients

1/4 cup of olive oil or water sauté

1 onion, chopped

1 bell peppers, red chopped

4 garlic cloves, chopped

1 cup of yellow split peas

4 qts of vegetable broth

2 medium carrots, peeled and chopped

1 cup mushrooms, buttons quartered

1 cup cassava (yuca root), peeled and cut into small pieces

1 cup malanga (yautía root), chopped

1 cup West Indian pumpkin, chopped

1 cup yams, chopped

1 corn on the cob, cut into 1/2" slices

1 Tbsp of dry oregano leaves

1 Tbsp chili powder

A bunch of cilantro and parsley, chopped

Salt to taste

pepper to taste

Directions

1. In a large boiling pot, sauté the onions and bell peppers for about 5 to 7 minutes until onions are golden.

2. Add the garlic and sauté for 30 seconds.

3. Add the remaining ingredients, except for the cilantro and parsley. Simmer for about 45 minutes to an hour. Everything should be tender.

4. Add the cilantro and parsley.

5. Season with salt and pepper to taste.

Chef Notes:

Traditionally this dish would be served with spicy bitter orange vinegar and white rice on the side. As far as the roots, and pumpkin, you can really use any roots like taro, and any winter squash works well too. If you're adding potatoes, use more dense potatoes like baby reds or yukon, or chopped fingerlings with the skin on are fabulous both for presentation and texture.

Serves: 8

Prep time: 30 min

Cook time: 2 hours

Total time: 2.5 hours

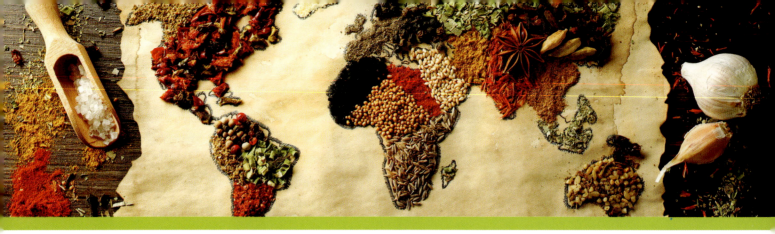

LATIN AMERICAN RECIPES

Brazilian Cocadas

Cocadas vary greatly from country to country. The Brazilian version resembles a macaroon. This vegan version is so good, you will start making double batches.

Ingredients

3 cup of shredded coconut

2 1/2 Tbsp of corn starch

1 tsp of cinnamon

1/4 tsp of salt

1/2 cup of walnuts, finely chopped

1 cup of vegan condensed coconut milk

Directions

1. Preheat oven to 375 degrees.

2. Meanwhile in a medium mixing bowl combine all the ingredients except the condensed milk.

3. Stir thoroughly making sure to break up any clumps.

4. Pour in the condensed milk and stir to coat evenly.

5. Cover cookie sheet with either parchment paper.

6. Using two tablespoons, drop rounded mounds onto the cookie sheet. they should be tighter on the insides, and have pieces of coconut hanging out here and there on the outsides. Make sure to give them a 1 inch space.

7. Bake for around 10-15 minutes or until light to golden brown.

8. Allow to cool before moving.

Chef's Notes:

For sweet and condensed coconut milk, I use 'Let's Do Organic' brand. Or here is a recipe (*see next page*) for making your own. It just takes time, but can be done at home.

Serves: 6

Prep time: 10 min

Cook time: 15 min

Total time: 25 min

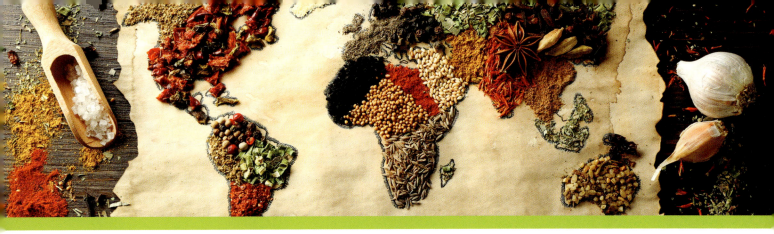

LATIN AMERICAN RECIPES

Vegan Condensed Milk

A popular ingredient in many dessert recipes is sweetened condensed milk. This can be done vegan, if you're up for the challenge. By swapping almond milk for cow's milk you get a vegan alternative to condensed milk that works perfect in any recipe that calls for sweetened condensed milk.

Ingredients

2 cups almond or soy milk

1 cup maple syrup

1 tsp of vanilla extract

oil

Directions

1. Using a paper towel spread layer of oil around the inside of the saucepan. This will help keep the sugars and the milk from sticking to the pan.

2. Pour milk into the pan and heat on medium heat until the milk begins to simmer.

3. Add in the sweetener of choice and vanilla extract. Lower heat to low and stir consistently for about an hour.

4. It is done when it has thickened. It should be reduced by at least half. Let cool.

5. The condensed vegan milk will continue to thicken as it sits.

6. You can refrigerate if not using the same day.

LATIN AMERICAN RECIPES

Banana and Black Bean Empanadas

This is a healthier version of the classic Argentinean pastry. These Empanadas are made with some added whole-wheat flour, and are baked instead of fried.

Ingredients Crust:

1½ cups whole-wheat flour

1 cup all-purpose flour

1½ tsp salt

½ tsp chili powder

4 Tbsp cold vegan margarine, cut into 1/2-inch cubes

½ cup unsweetened applesauce

1 Tbsp apple cider vinegar

Directions for Crust:

1. Sift flours, salt, and chili powder in bowl.

2. Cut in margarine with fork until mixture resembles coarse meal.

3. In separate bowl, whisk together applesauce, vinegar, and 1/3 cup cold water.

4. Stir applesauce mixture into flour mixture until textured dough forms. Add up to 1/4 cup more water, if necessary.

5. Knead on lightly floured surface until dough comes together. Form into ball, wrap in plastic wrap, and chill 1 hour, or overnight.

Ingredients Filling:

1 Tbsp olive oil or water sauté

1 medium onion, chopped (1 cup)

1 cup cooked black beans

1 clove garlic, minced (1 tsp)

2 bananas, peeled and diced (1 cup)

1 tsp ground cumin

¼ tsp cayenne pepper

¼ tsp ground coriander

2 Tbsp chopped fresh cilantro

1 tsp red pepper sauce, such as Tabasco

Direction for Filling:

1. Sauté onion 4 to 5 minutes, or until soft and translucent.

2. Add beans and garlic, reduce heat to medium, and cook 3 minutes.

3. Stir in bananas, cumin, cayenne, and coriander, and cook 2 minutes, or until bananas begin to break down and spices are fragrant.

4. Remove from heat, and stir in cilantro and red pepper sauce.

LATIN AMERICAN RECIPES

Direction Putting them Together:

1. Preheat oven to 400°F.

2. Divide dough into 12 balls.

3. Coat baking sheet with cooking spray.

4. Roll out each ball to 6-inch round (1/4-inch thick) on lightly floured work surface.

5. Fill with 2 tablespoons of filling, and brush edges of pastry with water.

6. Fold dough circle in half, press to close, and crimp edges with fork to seal.

7. Transfer to prepared baking sheet, and repeat with remaining dough balls and filling.

8. Bake Empanadas 20 minutes, or until golden brown and crusty.

9. Cool 5 minutes on baking sheet before serving.

Serves: 12 Empanadas

Prep time: 20 min

Cook time: 30 min

Total time: 50 min

BONUS FILLING #2

Sweet Potato, Chickpea, & Spinach Empanadas

Ingredients

2 cups water

2 medium sweet potatoes, finely diced

2 medium shallots, peeled and diced

2 garlic cloves, peeled and minced

1/2 cup canned light coconut milk

1 1/2 tsp curry powder

2 cups spinach fresh, chopped

1 - 16 oz can chickpeas, drained and rinsed

1/4 cup fresh cilantro, roughly chopped

1 tsp salt

1/2 tsp ground nutmeg

1/4 tsp red pepper flakes

Directions for filling:

1. In a medium boiling pot, simmer water and sweet potatoes until water is almost evaporated.

2. Add shallots and garlic and sauté for a minute.

3. Add remaining ingredients and stir well, until the mixture is tight and not runny.

4. Use this mixture for the filling.

Mediterranean

Mediterranean Cuisine is without a country to call home. It's a culinary concept that was created out of thin air. Some of the countries around the Mediterranean Sea are Spain, France, Italy, Greece, Syria, Lebanon, and Israel. All of these countries have their own distinct styles of food and cooking. And none of them are exclusively 'Mediterranean Cuisine'.

The largest common denominator of Mediterranean Cuisine is olive oil.

There is a perception that the Mediterranean Diet is healthy and it is often attributed to their use of olive oil. We need to consider the other elements and not give the credit exclusively to olive oil. First, even the Mediterranean people don't use excessive amounts of oil. Secondly, they have better portion control than typically found in other cultures, and they also eat an abundance of fruits and vegetables, and whole grains.

 And that's what we are going to stick to when it comes to achieving Simply Incredible Mediterranean Flavor.

Mediterranean

GOOD
These items go well with this cuisine.

asparagus	raisins
basil	salt
beans	savory
bell pepper	thyme
cheese	zucchini
chocolate	
cinnamon	
citrus	
fennel	
grapes	
greens	
honey	
marjoram	
Marsala	
olive oil	
oranges, zest	
oregano	
parsley	
pasta	
peppermint	
pestos	

BETTER
Even better pairing.

- artichokes
- chili peppers
- eggplant
- garlic
- herbs
- lemon juice
- nutmeg
- olives, black, green
- potatoes
- rice
- rosemary
- saffron
- sage
- spinach
- sun-dried tomatoes
- tomatoes and sauces
- vinegars, all

BEST
The WOW factor!

- **CAPERS**
- **KALAMATA OLIVES**
- **LEMON**
- **VEGETABLES**

SIMPLY INCREDIBLE PAIRINGS

asparagus + garlic + lemon + tomatoes + onion

eggplant + garlic + tomato

garlic + herbs + lemon

marjoram + rosemary + savory + thyme

MEDITERRANEAN RECIPES

Easy Mediterranean Orzo Pasta

Ingredients

2 Tbsp olive oil or water sauté

1 large onion, diced

3 cloves garlic, minced

1 1/2 cups orzo

4 cups vegetable broth

1 cup parsley, minced

1 cup marinated artichokes, drained and roughly chopped

1/2 cup pitted Kalamata olives, finely chopped

1/2 cup sun-dried tomatoes, finely chopped

1/4 cup toasted pine nuts (optional)

Directions:

1. In a high-sided 10-inch skillet, sauté onions for about 5 minutes.

2. Add the garlic and sauté for 30 seconds.

3. Add the vegetable broth and orzo, and bring to a boil.

4. Reduce heat and simmer, stirring frequently. Make sure the orzo doesn't stick to the bottom of the pan.

5. Continue cooking until the orzo is al dente and broth has thickened, 10 to 15 minutes depending on your brand of orzo.

6. Add the artichokes, olives, sun-dried tomatoes, and parsley, and stir until well combined.

7. Remove from heat, cover and allow flavors to blend for 5 minutes.

8. Garnish with pine nuts.

Serves: 4 to 6

Prep time: 10 min

Cook time: 20 min

Total time: 30 min

MEDITERRANEAN RECIPES

Mediterranean Spiced Freekeh Salad

This salad is the perfect combination of ingredients that not only looks and tastes great, it also provides high energy nutrients. Freekeh is a cereal food made from green durum wheat that is roasted and rubbed to create its unique flavor.

For the salad:

1/4 cup sesame seeds

1 cup Freekeh

1 bunch kale, de-stemmed, chopped small (about 2 cups)

1 cup chickpeas, rinsed and drained

1 small fennel bulb, quartered, cored and thinly sliced

Directions

1. Warm a small, dry saucepan over medium heat and add the sesame seeds. Toast until fragrant and light golden-brown, 6 to 7 minutes.

2. Shake the pan periodically to avoid burning. Once toasted, pour the seeds onto a clean plate and aside to cool.

3. Bring a medium size pot with 2 1/2 cups of water to a boil.

4. Add the Freekeh. Bring back to a boil, then cover the pot and reduce the heat to low for 15 minutes.

5. Remove from heat, and keep covered for another 15 minutes.

6. Drain any excess water.

7. In a large bowl, combine cooked Freekeh, collard greens, chickpeas, and fennel.

8. Toss the salad with the dressing, season with additional salt and pepper as needed. Sprinkle the sesame seeds over top before serving.

9. Enjoy room temperature or cold. Cover and refrigerate leftovers for up to three days.

For the dressing:

2 garlic cloves, minced

3 Tbsp extra-virgin olive oil

3 Tbsp tahini

1 lemon, juiced

1 Tbsp apple cider vinegar

2 1/2 Tbsp za'atar

1 tsp ground coriander

1/2 tsp ground allspice

Pinch sea salt and ground pepper

Directions

1. In a small bowl, whisk together all the ingredients.

2. Season with salt and pepper.

Chef's Note:

If you do not find Freekeh, use Bulgar Wheat, and add a tablespoon of soy sauce to the water.

Serves: 6 » **Prep time:** 20 min

Cook time: 40 min » **Total time:** 60 min

MEDITERRANEAN RECIPES

Mediterranean Cauliflower Couscous Salad
WITH ROASTED CHICKPEAS & LEMON DIJON DRESSING

For the salad:

1 large head cauliflower, cut into florets

1 1/2 cups cherry tomatoes, sliced in half

1/2 red onion, diced

1/2 cup Kalamata olives, chopped

1 English cucumber, diced

1 cup parsley, finely chopped

1/4 tsp crushed red pepper flakes

Salt and pepper to taste

Lemon Dijon Dressing (see recipe)

Roasted Chick peas (see recipe)

Directions:

1. In a food processor, place the cauliflower florets and pulse into 'couscous'. Be careful not to over process, just pulse, you don't want cauliflower puree.

2. Transfer the cauliflower to a large bowl and combine with the cherry tomatoes, onion, olives, cucumber, parsley, and crushed red pepper flakes. Toss well. Slowly drizzle with dressing and season to taste with salt and pepper.

3. Top with roasted chickpeas and serve.

Chef's Notes:

The salad can be made a day ahead of time, but the roasted chickpeas won't stay crispy after a day, so enjoy them right away.

Serves: 4 to 6 » Prep time: 10 min
Cook time: 40 min » Total time: 50 min

For the Lemon Dijon Dressing:

2 Tbsp fresh lemon juice

1/2 tsp dijon style mustard

1 garlic clove, minced

1/2 tsp sea salt

1/4 cup olive oil

To make the dressing:

1. Mix the lemon juice, mustard, garlic and salt in a bowl.

2. Drizzle in olive oil while whisking continuously. Taste and adjust seasonings if needed.

For the Roasted Chickpeas:

1 1/2 cups chickpeas, cooked, and patted dry

1 Tbsp olive oil

1/2 tsp ground cumin

1/4 tsp sea salt

1/8 tsp cayenne pepper

Directions:

1. Preheat the oven to 400 degrees.

2. In a bowl, mix the chickpeas with spices and oil.

3. Lay them on a parchment-lined baking sheet and bake in the oven until browned and crisp, about 35 to 40 minutes. Shake chickpeas halfway through to cook them evenly.

MEDITERRANEAN RECIPES

Matbucha

Matbucha is a spicy roasted tomato-based spread that makes a perfect topping for any Mediterranean dish.

Ingredients

8 tomatoes, large vine-ripened

2 green peppers

2 onions

6 garlic cloves

2 onions

1/4 cup olive oil

1/2 tsp sea salt

1/4 tsp pepper, ground

1 lemon, juiced

1 Tbsp tomato paste (2 if needed)

1 tsp schug (see recipe on next page)

Directions

1. Preheat oven to 375.

2. Line a baking sheet with parchment paper.

3. Cut peppers in quarters.

4. Remove the core of the tomatoes sliced into quarters.

5. Cut onions into quarters.

6. Toss all vegetables and garlic in a large bowl with olive oil, salt and pepper.

7. Spread out onto parchment paper and roast for 30+ minutes, until browning well.

8. Allow to cool. Then pulse briefly in food processor with 1 to 2 tablespoons tomato paste, a drizzle of olive oil, fresh lemon juice and schug. This sauce should be chunky, so don't over process.

Chef's Notes:

This is honestly one of the best flavors the Mediterranean has to offer. The worlds most wonderful ingredients all combined into one.

Yield 3 cups

Prep time: 20 min

Cook time: 30 min

Total time: 50 min

MEDITERRANEAN RECIPES

Schug

Schug, or Skhug, or Sahawiq, or Zhug, or a dozen other names, actually originated in Yemeni. Today, it is a popular Mediterranean staple. Most preferred is this green version, and you can also create red or smoked versions. This is the perfect middle of the road recipe, that can be tweaked a lot of different ways. That's the way I love to cook. So you can keep the flexibility in your own creations.

Ingredients

10 jalapeño peppers

8 garlic cloves

2 cups roughly chopped cilantro

2 cups roughly chopped parsley

2 Tbsp olive oil

1/2 lemon, juiced

1 tsp salt, or more to taste

1/4 tsp cumin

1/8 tsp cloves, ground

Pinch of black pepper

Directions:

1. Remove the stems and seeds from the jalapeño peppers. I suggest wearing gloves for this. The peppers will leave a layer of capsaicin on your skin for up to two days.

2. Place all ingredients into a food processor. Pulse, scraping the sides a couple times. Don't over blend. You still want a little gritty body to it.

3. Add salt and pepper to taste Careful, it's spicy.

Chef's Notes:

For a milder version, simply reduce the jalapeño and garlic. Adding a pinch of sugar gives it a totally different flavor. And adding this to a couple cups of diced tomatoes, it's a Mediterranean salsa.

Yield 1 cup

Prep time: 15 min

Total time: 15 min

MEDITERRANEAN RECIPES

Olive and Sun Dried Tomato Tapenade

Ingredients

1 cup black olives, pitted

1 cup green olives, pitted

1/2 cup sun dried tomatoes, in juice, chopped

1/4 cup olive oil

1 Tbsp capers

2 garlic cloves

1 Tbsp basil fresh, chopped

Directions

In a food processor, combine all the ingredients. Using the pulse button, do not over blend, you want a fine chop. Refrigerate in a covered container. Use as needed.

Chef's Notes:

Some of the gourmet chefs may try to convince you to use the high end olives like Niçoise olives, Picholine olives, or Kalamata olives, but it's really not necessary. While you can get some unique flavors there, the real flavor from this recipe comes from the capers and dried tomatoes.

Yield 1 1/2 cups

Prep time: 10 min

Total time: 10 min

MEDITERRANEAN RECIPES

Baked Red Lentil Falafel Salad

For the Salad:

3 cups shredded kale

3 carrots, shaved into ribbons

1/4 cup thinly slivered red onion

1 Tbsp lemon juice

Baked Falafel (recipe below)

Tahini Dressing (recipe below)

Directions:

Toss the kale, carrots, and red onions. Splash with lemon juice prior to serving.

To serve: Plate the Falafels over a bed of kale & carrot salad with a heaping dollop, or two, of tahini dressing.

For the Balsamic Tahini Dressing:

1/3 cup tahini

1 lemon, juiced

3 Tbsp vinegar, balsamic

1 garlic clove, minced

1/4 cup parsley, flat Italian, chopped

1/2 tsp paprika

Salt and freshly ground pepper, to taste

Directions:

To make the tahini dressing, whisk all the ingredients together. Salt and pepper to taste.

For the Falafels:

1 cup dry split red lentils

2 cups parsley leaves, stems removed

2 cups cilantro leaves, stems removed

5 garlic cloves

1 red onion, chopped

1 Serrano pepper, chopped

1 1/2 Tbsp tahini paste

1 1/2 Tbsp olive oil

1 tsp salt

1 tsp ground cumin

1 tsp ground coriander

1/2 tsp baking soda

1-3 tsp chickpea flour (or whole spelt or whole wheat all-purpose)

Olive oil spray

MEDITERRANEAN RECIPES

Directions

1. Soak the lentils in water overnight.

2. Strain and rinse the soaked lentils.

3. In a food processor, pulse the lentils until they are coarsely ground, just 3 or 4 times.

4. Add the parsley, cilantro, garlic, onion, and Serrano pepper, and pulse another few times.

5. Add the tahini paste, olive oil, spices, salt and pepper, and blend until NOT smooth. Make sure not to over blend, you want some crumb and texture to it.

6. Transfer to a large bowl.

7. Taste the mixture, and adjust the seasoning according to your liking.

8. Add the baking soda and the chickpea flour. Start by adding 1 tablespoon of chickpea flour at a time. If the mixture is still too wet add another. The mixture should be fairly moist, and if you add too much flour, the Falafels will become too dry and hard when baked. I wouldn't add more than 3 tablespoons.

9. Refrigerate mixture for 30 minutes.

10. Preheat your oven to 375° F.

11. Using a tablespoon measure, scoop out 2 tablespoons of the Falafel mixture into the palm of your hand. Roll into a ball and place on a parchment-lined baking sheet. Repeat with the rest of the mixture.

12. Coat the Falafels with olive oil spray.

13. Bake until golden brown, 18 to 20 minutes. Make sure not to over cook these. You don't want them too dry.

Serves: 20 falafels and 2 salad servings.

Prep time: 20 min

Cook time: 20 min

Total time: 40 min

Middle Eastern

While the term 'Middle Eastern' includes countries like Iran, Saudi Arabia, Turkey, and Israel, the culinary region extends into the northern African countries of Morocco, Algeria, Libya, and Egypt.

Historically, the diet was based on what ever was available in the local marketplace. And even today, availability plays a huge role in the cuisine. Especially when it comes to preserving foods for out of season usage. Spices have a long shelf life, so they were needed to enhance the grains when fresh foods were not available.

Here are the basics for achieving Simply Incredible Middle Eastern Flavor.

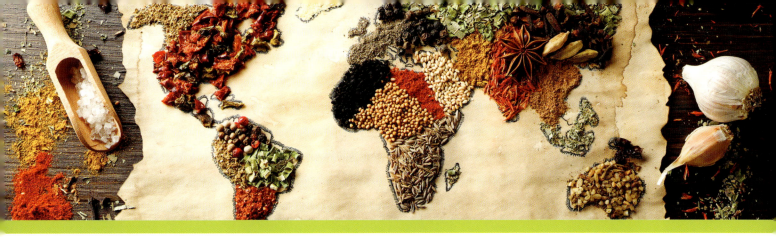

Middle Eastern

GOOD These items go well with this cuisine.		BETTER Even better pairing.	BEST The WOW factor!
almonds	oregano	**beans, fava**	**CHICKPEAS**
apricots	parsley	**cinnamon**	**LEMON**
basil	pepper	**coriander**	**LENTILS**
beans	pine nuts	**couscous**	**TAHINI**
cheese, feta	pistachios	**dates**	
cloves	plums	**eggplant**	
cumin	pomegranates	**figs**	
dill	poppy seeds	**garlic**	
fruits	raisins	**nutmeg**	
ginger	saffron	**olives**	
honey	sesame seeds	**rice**	
lemons, preserved	sumac	**sesame oil**	
mint	tomatoes	**turmeric**	
nuts	walnuts		
olive oil	yogurt, vegan		
onions			

SIMPLY INCREDIBLE PAIRINGS

cardamon + cinnamon + cloves + cumin
chickpeas + garlic + lemon + tahini + salt
chili peppers + garlic + olive oil + salt (harissa)
cilantro + cumin + ginger + red pepper
cinnamon + cloves + ginger + nutmeg
cinnamon + coriander + cumin
cinnamon + lemons + tomatoes
cinnamon + tomatoes
coriander + cumin + garlic
coriander + cumin + garlic + onions + parsley
eggplant + onions + tomatoes
eggplant + cinnamon + mint
garlic + coriander
garlic + lemon + mint
garlic + lemon + oregano
garlic + lemon + parsley
lemon + parsley
oranges + honey + mint
parsley + lemon juice
yogurt + mint

MIDDLE EASTERN RECIPES

Amazing Shawarma White Sauce

This is a staple Middle Eastern compliment for all types of sandwiches. It is also a great starter for hundreds of dips and sauces, and also stands well all on its own.

Ingredients

1 cup vegan yogurt (or sour-cream)

Juice of 1 lime

2 Tbsp Tahini

5 garlic cloves, minced

3 Tbsp fresh dill, chopped

1 Tbsp mint leaves, chopped

1/2 teaspoon salt

Directions

Place all the ingredients in a food processor or blender and process for 1 minute or until light and fluffy.

Store in the fridge, in an air tight container.

Yield: 1 1/2 cups

MIDDLE EASTERN RECIPES

Middle Eastern Potato Garlic Sauce

ingredients

3 medium russet potatoes, peeled

8 garlic cloves, peeled and crushed

1 1/2 tsp salt

1/3 cup lemon juice

1/2 cup olive oil

Directions

1. Place the potatoes into a large pot and cover with water, bring to a boil. Reduce heat to medium and boil until tender, 15 to 20 minutes.

2. Drain, transfer to a bowl, and mash until smooth. Set aside to cool.

3. Put garlic, salt, and lemon juice and just 1 tablespoon of olive oil in a blender. Blend until smooth.

4. Blend mixture on high, and slowly stream the remaining olive oil through the top opening while running. Blend until mixture is smooth.

5. While the blender is running, add the mashed potatoes, about 2 to 3 tablespoons at a time,

6. Continue adding potatoes until all are incorporated. This should be a thick, but pourable sauce. And creamy too. Do not add too many potatoes.

7. Transfer sauce to a bowl and refrigerate until chilled, 1 hour to overnight.

8. After chilled, it may thicken a little. If too thick, you can thin by whipping a little water into it.

Yield 2 cups

Prep time: 10 min

Cook time: 20 min

Total time: 30 min

Healthy Hummus at Home

Hummus is a staple in almost every healthy environment. It really isn't necessary to pay top dollar for store bought hummus that is loaded with oil when it is so easy to make a healthier version yourself.

THE BASIC HEALTHY HUMMUS CONCEPT:

To make healthy hummus at home, you need literally one ingredient. And that would be chickpeas, Or garbanzo beans, as I was raised to call them.

You can literally make hummus by tossing a couple cans of chickpeas into a food processor and blend until smooth. Drain the juice but save it. And when you turn on the food processor with the chickpeas, drizzle the chickpea juice in it until the product is flowing freely. Keep it as thick as you can, and then let it process for a couple minutes until smooth, and you're done. That easy.

This may be a little plain compared to the hundreds of versions we could show you, but it does have the salt in it from the juice, so it will have good flavor.

Now for the Standard Healthy Hummus, you would need to add tahini, garlic, lemon juice, and perhaps some oil. There is really no need for the oil, it adds unnecessary calories. Oil can make it creamier, but so does the chickpea juice.

You should have your chickpeas fully cooked and even overcooked a little. This will help dramatically in the blending process. In fact, I have tried a dozen brands of chickpeas, and find that a lot of them are too firm to make a good hummus. So I cook my own. You can do this by simply filling a crockpot 1/3 full of dried chickpeas, fill it up with water, turn on medium or low. And cook until they are soft. Blending the chick peas while still warm makes the hummus very creamy.

Now for the variations of hummus that will get you Simply Incredible Hummus flavor.

The Standard Healthy Hummus Recipe

Fill your food processor 1/2 full with chickpeas.

ADD:

3 cloves of garlic

2 Tbsp tahini

2 Tbsp lemon juice

AND then add the chickpea juice or water until thick but freely flowing in the processor. Salt to taste. Process for a couple minutes.

AND for Heat: add a pinch of cayenne pepper to taste.

MIDDLE EASTERN RECIPES

Simply Incredible Hummus Pairings

Here are items to add to your standard healthy hummus. Or you can use other types of beans for endless creations.

MIX IN WITH, OR SUBSTITUTES FOR CHICKPEAS

avocado
black beans
white beans
edamame
cauliflower, roasted
eggplant. roasted
roasted carrots
pumpkin
lentils

ADDED FLAVORS

artichokes
avocado + artichoke + kale
avocado + coriander + lemon
black beans + lime + cumin
basil
caramelized onions
cayenne
celery + hot sauce
chili powder
chipotle
cilantro
cilantro + jalapeno
curry
figs
garam masala
GARLIC
garlic, roasted
garlic + rosemary
garlic + green olive
green olive
hot sauce
lemon
lemon juice
lentil + curry
lime
LEMON
mushroom
pinenuts
pumpkin
RED PEPPER, ROASTED
roasted carrots + cumin
SALT
spinach + lemon
Sriracha
sugar
sun-dried tomato
thyme
white bean + rosemary
zucchini

ARE YOU GETTING THE IDEA?

MIDDLE EASTERN RECIPES

Easy Tahini Recipe
BETTER THAN STORE-BOUGHT

It's easy to make tahini at home, and much less expensive. I suggest looking for sesame seeds in bulk bins, or try Asian and Middle Eastern food stores. Tahini can be made from unhulled, sprouted, or hulled sesame seeds, I prefer to use the hulled sesame seeds. Tahini can be kept in the refrigerator for months.

Ingredients

2 cups sesame seeds, (hulled is best)

1/2 cup of a light olive oil OR use 1/2 water and drizzle olive oil.

1/4 tsp salt

Directions
TOAST SESAME SEEDS

1. Add sesame seeds to a dry skillet on medium-low heat and toast, stirring constantly until the seeds become fragrant and very lightly colored, 3 to 5 minutes.(Careful, sesame seeds can burn quickly)

2. Transfer toasted seeds to a baking sheet or large plate and cool completely..

3. In a food processor, add sesame seeds and then process to a crumbly paste, about 1 minute.

4. Add 1/4 cup of the oil and process for 3 minutes or more, stopping to scrape the bottom and sides of the food processor a couple times.

5. Check the tahini's consistency. It should be smooth, not gritty and should be pourable, but thick. You may need to process for another minute or add the additional tablespoon of oil.

6. Taste the tahini for seasoning then add salt to taste. Process for another minute to mix it in.

7. Store tahini covered in the refrigerator.

Yield 1 cup

Prep time: 10 min

Cook time: 5 min

Total time: 15 min

MIDDLE EASTERN RECIPES

Muhammara
RED PEPPER AND WALNUT DIP

Need a break from good old hummus? Here is a great solution. It is pronounced 'mmmhamara' and means 'very red'. This beautiful, bright colored dip will be ready to serve in 5 minutes. Muhammara is a hot pepper dip originally from Aleppo, Syria. It is found in Levantine and Turkish cuisines.

Ingredients

2 cups roasted red peppers

2 cups walnuts

1 cup chopped scallions

2 tsp lemon juice

1 tsp cumin, ground

2 tsp red pepper flakes,

1 1/2 Tbsp pomegranate molasses

1/4 cup olive oil

1/4 tsp salt to taste

water to thin

1/4 cup bread crumbs

Pita bread, for serving

Directions:

1. In a food processor, combine the peppers, walnuts, scallions, lemon juice, spices, molasses, olive oil and salt.

2. Process until smooth adding a drizzle of water until you get your desired consistency. Process until smooth.

3. Add the bread crumbs, pulsing until the desired consistency. You can always add more breadcrumbs or water if you want it thicker or thinner.

4. Transfer to a bowl and sprinkle some crushed walnuts over the top. Serve with pita bread or pita chips.

Chef's Notes:

This is my healthier version made with 1/2 the fat that most people would use. If you want no fat, eliminate the oil all together and add more water. If you don't have pomegranate molasses, you can use cranberry juice concentrate. Grenadine is an alternative also, but a little too sweet for this recipe.

Yield 3 cups

Prep time: 5 min

Total time: 5 min

MIDDLE EASTERN RECIPES

Homemade Za'atar

Za'atar commonly refers to a spice blend made with ground dried thyme, oregano, marjoram, toasted sesame seeds, salt, and the unique spice sumac. Sumac is a flowering plant. The fruits form clusters of reddish drupes called sumac bobs. These dried drupes are ground to produce a tangy crimson spice.

Ingredients

1/4 cup sumac

2 Tbsp thyme

2 Tbsp marjoram

2 Tbsp oregano

1 Tbsp roasted sesame seeds

1 tsp sea salt

Chef's Notes:

Ground Sumac is a great seasoning for vegetable dishes, and homemade hummus. Sumac mixes well with most nuts, such as walnuts and pine nuts. And brings a mouth-watering element when added to eggplant dishes.

The flavor of Sumac is quite surprising. It has levels of tart and fruity flavors as an element of lemony goodness. This sweet but sour taste is followed by a powerful taste bud punch. It blends exceptionally well with other spices such as: allspice, chili, thyme, and cumin.

Yield 3/4 cup

MIDDLE EASTERN RECIPES

Baba Ganoush

A Middle Eastern favorite. This base recipe is perfect just the way it is. It's also flexible enough for adding any personal flair you want.

Ingredients

1/2 cup tahini

5 garlic cloves, minced

1/4 cup lemon, juice, fresh

1/4 tsp cumin, ground

1/2 tsp salt to taste

1/8 tsp liquid smoke

Chef's Notes:

While this is an easy basic recipe that everyone will love, I do want to point out that most Baba Ganoush recipes will actual charbroil the eggplants. But realistically, firing up the outdoor grill to cook one or two eggplants is just not practical. Plus the gas and charcoal grills are never going to give you the smoky flavor needed from a real wood fire. So I simply use a splash of liquid smoke, and it's there.

Directions

1. Preheat an oven to 375°F.

2. Prick the eggplant with a fork in several places and bake until very soft, about 30 minutes.

3. Remove from the oven, let cool slightly. Peel off and discard the skin.

4. In a food processor, add all the ingredients, until it is smooth and creamy.

5. It's ready to serve at room temperature. You can garnish with chopped parsley and pitted kalamata olives.

Yield 3 cups

Prep time: 10 min

Cook time: 30 min

Total time: 40 min

MIDDLE EASTERN RECIPES

Harira
A TRADITIONAL MOROCCAN SOUP

Ingredients

2 Tbsp olive oil or water sauté

1 onion, finely chopped

8 cups water

3/4 cup tomato paste

1/2 cup lentils

1 cinnamon stick

2 tsp coriander

1 tsp paprika, smoked

1/2 tsp ginger

A pinch of saffron (optional)

1 bunch parsley stems tied together

1 bunch cilantro stems tied together

1 - 15 oz can chickpeas, drained

Slurry with 3Tbsp corn starch and 1/2 cup water

Salt and pepper to taste

Chopped cilantro and lemon wedges for garnish.

Directions

1. Sauté onion until translucent. You can do this with a olive oil, OR do a water sauté.

2. Add spices, tomato paste, lentils, and 8 cups of water.

3. Stir well, bringing to a boil.

4. Add parsley and cilantro tied together.

5. Reduce heat to low, cover, and simmer for 30 minutes.

6. After 30 minutes, add the cooked chickpeas.

7. Remove the parsley and cilantro stems.

8. Make a slurry with corn starch and 1/4 cup of cold water, and add to the soup, stirring well.

9. Simmer for another 10 minutes.

10. Add as much salt and pepper as you deem necessary.

11. Ladle into bowls and garnish with chopped cilantro leaves and wedge of lemon.

Servings 6

Prep time: 10 min

Cook time: 45 min

Total time: 55 min

Mexican

There are 7 regions for Mexican Cuisine. The most familiar region would be El Norte, which stretches 2,000 miles from the Pacific Baja Coast to the Gulf of Mexico. The average person would really never recognize the subtle differences between the different regions. Most have simply adjusted to the availability of food. Coastal regions adapted more seafood, southern regions incorporated the bananas and plums that grow so well there. Fortunately today, even in Mexico, products are readily available throughout the country. Regional food supplies are no longer limited, and seasonal restrictions have been broken.

Now, Mexican food is not the food of yesterday. In Mexico, cooking creativity has exploded. By parring some of these ingredients, you too will achieve Simply Incredible Mexican Flavor.

Mexican

GOOD These items go well with this cuisine.	BETTER Even better pairing.	BEST The WOW factor!
annatto seed	**chili powder**	**BEANS**
avocados	**cilantro**	**CHILE PEPPERS**
bananas	**coriander**	**CUMIN**
bell peppers	**corn**	**RICE**
cheese - jack and cheddar	**green chillies**	**SALSA**
chocolate	**lime**	
chorizo	**onions**	
cinnamon	**oregano**	
coconut	**sour cream**	
epazote	**tomatoes**	
garlic	**tortillas**	
kiwi		
lemon		
mint		
nuts		
oranges		
plums		
saffron		
scallions		
seeds		
squash		
vanilla		

SIMPLY INCREDIBLE PAIRINGS

beans + rice

chili peppers + lime

chili peppers + tomatoes

chili powder + cumin

cilantro + lime

coconut + corn

green chilies + tomatoes

kiwi + lime

salsas + sour cream

MEXICAN RECIPES

Simple Fat Free Tortillas

Ingredients

3 cups all-purpose flour

2 tsp baking soda

1 tsp salt

1 cup warm water

Directions

1. In a mixing bowl, stir dry ingredients together

2. Add water gradually to form a crumbly dough, turn out on flat surface board and knead until smooth.

3. Divide into 12 equal pieces.

4. Shape each into balls then cover lightly in plastic and let rest 15 to 20 minutes. Do not skip this step or dough will not roll well.

5. Roll out each ball into round tortilla shape. As thin as possible, the thinner the better.

6. In a heavy wide frying pan on medium-high heat, cook just long enough on each side to blister.

7. Place them immediately in a covered container or wrap in a dish towel, serve while warm.

Chef's Notes:

You can also bake these on parchment lined baking sheets at 375, flipping after about 5 minutes.

These tortillas can be refrigerated and frozen also.

Servings 12

Prep time: 30 min

Cook time: 30 min

Total time: 60 min

MEXICAN RECIPES

Serrano Salsa

Ingredients

2 lb. tomatillos, husked and rinsed

8 serrano chiles, stemmed

6 cloves garlic, peeled

2 tsp kosher salt

1/2 cup finely chopped cilantro

1/4 cup white onion, chopped

2 Tbsp fresh lime juice

Directions

1. Position an oven rack 4" from broiler, heat to high.

2. Place tomatillos, chiles, and garlic on a foil-lined baking sheet and broil. Turning occasionally. This will take about 10 minutes for the garlic and chiles, and about 15 minutes for the tomatillos, remove each ingredient as it finishes cooking. They should be browned and broiled well, without burning.

3. Place roasted chiles, garlic, and salt in a food processor and puree until smooth.

4. Add tomatillos, cilantro, onion, and lime juice. Pulse until roughly chopped. Transfer to a serving bowl.

Yield 2 cups

Prep time: 10 min

Cook time: 25 min

Total time: 35 min

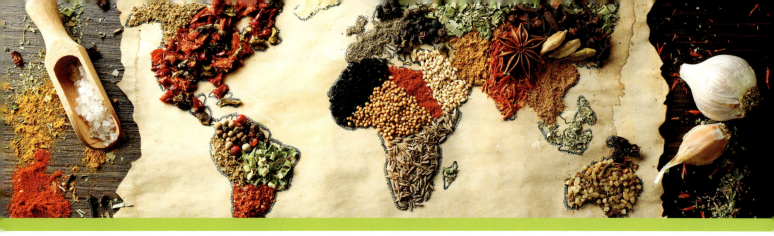

MEXICAN RECIPES

Salsa De Piña Picante

Ingredients

2 cups fresh pineapple, chopped fine (tidbit)

1/2 red onion, diced fine

2 jalapeños, stemmed, seeded and minced

1/2 cup cilantro, finely chopped

3 Tbsp lime juice

3 Tbsp orange juice

1 tsp sea salt

Directions

In a large bowl, mix together all ingredients.

Yield 2 1/2 cups

Prep time: 10 min

Total time: 10 min

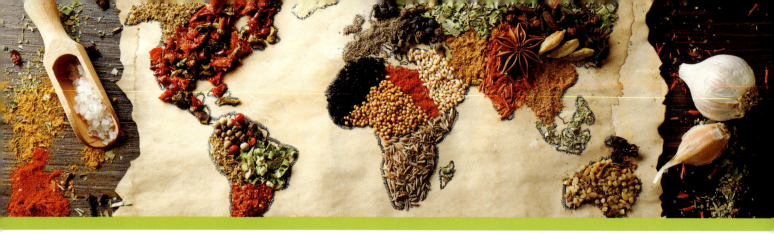

MEXICAN RECIPES

Guacamole

I truly believe that the best guacamole is simply mashed avocados and garlic salt. In fact many years ago in Las Vegas, I knew a chef who took first prize for the best guacamole by using only avocados and salt. But for those of you who feel the absolute need for more than two ingredients to consider it a recipe,

Here is my 30 year old recipe that is always sure to please.

Ingredients

3 avocados - peeled, pitted, and mashed

2 roma tomatoes, diced

Juice of 1 lime

1/2 cup red onion, finely diced

3 Tbsp cilantro, fresh chopped

1 garlic clove, minced

1 tsp salt

1 pinch cayenne pepper

Directions

Mix all the ingredients together. Serve immediately.

Chef's Notes:

Guacamole tends to turn brown very fast in the fridge. The Mexican tradition is to put an avocado pit in with the guacamole. While this seems to create a longer shelf life, I find the best thing to do is cover with saran wrap, pressing out all the air. If you have eliminated all the oxygen, the guacamole will last much longer.

Yield 3 to 4 cups
Prep time: 15 min
Total time: 15 min

MEXICAN RECIPES

Brown Sugar Fajita Seasoning

Like guacamole, my go to recipe for fajita seasoning has only 2 ingredients, and that's Lawry's seasoning and cayenne pepper. That's it. I have used that exact combo at a dozen different restaurants, with customers raving over the best fajitas they have ever had. Now for a more traditional fajita, you are going to have to try my brown sugar recipe. It's the secret ingredient, along with the traditional oregano.

Ingredients

2 Tbsp chili powder

2 tsp salt

2 tsp paprika

2 tsp brown sugar

1 tsp oregano

1 tsp cumin, ground

1 tsp onion powder

1/2 tsp garlic powder

1/2 tsp black pepper, ground

1/2 tsp cayenne pepper

Directions

Mix all ingredients together. Store in an airtight container.

Chef's Notes:

My favorite meat substitute to use for fajitas is Butler Soy Curls. They are available in the resources section of this book.

Yield 1/4 cup

MEXICAN RECIPES

Taco Seasoning

This is a basic recipe that works great for seasoning your tacos.

Ingredients

2 Tbsp chili powder

1 Tbsp ground cumin

1 tsp paprika

2 tsp sea salt

1 tsp black pepper

1/2 tsp garlic powder

1/2 tsp onion powder

1/2 tsp crushed red pepper flakes

1/2 tsp dried oregano

Directions

Mix all ingredients together.

Store in an airtight container.

Chef's Notes:

If I'm not going to use fresh chopped onions in my cooking recipe, I will add dehydrated chopped onions.

Yield 1/4 cup

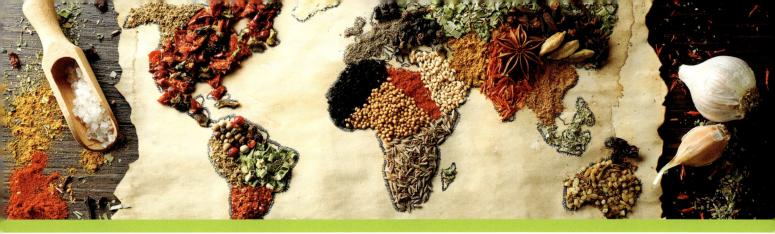

MEXICAN RECIPES

No Salt Mexican Spice Blend

This flavorful spice blend is great for any dish from simple rice and beans to tofu tacos or a creamy squash soup.

Ingredients

2 Tbsp paprika

2 Tbsp chili powder

2 tsp ground cumin

1 1/2 tsp onion powder

1 tsp garlic powder

1 tsp ground black pepper

1/4 tsp cayenne or ground chipotle pepper (optional)

Directions

Mix all ingredients together.

Store in an airtight container.

Chef's Notes:

I use this as a no salt recipe for a lot of different foods. I always want to test something before adding salt. If you are going on a no salt or low salt diet, you can add dried lemon or lime zest. Simply zest a bunch of lemons or limes, dry them, and then pulverize them in a coffee grinder, then add to recipes for a salt sensation.

Yield 1/4 cup

MEXICAN RECIPES

Quick Enchilada Sauce

This is the easiest way to create a Simply Incredible enchilada sauce.

Ingredients

2 cups tomato sauce

1 Tbsp chili powder, dark

1 tsp onion powder

1/2 tsp garlic, powder

Directions

Mix well and it's ready for your favorite dishes.

Chef's Notes:

I prefer the dark chili powder for this recipe. It will give a far more robust flavor. Generally, if there's time, I would also want to simmer this on low heat for some time in order to blend the flavors.

Yield 2 cups

MEXICAN RECIPES

Pico de Gallo

Simple fresh ingredients always produces Simply Incredible Flavor.

Ingredients

8 roma tomatoes, chopped

1 red onion, finely diced

1 cup cilantro, fresh chopped

2 jalapeño, seeded and finely diced

Juice of 1 lime

Salt

Directions

1. After all the ingredients are diced, mix together well.

2. Allow to rest for ten minutes or so and mix again.

3. Adjust according to your taste.

Chef's Notes:

The general rule of thumb is to have equal parts of onions to tomatoes. I personally have always had a greater tomato presence. Two parts tomatoes to one part onion seems to be a more acceptable ratio for most.

Yield 4 to 6 cups

MEXICAN RECIPES

Salsa Verde

A staple in every Mexican kitchen is this simple Salsa Verde, commonly referred to as 'GreenSauce'. Simple to make from readily available ingredients.

Ingredients

1 pound tomatillos

1 medium white onion, quartered

3 Serrano chiles

4 garlic cloves

1/4 cup cilantro, fresh leaves

1 tsp salt

Directions

1. Remove the husks from the tomatillos and rinse. There can be sticky residue on them.

2. In a large pot, add all of the ingredients except for the cilantro and salt, and add just enough water to cover.

3. Bring the water and ingredients to a boil and then simmer for 10 minutes.

4. In a food processor, blend the cooked ingredients and the cilantro with just some of the cooking water. Blend until smooth. (About 30 seconds) It should be like a smooth sauce. Add more water if necessary.

5. Pour the blended salsa back into the pot and simmer for 20 minutes.

6. Add the salt and adjust if necessary.

Chef's Notes:

You do not have to seed the Serrano chiles, unless you want an extremely mild sauce. You can also use jalapeños. This salsa freezes well, so make a triple batch, and freeze for later.

Yield 4 cups

Prep time: 10 min

Cook time: 20 min

Total time: 30 min

Russian

Russian cuisine is influenced by Central Europe, Central Asian, and Middle Eastern countries. While pork, poultry, fish, and caviar were readily available, whole grains such as wheat, barley, rye and millet also dominated the culture.

Cabbage and potatoes were and still are a staple, and many other vegetables were pickled. These are still reflected in the style of food found in Russia today.

Keep reading for tips to create Simply Incredible Russian flavor.

Russian

GOOD These items go well with this cuisine.		BETTER Even better pairing.	BEST The WOW factor!
barley	ginger	**beets**	**PICKLING SPICE**
caraway seeds	lentils	**cabbage**	**POTATOES**
carrots	mint	**mushrooms**	**TOMATOES**
celery	nutmeg	**onions**	**VINEGAR**
cilantro	paprika	**radishes**	
cinnamon	parsley	**sour cream**	
cloves	peas	**tarragon**	
cucumbers	pepper	**thyme**	
cumin	pickles		
dill	poppy seeds		
fruits	saffron		
fruit sauces	sage		
garlic	yogurt		

SIMPLY INCREDIBLE PAIRINGS

mushrooms + cloves + pepper + vinegar

RUSSIAN RECIPES

Russian "Olivie" Salad

This is probably one of the most traditional Russian dishes. Often made for holidays and parties. The trick to this dish is simply to make sure all the vegetables are cut into uniform, very small diced shapes.

Ingredients:

3 potatoes

4 carrots

8 pickles

2 cucumbers

1 onion

2 cups frozen peas

1 1/2 cups vegenaise

fresh chives

Directions:

1. Boil off the potatoes with the carrots ahead of time. Do not overcook, just until tender. We want some firmness. And then chill to tighten them up.

2. Cut the potatoes, carrots, pickles, cucumbers and onions, into small ¼ inch dice.

3. Mix all the ingredients with the mayonnaise.

4. Salt and pepper if desired.

5. Garnish with fresh cut chives.

Chef's Notes:

In the original salad, cooked wild meat was used, but now most people use bologna or some other type of sausage meat. You can use any vegan meats, or just keep it a simple vegetarian dish.

Yield 10 - 12 cups

Prep time: 20 min

Cook time: 20 min

Total time: 40 min

RUSSIAN RECIPES

Vegan Borscht

Borscht is a sour soup popular throughout all of Russia and Eastern European countries. The beetroot borscht was invented in what is now Ukraine. Today, several ethnic groups claim borscht as their own national dish, and many consume borscht as part of ritual meals within Orthodox, Catholic, and Jewish religions.

Ingredients

3 large beets, peeled and cut into matchsticks

1/2 large cabbage, cut thinly into shreds

2 onions, slivered

2 large carrots, peeled and cut into matchsticks

2 Tbsp olive oil

2 cloves garlic

5 cups vegetable stock

salt to taste

juice of 1/2 a lemon

black pepper

vegan sour cream

chives

Directions

1. Peel and cut the onions, carrots, beets and cabbage.

2. In a large soup pot, sauté vegetables over medium-high heat with a pinch of salt. About five minutes, adding garlic at the end.

3. Add vegetable stock bring to a boil, then simmer for 25 minutes.

4. Season to taste with salt and pepper,

5. Then add the lemon juice.

Chef's Notes:

This dish is often garnished with sour cream, black pepper and chives.

Servings 4 to 6

Prep time: 15 min

Cook time: 30 min

Total time: 45 min

RUSSIAN RECIPES

Vegan Rassolnik
LENTIL AND BARLEY SOUP WITH PICKLES

This old family recipe comes from my mom's side of the family tree, who were of Russian descent. Generally this soup is made with pork or beef. But during lent, we made this version without meat. The pickles offer a zingy contrast to the hearty vegetables in this traditional Russian soup.

Ingredients

2 tsp olive oil

4 cloves garlic

2 Tbsp tomato paste

12 cups vegetable stock

3/4 cup barley, dry

1 cup lentils, dry

1 lb beets, peeled and diced

2 carrots, peeled and diced

4 large potatoes, cubed 1 inch size

1 onion, dice

2 stalks celery, dice

6 bay leaves

2 tsp allspice

1 tsp black pepper

2 tsp sea salt

1 bunch parsley, flat leaf chopped

2 bunches fresh dill, chopped

1/2 cup pickle juice

1½ cups pickles, chopped

Directions

1. In a large heavy bottom stock pot, heat the oil over medium high heat. Add the garlic, sauté for 30 seconds.

2. Add the tomato paste and stir constantly for 45 seconds.

3. Add the stock, barley, lentils, beets, carrots, and potatoes, stir gently, cover, and bring to a boil.

4. Reduce heat to a simmer and cook for 30 minutes.

5. Add the onion, celery, the bay leaves, allspice, salt and black pepper.

6. Cover and simmer for 15 minutes, until all the vegetables are tender.

7. Remove the bay leaves.

8. Add the parsley, dill, pickles and juice.

9. Often served with sour cream.

Chef Notes:

It's a good idea to wear disposable gloves when cutting the beets, and wash the cutting board immediately to prevent staining. The only way to handle beets is to use disposable gloves…or be prepared to live with pink fingers.

Yield 12 » Prep time: 30 min
Cook time: 55 min » Total time: 1.5 hours

RUSSIAN RECIPES

Mushroom Stroganoff

Ingredients

10 ounces uncooked ribbon noodles

2 Tbsp olive oil

1 onion, diced

1 clove garlic, minced

3 Tbsp whole wheat flour, divided

2 cups beefless beef broth or vegetable broth

1 Tbsp soy sauce

1 tsp lemon juice

1 tsp tomato paste

3 pounds mushrooms cut into chunks

1 tsp dried thyme

1/2 teaspoon dried sage

1/2 teaspoon salt

1 Tbsp apple cider vinegar

1 cup vegan sour cream

10 turns of fresh ground, black pepper

1/4 cup flat-leaf parsley, minced

Directions

1. Cook the noodles…. under-cooked just a bit. Run cold water over pasta, drain and set aside.

2. In a large saucepan over medium heat, add the olive oil and sauté the onions for about 5 minutes.

3. Add garlic and sauté for 30 seconds.

4. Add the flour swirling constantly for a minute, making a roux.

5. Gradually add the broth, soy sauce, lemon juice, and tomato paste, while stirring at the same time.

6. Stir over heat until mixture becomes thick and bubbly.

7. Add the mushrooms, thyme, sage, and salt. Cook for 5 minutes, stirring frequently..

8. Add the vinegar, noodles, sour cream, black pepper, stir in and cook on low for an additional 5 minutes.

9. Garnish with parsley.

Servings 4 to 6

Prep time: 10 min

Cook time: 20 min

Total time: 30 min

Spanish

Spain is a highly agricultural country. Known as "Europe's Orchard", some of the healthiest food in the world originates in this region. It is easy to achieve Simply Incredible Spanish Flavor with the variety of fresh produce and seasonings that allow for so much flexibility when creating these healthy dishes.

Spanish

GOOD These items go well with this cuisine.		BETTER Even better pairing.	BEST The WOW factor!
anise	thyme	**almonds**	**EGGPLANT**
bay leaf	turmeric	**chili peppers**	**OLIVES**
beans	vanilla	**chorizo**	**PAPRIKA, SWEET**
breads	walnuts	**cilantro**	**SAFFRON**
cinnamon	zucchini	**kale**	
custards		**lemon**	
fruits		**peppers**	
garlic		**potatoes**	
hazelnuts		**rice**	
olive oil		**tomatoes**	
onions		**vegetables**	
orange		**vinegar**	
parsley			
pine nuts			
pomegranates			
roasted red peppers			
soups			
squash			
stews			
tamarind			

SIMPLY INCREDIBLE PAIRINGS

almonds + garlic + olive oil

garlic + kale + onions + potatoes

garlic + lemon + salt

garlic + onions + paprika + rice + saffron

garlic + onions + parsley

peppers + onions + tomatoes

tomatoes + almonds + roasted red peppers

SPANISH RECIPES

Crockpot Cocido

Cocido, also known as Cocido Rojo Madrileno, is a hearty stew or soup that has its origins in the Middle Ages and is now widespread through all of Spain. It is a national dish of Spain often made with chicken beef or blood sausage. This is my vegan version.

Ingredients

2 quarts water

1/2 cup tamarind paste

1/2 cup white miso paste

4 cups crimini mushrooms, sliced thick

2 lbs red potatoes, quartered

1 white onion, chopped

2 large carrots, chopped

1 large ear of corn, cut across the cob into 1 inch pieces

1 cup kale, chopped

3 garlic cloves, minced

2 jalapeño peppers, seeds removed, chopped

1 tsp salt added to taste

2 summer squash cut into 1 inch slices - about 3 cups

1/2 cup fresh cilantro leaves

Directions

1. In a large crock pot on high, add most ingredients... expect the squash and cilantro.

2. Once the crockpot is hot, mix well to ensure smooth separation of the miso and tamarind paste.

3. Put crockpot on low and cook for 5 hours.

4. Add squash and cook for one more hour.

5. Salt and pepper to taste.

6. Garnish with generous portions of cilantro.

Chef's Notes:

You can serve this as a soup, or turn this into a stew by thickening with a cornstarch slurry or roux.

Servings 12

Prep time: 20 min

Cook time: 6 hours

Total time: 6.2 hours

SPANISH RECIPES

Tombet

Tombet is a traditional vegetable dish from Majorca. It is widely available at almost every restaurant on the island. Tombet is often served along with fish or meat. Similar to ratatouille, fresh vegetables make it a fantastic vegan dish.

Ingredients

2 lbs. red potatoes, sliced thick or quartered

1 large onion, slivered

2 zucchini, sliced 1/2 inch

1 yellow squash, sliced 1/2 inch

1 green bell pepper, cut into strips

1 red pepper, cut into strips

1 eggplant, diced large

2 cups tomato sauce

1 lemon, juiced

5 garlic cloves, chopped

1/2 tsp sea salt

1 tsp thyme

Directions

1. Preheat oven to 425 degrees.

2. Take all the above vegetables and bake for 25 minutes, browning well. You can do this in one pan or two pans at a time if necessary.

3. Meanwhile, mix together the tomato sauce, lemon juice, garlic, salt, and thyme.

4. In a large casserole baking dish, gently mix all the vegetables with the tomato sauce mixture.

5. Bake at 350 degrees for about 30 minutes.

Chef's Notes:

This is an extremely healthy version, packed with great flavor. Normally this dish is fried with a bunch of oil, and then layered in the casserole dish.

Servings 6

Prep time: 20 min

Cook time: 1 hour

Total time: 1.3 hours

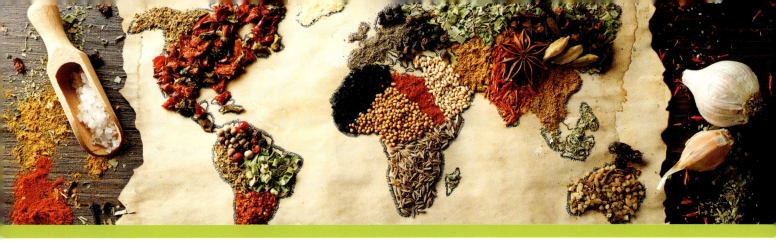

SPANISH RECIPES

Fabada Asturiana

Often simply known as Fabada, it is a rich Spanish bean soup or stew. This is a fast easy recipe that will capture the flavor without the fat.

Ingredients

6 cloves of garlic, sliced

2 onion, chopped

3 - 15 oz cans of cannellini beans, drained

2 cups water

2 Tbsp paprika, sweet

1 tsp turmeric

2 bay leaves

1 tsp sea salt and

black pepper to taste

Directions

1. Water sauté the onions and garlic with 1/2 cup of water, until the water is gone. And then add another 1/2 cup - sautéing till gone, and repeating the process until onions are caramelized.

2. Blend until creamy smooth, the onions, garlic and half of the water with 1/3 of the beans.

3. Pour the mixture into a medium heavy bottom cooking pot.

4. Add the remaining ingredients and heat on medium high heat for 10 minutes.

Chef's Notes:

There is an actual 'fabada' bean. It is an extra long white bean. Hard to find in America, and very expensive, that's why I use the canned cannellini beans. Any white bean would work.

Servings 4

Prep time: 5 min

Cook time: 20 min

Total time: 25 min

SPANISH RECIPES

Papas Arrugadas Con Mojo Verde
(CANARY ISLANDS WRINKLED POTATOES)

'Wrinkled' potatoes with a fresh cilantro 'Mojo sauce' is a traditional dish in the Canary Islands. It is a great side dish, snack, or even a light dinner.

Ingredients

3 lbs. baby potatoes - baby Maris Pipers or fingerlings

1/4 cup sea salt

water

For The Mojo Sauce:

2 large bunches of cilantro

4 cloves garlic, peeled

1 tsp salt

1/2 tsp ground cumin

1/4 cup water

2 Tbsp vinegar,

1/2 cup olive oil

Directions

1. Wash the potatoes and place them in a pot with the salt and just enough water to cover them. Bring them to a boil and simmer until the potatoes are cooked - about 20 minutes.

2. In the meantime, let's make the mojo sauce. In an electric blender, add the remaining ingredients, except the olive oil.

3. After everything is blended extremely well, continue blending on a medium speed, and slowly drizzle the oil in until smooth and creamy.

4. Once the potatoes are cooked, drain all the water and return the pot to the hot heat.

5. When all the moisture has evaporated, a thin coating of white salt will start forming as the potatoes are getting crispy. Keep cooking.

6. Shake or stir the pot to stop them from sticking - when the potatoes start to brown and wrinkle slightly, they are done.

7. Serve hot, topped with the mojo sauce.

Servings 2 to 4

Prep time: 5 min

Cook time: 30 min

Total time: 35 min

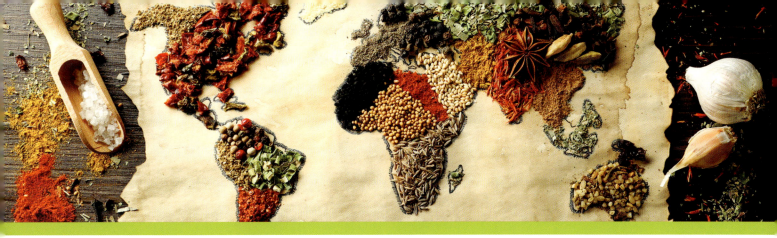

SPANISH RECIPES

Patatas Bravas
HOME FRIES WITH ROASTED TOMATO AIOLI

Ingredients

6 large russet potatoes, boiled and chilled, or baked.

2 large plum tomatoes, halved, seeded

1/2 red onion, chopped and separated

4 cloves garlic, chopped

1 Tbsp paprika, smoked

3/4 cup veganaise

Splash of apple cider vinegar

Dash hot pepper sauce

Salt and pepper to taste

Directions

1. Boil off the potatoes until fully cooked, but not over cooked.

2. Refrigerate overnight uncovered.

3. Preheat the oven to 375 degrees.

4. Cut the potatoes into wedges. Place on baking sheets, and spray with a little vegetable oil.

5. Cook potatoes for about 40 minutes, until crispy.

6. Plate up the potatoes and drizzle with the aioli sauce.

Directions for the Roasted Tomato Aioli Sauce

1. In the 375 degree oven, roast the tomatoes, onions, and garlic, for 45 minutes.

2. Allow to cool.

3. In a food processor, combine the roasted onions, garlic, and tomatoes along with the remaining ingredients.

4. Ready to serve or chill in an airtight container.

Chef's Notes:

This is the healthy version of Patatas Bravas, which are normally deep fried. Even the oil in the veganaise can be eliminated it you want a fat free dish. Just triple the tomatoes and you will have a roasted garlic tomato sauce. You can always use day old baked potatoes.

Servings 4 to 6

Prep time: 20 min

Cook time: 1 hour

Total time: 1.3 hours

SPANISH RECIPES

Gazpacho

Ingredients

1 english cucumber, halved and seeded, but not peeled

2 red bell peppers, seeded

4 plum tomatoes

1 red onion

3 garlic cloves, minced

3 cups tomato juice

1/4 cup apple cider vinegar

1 Tbsp soy sauce

1/2 Tbsp kosher salt to taste

1 tsp black pepper to taste

1/2 tsp oregano

1/2 tsp cumin

Directions

1. Roughly chop all the vegetables and garlic, and place in a food processor.

2. Pulse until it is coarsely chopped. Do not over process. You want this to be chunky.

3. Add the remaining ingredients and stir well.

4. Allow to chill for hours or a day before serving.

Servings 4 to 6

Prep time: 20 min

Chill time: 3 hours

SPANISH RECIPES

Vegan Paella

Paella is a Spanish dish of rice, saffron, and meats or vegetables. It's cooked and served in a large shallow pan, which is also called a Paella pan. While the Paella pan is the standard for cooking and presentation, it is not necessary. Any regular large skillet will work just fine.

Ingredients

2 1/2 cups vegetable stock

1/2 tsp saffron threads

1 1/2 Tbsp olive oil or water sauté

1 large red onion, sliced

1 yellow bell pepper, sliced

1 red bell pepper, sliced

3 cloves garlic, minced

1 cup mushrooms, sliced

1 cup Bomba rice

2 roma tomatoes, diced

1 1/2 tsp smoked paprika

1/2 tsp salt to taste

1/4 tsp pepper to taste

1 cup green peas

1 can artichoke hearts, quartered and drained

1/2 cup parsley, chopped

Directions

1. In a medium saucepan, combine the vegetable stock and saffron threads. Bring to boil over high heat, then simmer on low.

2. In a heated Paella pan or large skillet, sauté onions and peppers for 5 minutes.

3. Add the mushrooms and garlic and sauté for another 5 minutes.

4. Add Bomba rice, tomato, smoked paprika, salt and pepper. Stir well.

5. Add one-third of the saffron infused stock, and let simmer uncovered for 5 minutes, until liquid is absorbed.

6. Add the next third of the stock and cook for 5 minutes uncovered, until the liquid is absorbed.

7. Add remaining third of stock and simmer for 10 minutes uncovered.

8. Cover entire pan with foil or lid and cook on low heat for another 10 minutes.

9. Add the peas and artichoke hearts to the top, don't stir in.

10. Shut heat off. Cover the pan tight with foil or lid. Let set for 15 minutes.

11. Remove foil and garnish with parsley.

Chef's Notes:

Bomba is a short grain rice commonly found in Spain. You can use any short grain rice, or in reality, any rice will create a wonderful dish.

Servings: 4 » Prep time: 10 min

Cook time: 30 min » Total time: 40 min

Swedish

A Swedish kitchen is an active place where families gather to socialize at the end of the day. Summertime draws the activity outdoors for picnicking or harvesting locally grown mushrooms and berries. Sweden has a long dark winter which limits access to fresh produce so the preservation of food is essential. While dairy consumption is the highest per capita of any country in the world, alternatives to dairy are also popular. Lets take a look at what makes Simply Incredible Swedish Flavor.

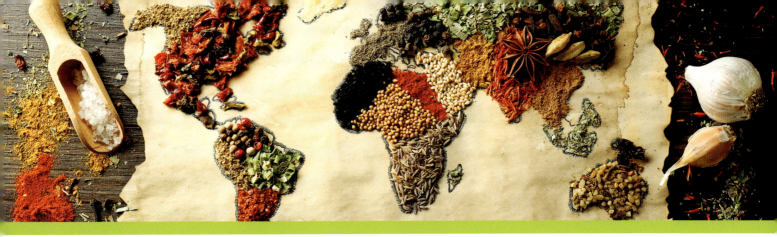

Swedish

GOOD These items go well with this cuisine.		BETTER Even better pairing.	BEST The WOW factor!
allspice	horseradish	**cream sauces**	**DILL**
apples	lingonberries	**mushrooms**	**SOUR CREAM**
bay leaf	mustard	**onions**	
breads	nutmeg	**potatoes**	
cardamom	pears		
chocolate	peas		
cream	pepper		
cream cheese	pickling	**SIMPLY INCREDIBLE PAIRINGS**	
cinnamon	vegetable stock	bay leaf + dill + nutmeg + onion	
cloves	vinegar	cream + mushrooms + onions	
fennel		cream + onions + potatoes	
ginger		horseradish + mustard + sour cream	

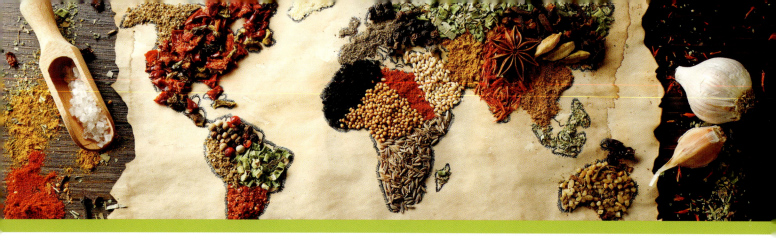

SWEDISH RECIPES

Inkokta Päron
SWEDISH POACHED PEARS

Ingredients

3 1/3 cups white grape juice

1 cup water

3/4 sugar, natural

2 whole vanilla beans, split and scraped

4 firm Anjou, Bartlett, or Bosc pears

Directions

1. In a 4-quart saucepan over medium-high heat, place the white grape juice, water, sugar and vanilla bean, bring to a boil.

2. Peel the pears, leaving the stem intact.

3. Core the pears from the bottom. Reduce the heat to medium low and place the pears into the liquid, cover and cook for 30 minutes or until the pears are tender but not falling apart.

4. Remove the pears to a serving dish. Stand them upright, and place them in the refrigerator.

5. Remove the vanilla bean from the saucepan.

6. Increase the heat to high and reduce into a syrup. About 20 to 25 minutes. Should be about 1 cup of liquid. Do not allow the syrup to turn brown. Place the syrup in a heatproof container and place in the refrigerator until cool, approximately 1 hour.

7. Remove the pears from the refrigerator, pour the sauce over the pears and serve.

Chef's Notes:

If you don't have vanilla beans, use 2 tablespoons of real vanilla.

Servings: 4

Prep time: 10 min

Cook time: 1 hour

Chill time: 1 hour

Total time: 2.2 hours

SWEDISH RECIPES

Kroppkakor
STUFFED SWEDISH POTATO DUMPLINGS

Kroppkakor, are hearty mashed potato dumplings stuffed with an allspice-laden filling. They are a specialty of Oland, an island off the southern coast of Sweden.

Ingredients

3 lbs russet potatoes, peeled and cut into 1" pieces

2 1/2 cups flour, plus more for dusting

1 tsp baking powder

1/2 tsp salt

1 Tbsp olive oil or water sauté

1 onion, yellow large, diced

1 lb mushrooms, sliced

1 clove garlic, minced

1 Tbsp allspice, ground

sour cream, for serving

Directions

1. In a 4-qt. saucepan of salted water, boil the potatoes until tender, about 20 minutes.

2. Drain potatoes and let cool completely, then transfer to a bowl and mash until smooth.

3. Mix the flour, baking powder, and salt well.

4. Add the mashed potatoes, knead well into a smooth dough. Cover with plastic wrap and chill dough 30 minutes.

5. Sauté onions and mushrooms until tender. Add the garlic and allspice, and stir well. Let cool.

6. Fill an 8-qt. wide saucepan 2/3 full of salted water and bring to a boil.

7. On a lightly floured surface, divide dough into sixteen balls.

8. Work with 1 dough ball at a time, press index finger into center of ball to create a pocket. Place about 2 tablespoons of the onion mixture into the pocket and pinch edges of dough to seal. Then roll into a smooth ball and flatten into a 2 inch wide patty about 1 inch thick.

9. Add dumplings to boiling water. When dumplings start floating, reduce the heat to medium and simmer until firm, about 30 minutes.

10. Using a slotted spoon, transfer to serving platter.

11. Serve with sour cream and apricot fruit dip.

Chef's Notes:

Apricot fruit dip is so easy to make. Just take a jar of apricot preserves and whip in a little white grape juice, or water.

Servings: 6 to 8 » **Prep time:** 20 min

Cook time: 1 hour » **Total time:** 1.7 hours

SWEDISH RECIPES

Rabarberkompott
RHUBARB COMPOTE

This is a fantastic sauce to pour over ice cream.

Ingredients

6 rhubarb stalks

1 cinnamon stick

3/4 cups of sugar

1/2 cup of water

Directions

1. In a medium size heavy bottom pan, combine the rhubarb, cinnamon, sugar and water. Bring to a boil.

2. Reduce to a simmer for about 10 minutes until the rhubarb is soft.

3. The longer you cook this the thicker it will get. Just don't burn it. Some rhubarb can be low in pectin and you may want to thicken with a slurry made of cornstarch and water.

Chef's Notes:

Great on ice cream, or serve with Créme Fraiche sweetened with sugar or vanilla. You can always thicken this mixture with a cornstarch and water slurry, and then you have a great product for pies and spreads.

Yield: 3 cups

SWEDISH RECIPES

Vegan Crème Fraîche

Ingredients

1 cup whole raw cashews

1 Tbsp lemon juice, fresh

pinch salt

1/2 cup water

1/4 cup powdered sugar (optional. For a sweet version)

1/4 tsp vanilla, (optional)

Directions

1. Cover the cashews in water. Let sit for 30 minutes, or even overnight.

2. In a blender, combine the drained cashews, lemon juice, salt, and water. Scrape down the sides as necessary.

3. If the cream is too thick, then add more water - 1/2 tablespoon at a time while blending, until desired consistency is reached.

4. For sweet dishes, stir in powdered sugar.

Use immediately, or cover and store for up to a few days in the fridge.

Yield: 1 cup

Conclusion

Healthy living is a result of choices, every single meal, every single day. Only you can decide what to eat and how much is best for you. Simply eat whole natural foods. Eat something that **IS** a plant, not something that was manufactured **IN** a plant.

Pray for discernment and wisdom. Remember that your body is an amazing instrument, created by God to do amazing things. Give Him full control of everything you do. Make choices that are best for your body, not your appetite.

Some of us have to make some serious changes in our lifestyle, and we just need to take those steps. We need to train our bodies. Actually, we need to RETRAIN ourselves because we were not trained right the first time. And once we get our bodies RETRAINED, into the way we should have been eating all along, we will see mighty transformations. I can't believe I used to eat the way I used to eat. But every change I've made has led to positive results.

Take one day at a time and keep your focus on Christ.

MANY BLESSINGS,

Mark Anthony

AND DON'T FORGET TO READ
THESE BOOKS ABOUT GETTING HEALTHY:

THE STARCH SOLUTION *by Dr. McDougall*

THE LOW CARB FRAUD *by T. Colin Campbell*

AND THE LOW CARB MYTH *by Doctor Ari Whitten and Wade Smith*

RECIPE Index

1 Hour Shepherd's Pie	359
4 Ingredient Quinoa	185
Acorn Bread	274
Alfredo Sauce	367
Almond Crusted Tofu Nuggets	223
Aloo Gobi	356
Amazing Lentil Sloppy Joe's	136
Amazing Shawarma White Sauce	392
Apple Mashed Potatoes	157
Avocado Sauce	90
Baba Ganoush	399
Baked Jalapeño-White Bean Flautas	115
Baked Red Lentil Falafel Salad	388
Balsamic Tofu	215
Banana and Black Bean Empanadas	378
Berbere Spice	246
Black Bean Brownies	91
Black Bean Enchilada Stuffed Shells	88
Black Beans and Rice	94
Black-eyed Pea and Acorn Squash Stew	236
Blackfeet Bread	273
Bo-Kaap Cape Malay Curry Powder	247
Brazilian Cocadas	376
Broccoli Quinoa Slaw	193
Brown Sugar Delicata Squash	239
Brown Sugar Fajita Seasoning	407
Bulgur Chili	230
Butternut Squash Barley Risotto	82
Butternut Squash Pancakes	240
Butternut Squash Taquitos	241
Buttery Lemon Rice	204
Cajun Spice Blend	260
Cannellini Bean and Roasted Red Pepper Dip	116
Caramelized Onion Mashed Potatoes	161
Caribbean Confetti Rice	202
Chana Masala	355
Chickpea & Edamame Salad with Lemon & Mint Dressing	119
Chickpea Blondies	125
Chickpea Pumpkin Granola Bars	124
Chickpeas, Mushrooms, and Caramelized Onion Risotto	120
Chipotle Ketchup	287
Chocolate Chickpea Cookie Dough	126
Cilantro Lime Rice	200
Cilantro Lime Sauce	286
Classic Southern BBQ	253
Coconut Chickpea Truffles	123
Coconut Lime Quinoa	183
Cold Barley Kalamata Salad	83
Confetti Mashed Potatoes	158
Cooking Millet	233
Corn Chowder	130
Corn Fritters	131
Cranberry Apple Pecan Wild Rice	208
Creamy Roasted Garlic White Bean Soup	112
Creamy Rosemary and White Bean Soup	114
Creamy Vegan Potato Leek Soup	168
Creamy Yuzu Sauce	301
Crispy Baked Garlic Tofu	221
Crispy Roasted Potatoes	173
Crockpot Cocido	421
Cuban Mojo Sauce	321
Dijon Tofu Burgers with Maple Mayo	224
Dirty Rice	263
Drunken Noodles	307
Duck Sauce	295
Easy Black Bean and Zucchini Burgers	92
Easy Crockpot Red Beans and Rice	279
Easy Homemade Oat Bread	144
Easy Mediterranean Orzo Pasta	382
Easy Tahini Recipe	396
Easy Tofu Eggless Salad	222
Easy Vegan Fried Rice	199
Energy Packed Blueberry Tofu Smoothie	219
Ethiopian Injera Bread	248
Fabada Asturiana	423
French Silk Pie	212
French Toast Bites	328
Fresh Herb Tofu Aioli	121
Fufu	250
Garam Masala Spice Blend	354
Garlic Mashed Beans	114
Gazpacho	426
Greek Cabbage Rolls	340
Greek Dolma	337
Green Garbanzo Patties with Fresh Herb Tofu Aioli	121
Guacamole	406
Gumbo	262
Harira	400

Hawaiian Poke Bowls	269
Hawaiian Rice	209
Healthy Hummus at Home	394
Homemade Ginger Sauce	294
Homemade Refried Beans	98
Homemade Za'atar	398
Hopi Corn Stew & Blue Dumplings	275
Hot German Potato Salad	331
Hungarian Lecso	346
Hungarian Tofu and Potato Goulash	348
Indian Dal	353
Inkokta Päron	430
Irish Soda Bread	361
Irish Stew	362
Jambalaya	261
Kansas City BBQ	257
Kidney Bean and Coconut Curry	104
Kidney Bean and Zucchini Cutlets	108
Kidney Bean Burgers	106
Kidney Bean Salad	107
Kidney Beans and Mushroom Rougaille	105
Kroppkakor	431
Leftover Mashed Potato Pancakes	170
Lentil and Quinoa Chili	135
Lentil Cookies	137
Lentil, Leek, and Sweet Potato Soup	139
Lentil Pâté	138
Lo Mein Sauce	296
Mark Anthony's Signature Hybrid Potato Wedges	163
Mashed Potato Bake	167
Matbucha	385
Mediterranean Cauliflower Couscous Salad	384
Mediterranean Quinoa Salad	186
Mediterranean Spiced Freekeh Salad	383
Memphis BBQ Sauce	254
Middle Eastern Potato Garlic Sauce	393
Minestrone Soup	370
Muhammara	397
Mushroom Barley Soup	81
Mushroom Stroganoff	418
Native Indian Flat Bread	272
No Bake Oat and Almond Bars	148
No Bake Oat Balls	145
No Salt Mexican Spice Blend	409
Oat & Lentil Pie	147
Oatmeal Carrot Cookies	146
Oil Free Homemade Potato Rolls	174
Oil Free Scalloped Potatoes	172
Okinawan Sweet Purple Potatoes	266
Olive and Sun Dried Tomato Tapenade	387
One Pan Mexican Quinoa	184
One Pot Mushroom Garlic Quinoa	187
Oven Baked Green Tomatoes	280
Overnight Oats in a Jar	142
Papas Arrugadas Con Mojo Verde	424
Paratha	351
Pareve Cholent	84
Patatas Bravas	425
Peanut Butter Cup Pie	216
Perfect Quinoa	182
Pico de Gallo	411
Pikliz	318
Pinto Bean Breakfast Sausage	101
Pinto Bean Quesadillas	99
Pique	320
Poi	267
Ponzu Sauce	300
Potato Pumpkin Mashed	159
Pumpkin Leather Recipe	242
Quick Black Bean Chili	95
Quick Enchilada Sauce	410
Quinoa Enchilada Bake	189
Quinoa Stuffed Bell Peppers	190
Rabarberkompott	432
Rainbow Quinoa Salad	192
Raw Vegan Sun-dried Tomato Olive Pate	326
Red Bell Pepper Parathas	352
Roasted Garbanzo Beans	119
Roasted Root Vegetable Bisque	325
Roasted Tomatoes and Cannellini Bean Bake	115
Roasted Vegetable Enchilada Stack	89
Russian "Olivie" Salad	415
Salsa De Piña Picante	405
Salsa Verde	412
Salt Free Southwest Seasoning	290
Samoan Poi	268
Sancocho	375
Sausage Stuffed Kolache	345

Schug	386
Scottish Oatcakes	360
Serrano Salsa	404
Simple Black Bean Dip	87
Simple Black Bean Salads	93
Simple Fat Free Tortillas	403
Simple Homemade Yuzu Dressing	301
Simple Lentil Burgers	134
Simple Miso Soup	303
Simple Oat Granola Recipe	143
Simple Pad Thai Recipe	308
Simple Pasta e Fagioli Recipe	369
Simple Pinto Bean Meatless Meatloaf	100
Simple Scrambled Tofu	218
Simple Seasonings for Wedges	163
Simple Sweet and Sour	294
Simple Teriyaki Sauce	299
Simple Wasabi Recipe	302
Simply Amazing Vegan Brats	334
Simply Incredible Hummus Pairings	395
Simply Incredible Waffles	313
Simply Incredible White Bean Chili	113
Slow Cooker Vegetable Barley Soup	80
Smashed Potatoes	169
Smashing Chickpea Avocado Salad	122
Smoky Black-eyed Pea & Sweet Potato Soup	281
Smothered Black Bean Burrito	90
Sopapillas	374
Southwest Black Bean Pie	285
Southwest Dip	288
Southwest Mayo Spread	288
Southwest Vegetable Broiling Rub	290
Spanakopita	338
Spanakopita Mashed Potatoes	160
Spanish Rice	201
Spicy Thai Rice	203
Spinach and Quinoa Salad	191
Squash Harvest Loaf	237
St. Louis BBQ	255
Stuffed Poblano Peppers in a Chipotle Sauce	284
Sugar Free Lemon Curd	214
Sugar-Free Quinoa Granola Bars	188
Sweet Potato Lasagna	177
Sweet Potato Nachos	178
Sweet Potato Pound Cake	179
Tabbouleh	231
Taco Seasoning	408
Texas BBQ Sauce	256
Texas Caviar	286
Texas Spice Blend	289
Tex-Mex Burgers	287
Thai Coconut Soup	306
Thai Peanut Sauce	309
The Simply Incredible Waffle Recipe	314
The Standard Healthy Hummus Recipe	394
Tofu Pancakes	220
Tombet	422
Traditional Native American Fried Green Tomatoes	276
Trinidad Green Seasoning	322
Turmeric Coconut Basmati Rice	206
Turos Csusza	347
Tuscan Spaghetti Squash	238
Tzatziki Sauce	339
Ugali	249
Ultimate Lasagna	366
Vanilla Lime Cheesecake	213
Vegan Borscht	416
Vegan Ceviche	373
Vegan Condensed Milk	377
Vegan Cornbread	129
Vegan Crème Fraîche	433
Vegan 'Fish' Sauce	310
Vegan French Crepes	327
Vegan Paella	427
Vegan Pesto	368
Vegan Potatoes Au Gratin	171
Vegan Rassolnik	417
Vegan Schnitzel	332
Vegetable Lo Mein	296
Wasakaka	319
White Bean and Mint Crostini	116
White Bean Hummus	111
Wild Rice and Mushrooms	207
Winter Squash Fruit Leathers	242
Yellow Jasmine Rice	205
Yuzu Dressing	301
Yuzu Sauces	301
Zaboca & Channa Bruschetta	317